You Don't Look Psychic

For our children and grandchildren,

our parents and grandparents,

our ancestors we know and the ones we don't.

For those who came before whose shoulders we stood upon,

and those who come after whom we offer ours.

 This book was printed in the United States of America

ISBN-13: 978-0-578-75034-7

Printed by Kdp Publishing, An Amazon.com Company

Book Design by Heather Holmstrom

Available from Amazon.com and other retail outlets.

You Don't Look Psychic

Your Essential Guide To
Tapping Into Your Natural Power

Lynnette Brown & Dr. Divi Chandna

You picked up this book for a reason.

Did you open to this page because you were drawn to it

or was it a coincidence?

Or was it energy, magic, and intuition at play?

You decide.

Stephanie was pregnant with her son; it was a time of new life and excitement within her family. But weeks leading up to her delivery, she kept seeing her death. It wasn't a single message; it kept repeating itself over and over again. She was going to need extra blood in the delivery room, and she was going to need extra equipment on hand to live. She saw it clearly weeks before her son came into the world. She felt it loud and clear, and she shared her visions with the doctors. Everyone warily listened to her requests, but they were quickly dismissed as preemptive fear. The night Stephanie gave birth, she died for 37 seconds before the doctors were able to bring her back to life with the extra blood and equipment stocked in the room.

On the other side of the country, Lynnette was sitting with a group of friends practicing their advanced intuitive tools. This particular day they were focusing on remote viewing. An intuitive practice of seeing and acquiring information about a remote unseen location. They decided they would connect with her friend, Jeremy who lived in Australia. Energetically she saw him in front of her in his home, a place she had never visited nor seen. In her vision, she took a feather and brushed it across his face to see if it would get his attention. Wanting to know if this was truly real she told him, "If you are feeling this and if you are seeing or thinking about me, call me right now." Literally 2 minutes later her phone rang, Jeremy's voice pierced the silence saying, "I have no idea why, but I had this insistent sense I had to call you. Also, there's this irritating feeling like a hair was stuck on my face that I couldn't get off. What's going on over there?"

In Canada, Divi noticed how she was being pulled into a bookstore with a friend one day after completing her doctor training. When she walked in, she saw Judith Orloff's book, *Intuitive Healing*. Her gut told her to buy it. Little did she know that in sixteen years she'd be on a TED stage talking about: intuition, health, and healing.

Steve Jobs attributes intuition to his success. He traveled to India when he was young, and said the people in the villages there relied deeply on their intuition; it was ingrained into the culture and their intuitions were strong. His intuition pulled him to read books that didn't directly impact his career, but for some reason, he felt drawn to them. Later, when he took his place as CEO, he said he owed his success to those books and classes that weren't in his field. They were the books that made a difference.

The list goes on: Joe attributes his business direction and multimillion dollar successes to intuition, Meredith knows she wouldn't be cancer free without hers, and Michelle knows she would still be working her dead-end job if she didn't listen.

The doctors called it a miracle when Stephanie walked away alive. Jeremy, a world away thought it a coincidence. Divi's friend called it fate. Meredith's doctors considered it a miracle. But Stephanie, Lynnette, Divi, Steve, Joe, and Meredith know deep within, it was intuition that got them to where they are today. **There are no coincidences.**

Contents

AUTHORS' NOTE

Aloha! Bonjour! Hello! Hola!

We are grateful you peeked into our book. We know there are no coincidences. You may be *thinking* it is happenstance that you turned to this page, but it isn't: it is every particle in the Universe aligning with perfect timing, allowing you to grace us with your presence. We thank you for your time and following your intuitive pull toward this book, and we welcome you to this journey of uncovering intuition and discovering how to use it each and every day.

We are two women—mothers, daughters, partners, leaders, and teachers—who found ourselves leaving our stable, respected careers for a different journey: the journey to the life of our dreams. Our stories are different, yet the same. Throughout this book, we will share the ups and downs and the ins and outs of how we came to understand this amazing gift called intuition.

Once you understand what intuition is, you may find that you've already used it unknowingly. Whether you've had a gut feeling to skip the lunch entrée that made everyone else sick or you thought about someone right before they called, that's your intuition talking. We all have it, and despite popular Hollywood portrayals of "seeing" the other realm, being intuitive doesn't look a certain way.

Intuition is you. As you are in this moment. And guess what? We've all been gifted with the superpower of intuition, and we all have this uncharted ability of knowing. You may think that you don't look psychic, but a psychic doesn't have a "look." You are psychic; I am psychic; humans are psychic. We all have an inner-knowing. The trick to this inner-knowing is learning how to tap into it every day.

The reason Divi and I were guided to write this book was because of the multitude of people who are being impacted unknowingly by *ignoring* their intuition. As a doctor of Western medicine, intuitive practitioner, and yoga teacher, Divi started to see that health issues were directly connected to our intuition, ignoring our inner-knowing could wreak havoc on our bodies. She started to see she could help people heal their lives by enabling them to awaken their own intuitive abilities, their natural gifts.

I, on the other hand, have had the benefit of personally experiencing the debilitating impact of ignoring my intuition. After years working alongside some of the most prominent attorneys in Houston, I found myself having to choose between my well-being and my career.

Spending my days watching how the lawyers twisted facts and numbers to arrive at their conclusions ate me up inside. Because of my intense sensitivity, I spent my breaks finding quiet places where I could stow away and cry. One day, my intuitive voice screamed, "Stop! This is *not* your way. There is a better way for you." At the time, I had no idea what the "better way" was. I just knew that if I didn't take off the golden handcuffs of this job I wouldn't last; I wouldn't live.

Walking away from that job opened up my entire life. Once we answer the call of our intuition, jump, and land on our feet, we reinforce our ability to trust it, and in turn, we continue to use it. I began trusting my intuition and soon had a thriving intuitive practice doing what I love: helping people.

It's not a coincidence that my and Divi's paths crossed. Soon after Divi started studying intuition, a friend suggested she consult me as an intuitive coach to support building the intuition side of her business. Over the years of working together, Divi and I found our lives had a common thread: we had both experienced the side effects from ignoring our intuition. When we ignore our intuition, we tend to shut down our true selves, and too often, that leads to depression, stress, disease, anxiety, and basically, a lackluster life of not doing what we love.

Today, we know the importance of tuning into ourselves and listening, and we acknowledge how our culture—with its many distractions, its focus on doing and achieving—encourages us to speed up rather than slow down and listen. When we aren't listening to our own voice, we get caught up with what others have to say, following what they expect of us, instead of our own true north. Listening to our intuition can change the trajectory of our lives, which is why we wrote this book and lead a course called Intuitive Coach Training (ICT) that helps people understand energy and tune into their intuition. We don't want anyone to have to go through hell before they reach their dream life, inner peace, power, and healing. There is a much easier way, and it starts with tuning into your intuition.

Intuition's First Whisper

Growing up, my family consisted of three people: my mom, brother, and me, Lynnette. That was it. My mom, a single parent, worked at least two jobs most of my early childhood to put food on the table (back in a time when women weren't meant to work or earn a living). She worked hard and loved even harder. One weekday morning as she was rushing around getting ready for her day and coaxing us to do the same, she asked me to pack up some of the brownies I had made so she could take them to the office to share.

As I was putting the brownies into the brown paper bag, I heard my mom say, "Charles has been having a rough go lately, maybe you could write him a note to cheer him up." At 10 years old, I didn't know much about cheering people up, but I could write something nice.

So I wrote, "I know things have been hard lately, but they'll get better. These brownies are just the beginning. Love, Lynnette." I put the note into the brown bag, rolled it up, and set it on the table for my mom to grab on her way out.

That evening when my mom came home she said, "Honey, what made you write that note to Charles that you put in the brownies?" I must have looked confused because I said, "You did mom. You told me to." Her face puzzled, she replied, "What do you mean?" I said, "You told me to pack up some brownies, and then you said to write Charles a note cuz he was having a tough week." Her face went white, and I don't think I'll ever forget it. As a 10-year-old, my mom was my world, and she was the only stability I had. She sat down and took my hand, "Honey, I don't know what to say, but I didn't say a word about writing a note to Charles."

A high-pitch sound started ringing in my ears. She grabbed me, squeezed me tight, and said, "Well honey, you must've been hearin' the angels cuz it truly touched Charles' heart, and mine too." When she let go of me, I could see tears running down her cheeks. She knew I was hearing my intuition, and I think it scared her a little. Still, she didn't show any fear. Instead, from that point on, she began fostering my skills by asking me questions about what I felt, saw, heard, or knew. That was the first time I remember using my intuition. Everyone's first experience with their intuition is different. It doesn't look a certain way, have a certain shape or smell, but it always has a certain feel.

For my partner in crime and co-author Divi, she shut down her intuition in her younger years. She grew up with her parents and three other siblings. She had a nuclear, immigrant family in a small-mid size town in Canada. Her upbringing was classic for a family from India, in that her parents emphasized culture, religion, and studies. Emotions and intuition were not encouraged and were thought to be a waste of time. Emotions were swapped for science, academics, and achievement.

Since then, she has realized she fostered her intuition as a child anyway. Her father would have migraines regularly. She was told that many things triggered his migraines, including her misbehaving. He was holding so much together—a marriage, raising four kids, being an immigrant, and leaving his mark as a new university professor. Because of his temper, Divi and her siblings would whisper to each other if he was in a BM or GM (bad mood or good mood) as a way of knowing how to behave in front of him. She found herself waking up and knowing his mood. She would walk into the kitchen where he sat drinking his morning tea and reading the newspaper, and tried to sense what mood he was in. She did this daily, moment to moment. It was a way of making sure she wouldn't upset him or trigger a migraine. Always paying attention to the energy in the house, allowed her to pick the perfect moments to tell a joke, knowing she could make him laugh. That's her first memory of using her intuition.

As adults, Divi and I find we use our intuition all day, every day. Today, using our intuition could be something as simple as calling a friend we can't stop thinking about or finding the best parking space. Perhaps you've had the same experience without realizing it. Entering the parking garage, we are open to be guided to the best spot. We listen, tune in, and follow whatever nudges we receive. Surprisingly (or not), we always find a great parking spot.

Since our first intuitive experiences as children, the media has turned intuition into an avalanche of confusion—one part smoke and mirrors and another part marketable fear. It is no wonder that we question intuition's existence.

When people find out that Divi and I are intuitive success coaches, they take one of two avenues: 1) They smile politely and excuse themselves from the conversation, or 2) They jump in and ask all types of questions, including what we can tell them about themselves.

Thankfully, intuition is becoming more and more accepted in our world, but we still have a way to go. Many folks are frightened by the idea of connecting with the unseen for guidance, and they fear it to be evil, a lie, or both. Because of these fears and misunderstandings, intuitives are sometimes perceived as vagabonds and scammers who are trying to cheat people out of their money, and we are often met with great skepticism.

Experiencing others' skepticism is a good thing because it trains intuitives, who are living the work, to understand that not everyone sees things the same way. We are here to be of service through our skills and talents, and not everyone wants to know what their deceased Uncle Fred thinks about their new job.

Of course, there's always the funny jokester that says, "If you're so intuitive, why don't you tell me the lottery numbers," or "Prove it." There will always be those who don't believe in intuition, in love, in faith, in trust, in the existence of individual atoms, in radio waves, in the world being round, in things they cannot see or understand. It's not our job to change their beliefs. One valuable skill to develop as a professional intuitive is tough, Teflon-coated skin. We can't shut down and withdraw in the face of another's disbelief or disagreement. We must know we don't require another person to validate our abilities and our intuitive connection.

For years, I came across people constantly wanting to joust with me and have me "prove" my talent, and I learned early on, through my teachers, not to take the bait. Doing so only cheapens my connection. We aren't here to prove to anyone that we are connected. We know we are, and our lives prove that. The joy in our hearts and the people we help are the only validation we need. When I was able to own that for myself, I no longer ran into people who wanted to joust about my intuition because I finally owned it as a part of me.

At the other end of the spectrum are the people who meet an open intuitive and want to sit down and ask a million questions about the art of intuition, readings, and themselves. They are fascinated by it and often are drawn to wanting to hear and learn more. Whether people want to joust or ask a million questions, we must know and practice our boundaries.

Before we step behind the curtain, delve deeper, and see intuition in its true light, we want to set the stage, and as with any good production, there must be context, clarity, and collaboration. And here's the tricky part: intuition may not look like we always imagined it would.

PART 1

Intuition

It May Look Different Than You Think

CHAPTER 1

Crystal Balls, Capes, And Wands, Oh My!

"The sixth sense is a sacred energy -
it taps you into the state of all-knowing."
- STUART WILDE

Intuition isn't wielding wizard cloaks and sitting in front of a crystal ball (unless you want to dress up for the occasion). Intuition happens ordinarily, right where we are; it is here in every moment, and it isn't rainbows and butterflies, green hair or purple eyes. Intuition looks like me navigating a new city, or creating a daily schedule that works for me. It is knowing who I want to hang out with and who I don't. It is picking out gifts for loved ones and friends. It is knowing when it is time to take on a new client or write a book. My family jokes that my intuition is my life-support since I have no sense of direction when wandering around new cities. As I sit here thinking about it, it is harder for me to think of a time when I don't use my intuition than of times when I do. I use my intuition every single second, consciously or not. I cannot separate myself from my intuition because it is me, and I am it. Yes, I deliberately turn its volume down when I'm traveling or in a massive group, but it's always there. It is never gone.

Intuition is within all of us, and that is why it has nothing to do with external appearances. It looks as simple as knowing what our body needs to eat for breakfast, and it can be as complex as knowing when someone is going to call us. Intuition is the line of communication that gives us the ability to know something without prior knowledge. Intuition bridges the gap between the conscious and unconscious parts of our mind, as well as the left (logic) and right (creative) lobes of our brain. Our intuition is continuously feeding our mind with information—whether we know it or not. It is what we commonly call a gut instinct, and it is a sensation we experience when we know that a parking spot is around the corner or that we should talk to a stranger standing across the room. Everything, every single thing, we feel, think, remember, dream, or notice has information, direction, and meaning for us. It may, at times, feel like we are playing charades trying to translate the messages, but the meaning is there. And that meaning is our intuition telling us what is best for ourselves in each moment.

Intuition is an energy, a heightened awareness, and much like light, we can't touch it, but we know it's there. It is something we all carry within us. It is a communication channel we can access at any moment. But we have been taught over time to ignore it. The key is not to ignore this energy, and that is what this journey is all about.

If we ignore this energy, we are denying our birthright and our innate self—the part of us that knows what is best for us.

In today's society, we tend to drown out our intuitive voice and the feelings that go along with it by surrounding ourselves with screens, social media, YouTube, drama, or the like. We desire (or unconsciously desire) to be distracted from our intuition—our Divine Guidance and natural GPS. Regardless of what you call it—"gut instinct," intuition, inner-knowing, Divine Guidance, natural GPS—it is an important aspect of our human evolution. Why would we drown out such a valuable part of our humanity?

Following our intuition requires us to stand up (and usually out). Sometimes it requires us to live our lives a little differently (since we are listening to what we need), and sometimes the price of this is ridicule and isolation. Fear of this ridicule and isolation leads us to deny our intuition so we can be accepted by our communities and families. And as we are finishing up our editing of this book, we are in the midst of the ultimate isolation: sheltering in place for the COVID-19 global pandemic. Isolation can tend to naturally happen for those in touch with their intuition since it can make people feel different. A government ordered isolation is a different creature for everyone, but one that presents many of the same challenges. And empaths are especially impacted due to the intensity of the situation: the fear and uncertainty. They are feeling the impact of seemingly uncontrollable situations—a virus. From buying groceries to taking vacations, conducting business, holding classes for school, the way we go about our lives has instantly shifted and the world is in a dirge, moving in a slow solemn rhythm. We are single focused on the same topic: our thoughts of staying safe while navigating this new world. And this new rhythm we've found amidst the pandemic is more aligned with the natural rhythm of Mother Earth, which is a denser, slower movement, like that of a boulder or massive oak.

As we shelter in place, we are seeing that those who are practicing their intuition and living the Universal Laws—while feeling a significant tidal wave of fear—are finding it easier to maintain a calm and peaceful mind without jumping into a mob mentality of fear and anger.

So even in difficult times such as the ones we are experiencing right now, our intuition comes through and supports us in ALL ways. As we start to emerge from our sheltering during this pandemic, there is still an incredible unknowingness about how the virus will continue to move. Having your Divine Guidance is the port in the storm. When you trust your intuition, you can follow your guidance with trust. Instead of waiting for someone else to tell you what you should do, you have instant access to Universal wisdom and know what is best for yourself. All the answers are there. So why worry?

The abandonment and denial of our intuition has a price: our freedom, joy, and power. As a doctor, Divi has seen patients lose their health and well-being by ignoring their intuition, their innate selves, and I nearly lost my life by ignoring this powerful inner-knowing. Though it may sound quite dramatic, this is the cost of ignoring our intuition.

Our health, well-being, and success are all at stake, and our modernized world isn't teaching us how to tap into our natural resources, our intuition. Quite the opposite; we are being trained to ignore our inner-knowing, our intuition, and pushed to follow a designated path and set of rules for living, whether they are right for us or not. And because of this, we are living in a world where people are slowly and unknowingly sacrificing their well-being, which the pandemic is bringing into the light. Stepping into the world of intuition doesn't look like you thought it would, does it? Crystal balls, tarot cards, or hoop earrings are not required accoutrements of the everyday intuitive. Intuition looks like you and me, and oh yeah, that guy over there too. And now that you've stepped completely into this new world, we'd better make sure you understand the lingo.

CHAPTER 2

A Peek Behind The Curtain

"The only valuable thing is intuition."
- ALBERT EINSTEIN

Years ago, I traveled to Italy with three of my friends. I remember being famished upon arrival; we immediately struck up a conversation with the first local we saw, and he sent us to a tiny place that, to this day, gave me one of the best meals of my life. Connecting with the locals deepens our experience of flavors, textures, history, and culture of a new land. Just as psychics don't all look the same, they also don't all speak the same way. So, to help you in this new uncharted territory, like my trip to Italy, Divi and I are going to be the locals for your journey into intuition. Because we know the lay of the land, we're going to make sure you have the best map, a little cheat sheet to assure you that we're on the same page, looking through the same spyglass, using a shared context, and speaking the same language. To fully experience any new place, you want to be able to understand and speak a bit of the language, at least enough to get the best recommendations.

Some of these are terms you might have heard before, and maybe you created your own definition or meaning of them. That is perfect! We aren't asking you to not believe your own definition; we are asking that you consider looking through the lens of our spy glass, for even a moment, and see this subject through a different lens, through the context and intent we are sharing with you.

So, without further delay, following Julie Andrews' lead—let's start at the very beginning, it's a very good place to start.

I used "psychic" a couple of times already and we use it in the title of this book. What does "psychic" mean?

The origins of the word psychic come from the Greek word *psychikos*, which has two meanings: "of the mind" and "soul," and from Latin *psyche* meaning "breath." When we use psychic in this book, we have two meanings attached to it: 1) a colloquial term to mean intuition, the ability to have knowledge or sense of something, without prior knowing or contact, and 2) an untrained everyday person who is receiving intuitive information (consciously or unconsciously).

Some people when referring to a practitioner, use the terms "psychic" and "intuitive" interchangeably; we **DO NOT**. We see the discerning differences between someone who has trained, focused, and honed their abilities compared to someone who randomly receives information. A person who has trained as an intuitive.

The tongue in cheek title we used for this book, *You Don't Look Psychic* is about addressing the belief and mindset that people who tap into their intuition have a stereotypical look. Psychics look like you and me and the man at the grocery store. There is no "look." We have enough differences in our world and enough bias and pain in need of radical forgiveness, atonement, and healing, so rather than talk about differences, we want to highlight our similarities in addition to our uniqueness.

"Intuition" is the energy of information that comes through your Divine intuitive channels also known as the four clairs, which you'll read about later.

When we use the word "Divine," we are speaking about energy that is Universal, some may call it God, others Allah, or Jehovah. We use the phrases "Divine," "Divine I AM," and "Universe" all to reflect an energy that is referred to in the *Kybalion* as "ALL THAT IS." We prefer using the words "Divine" and "Universe" because it feels ALL inclusive. If you feel differently, please substitute the verbiage that feels best to you.

You will notice us using the phrase, "Divine Guidance" throughout the book. We like using this term interchangeably with "intuition," because when we speak of intuition we are not talking about a psychic (someone who isn't trained to use their intuition). We are referring to a deeply connected space of Universal wisdom hence the term "Divine Guidance."

To split another hair, when we talk about Divine Guidance, it is NOT "channeling." There are different realms of thought as to what "channeling" actually is, whether it is allowing an energy to enter your physical body, or simply allowing your consciousness to provide information. Regardless of how you define it, we aren't teaching channeling per se. We are teaching you how to build an intuitive connection, and where you choose to go with it is 100 percent up to you. The options are endless.

Let's talk about "Universal wisdom." Now that sounds like a big order, right? With "Universal wisdom," we are referring to the Divine wisdom, the kind of wisdom that is far-reaching, beyond the grasp of the human mind. We have access to this Universal wisdom 24/7 through our intuitive connections. We will use Universal wisdom interchangeably with One Mind, which is synonymous with Universal wisdom.

Rather than attach the words "good" or "bad" to an experience, we use the word "contrast." It allows us to discuss our experiences without our minds attaching inherent meaning to them. Rather than saying, "Last week sucked; it was such a struggle." We can say, "This week is a contrast to what I've been going through." Not good or bad. Simply different.

We use the phrase "Divine Support Team" to reflect any and all Divine Masters, teachers—living or otherwise—who guide us through our soul's plan, the contrasts and lessons of life. Here are some leaders whose wisdom and way of life illuminate impeccable examples to give us direction to live a more expanded life: Kali, Jesus, Kwan Yin, Buddha, Angels, Mary Magdalene, Freyja, Pele, St. Francis. These guides span all divinities and faiths, Greek, Druid, Roman, Tibetan, Buddhist, Celtic, Catholic, Cabalistic, Jewish, New Age or Christian roots. You may also hear others referring to these Divine beings as "Guides," because they literally "guide" your exploration. Also, included in our Divine Support Team are our ancestors, the blood lineage into which each of us are born. These ancestors support our growth and learning through our life as we learn and move through our experiences. When we grow, we not only expand our consciousness but also heal and expand our ancestral lineage.

We all have connections to our ancestors. Who are they? They are our ancient forebears, generations of those who came before us. Whether we know them or not doesn't matter. We are connected to our ancestors not just through our biology but our spiritually too. Their DNA is embedded in our own, all of their experiences, fears, and talents echo throughout our own individualized bodies. As we heal and move through our own adventures, our ancestral DNA releases and shifts, impacting our lineage in all directions of time.

Throughout this book, we will share exercises and processes we recommend to enhance your intuitive connections. If you use them, you may have miraculous results. What do we mean by "miraculous"? It's not that we are overemphasizing the potential of these exercises; it is the natural power of miracles. What do we mean when we say "miracles"? We are referring to an actual shift in conscious awareness, a change that happens inexplicably through natural or Universal Laws. This can be as simple as seeing a circumstance from a completely different perspective.

Given the potential of miracles, it begs the question: where's the magic? What's behind the curtain? And what do we mean when we speak about magic? Magic is simply natural forces that cause change. Where does magic dwell? Within each of us. It is our power to focus and direct energy to create and allow. Magic is the synchronicities of life that perhaps you have let go unnoticed, until now.

Along with that magic comes a powerful energy field that surrounds every living person or thing. These individualized energy fields cocoon our bodies so subtly and naturally that we may not even be aware they exist. We call these personalized energy fields "auras." Auras are a great way to access and work with your personal energy.

As you proceed deeper into your journey of intuition you will hear us use the term "success habits." We use this term to mean any habit or action that leads you to feeling aligned with your purpose and desired accomplishments. They can be actions such as meditation, mindfulness, exercise, dance, body movement, journaling, or gratitude practice. All actions when practiced regularly create a fertile foundation for success. We recommend tracking your successes, somewhere you can "see" you are stepping forward daily towards success. Even if the only success you had was making your bed. It still counts! Because as humans we are geared to only seeing what we do wrong, tracking our successes, regardless of size, shows us in print (or cursive) that we are making progress.

As you travel through this new land to connect with your intuition, you may feel hesitant, because all the uncertainty of the unknown, the unseen. Because the territory of intuition can be complicated and confusing there are some people who try to take short cuts by not working through their personal wounds. Psychics, who ignore the work to heal their wounds, have a static-filled bandwidth which gives them a greater propensity to dish out what we call "dark readings." Dark readings are when a psychic (untrained intuitive) delivers ego-derived guidance instead of Divine Guidance. This ego-driven guidance often comes in the form of a cloud over their client's head, problem or trouble that will be coming their way. In complete contrast, a trained intuitive in the same circumstance would receive Divine Guidance regarding the possible challenges. The big difference is the message received by the intuitive would be in a way their client could receive it and be open to taking inspired action.

One additional suggestion before you push off from the shore and embark on your journey: We suggest you track and create your own Symbols Legend along the way. It will be your own map to your personal intuitive symbology. As you begin to practice your intuition you will begin to receive signs and symbols that will repeat themselves—an eagle, a new billboard put upon your daily commute, the color yellow, and numbers, just to name a few. These signs and symbols are the shorthand of the Divine that help us receive blocks of information all at once instead of individual words. They are quick intuitive access points. As you move through the exercises and processes, tracking your symbols, you will begin to see a pattern emerge. These are your own personal Divine symbols and language. These are for you alone to ascertain the meaning, a language just for you! Keeping track of these symbols and shorthand will build your confidence in your intuitive abilities. When we actually witness our successful hits, we have proof of our abilities. This allows us to relax, which in turn opens our intuitive channels even more. It's also helpful to write down personal messages and guidance you receive. This way, you can actually track where the Divine Guidance leads—was the eagle you saw on your drive an accurate symbol of how the rest of your day would go, or did it show you how you aren't seeing things from a higher perspective? All of this is to help us personally acknowledge and witness ourselves as successful intuitives, which amplifies our abilities.

We'll give you some specifics in more detail about all of these phrases later in the book. Remember, this is just some "cliff notes" on our lingo. Now that you can speak the language, you'll be able to navigate this new world of intuition a bit more easily, and we will be on the same page, in the following chapters and beyond.

CHAPTER 3

The Science

"Scientific research is proving that this feeling, our intuition, is real and can be studied."

Intuition started popping up in scientific studies as early as 1984. People were becoming more in tune and aware of this unconscious information that was contributing to human decision making, and scientists got curious and started conducting studies on the experience.

Within the world of science, intuition is defined as a brain process that gives people the ability to make decisions without the use of analytical reasoning. It is the influence of "unconscious emotional information" transmitted from the body or the brain, allowing us to have an instinctual feeling or sensation without consciously rationalizing the information we receive. Rather than thinking, we have a feeling. Scientific research is proving that this feeling, our intuition, is real and can be studied.

Intuition was brought to the forefront of scientific thought in the western world in 1984 when an article was published in the *Harvard Business Review* about intuition and senior managers. Daniel Isenberg studied senior managers from companies with large revenues, including many from the top Fortune 100 companies. Over two years, he interviewed and studied their thought processes. He made many interesting observations in his review, and one of them was that senior managers "frequently bypass rigorous analytical planning altogether, particularly when they face difficult, novel, or extremely entangled problems. When they do use analysis for a prolonged time, it is always in conjunction with intuition." This article showed that intuition is not something that people use in a back alley with their crystal ball. In reality, each of us use it on a daily basis, and these senior managers of big, successful companies were trusting their gut feeling more than first realized. Demonstrating data and intuition have both long been part of the boardroom.

Years later, researchers showed 20 college students black-and-white images of dots moving around on half of a computer screen. The researchers asked the students to decide whether the dots were generally moving to the left or to the right. As the participants made this decision, on the other half of the computer screen, there was a bright, flashing square of color. Sometimes, the researchers embedded an image into the square that was designed to trigger a positive or negative emotional response from them. The participants were not aware they were being shown these emotional images because they flashed at speeds too fast to be consciously perceived. These subliminal images were meant to simulate the type of information we receive through intuition—they were brief, emotionally charged and subconsciously perceived. Their experiment results revealed that when participants were shown positive subliminal images, they did better on the task and more accurately determined which way the dots were moving. These students also responded faster and reported feeling more confident about their choice. They were using their intuition to process the subliminal messages, and they were using that subconscious information to help them on the task. This information was not processed in their conscious brain, demonstrating that there is a lot of information our intuition gives us that can help us with tasks at hand.

This experiment also showed that over time participants became better and quicker at using their intuition. The use of the positive versus negative subliminal images also shows us that paying attention to our emotional energy is important when learning to trust our intuition. The participants' accuracy was higher and faster when the participants were intuitively feeling positive (when shown the positive images of babies and puppies). One of the researchers said, "It's all about learning to use unconscious information in your brain." Just as people get more comfortable making decisions using logic and reasoning over time, this study showed that people can become more adept at trusting their intuition when they use it more frequently. Intuition is something that we can all grow, build, and learn to trust.

In 2007, the United States Army released a report on developing intuition in their junior Army officers. They acknowledged that "great commanders intuitively appreciate the value of their sixth sense or gut feeling." Junior officers are trained in technical abilities and when to rely on their intuition. Both of these aspects are an important part of their leadership development. These leaders must not only be well-versed in the technical side but also practiced at using their intuition.

Over the years, Western science has caught onto the fact that intuition is regularly used in different areas of our lives: playing board games, purchasing a home, becoming a senior manager, and working in the army. It's becoming clear that intuition isn't some back-alley phenomenon practiced by vagabonds. It was being used far and wide all over the world from top executives to children on a playground. Intuition is a part of all of us, and if we ignore it, we may be less satisfied with our choices in life. It's clear that intuition exists, and we all have access to it. Being intuitive doesn't look a certain way—senior executives use it, the military uses it, children use it. The real mystery lies in knowing how to deliberately use this subconscious information on a daily basis. Knowing where it resides in our body is a key part in understanding and accessing it.

CHAPTER 4

The Anatomy

"Attention to the human body brings healing and regeneration. Through awareness of the body we remember who we really are."
- JACK KORNFIELD

There are specific parts of our body meant for intuition, and the parts we use for intuition, like any muscle, can be woken up and strengthened. Since we all have the same anatomy within our bodies, it means that all of us are intuitive. Yep, you guessed it. We are all psychic, and we are all capable of being intuitive. It doesn't look a certain way. The three main structures that are responsible for intuition are the brain, gut, and heart.

Brain

Each day many people rely on intuition to complete their jobs: police, physicians, auditors, judges, and many more. During Divi's medical training, she was taught that she should be able to walk into a room and within seconds be able to determine if the person in her office was really sick or not. This skillset is something our brains are wired with, but it takes practice to develop.

Neuroscience has shown us that parts of our brains become activated when we are using our intuition. So as a trained physician, when she walks into a room, the intuitive part of her brain starts to work. Neuroscientists in Japan performed a study on Shogi players (a game similar to chess) to discover the difference in brain flow patterns between amateur and professional players. Players who practiced and trained for 10 years were deemed professionals, and the theory was that experienced players have built a part of their brain that has "greater, faster, intuitive knowing" than amateur players. Using magnetic resonance imaging (MRI), they were able to determine where blood flow traveled in the brain of the professional players compared to a novice's. In the expert players, it was found that more blood went to certain parts of the brain—the precuneus region of the parietal lobe and the caudate nucleus—indicating that these players were using their brain when they accessed their intuition, showing the brain played a main role in intuition. Studying intuition using brain scans is still new, and the fact that we can locate a part of the brain with increased blood uptake shows us there are parts of the brain doing this specific task of intuition. It tells us that there are specific parts of us, parts we are born with, that can be awakened to perform the task of intuition. This is one of the many studies that shows a distinct blood flow difference in people using their intuition compared with people who may still be learning to use it.

In another study, researchers looked at mediums. Mediums are intuitives who can communicate with deceased loved ones. When looking at the brain of mediums, it was found that there was a measurable shift in their brain activity when they were tapping into their intuitive connection. During the study, scans were used to show brain activity for different parts of the brain. Both experienced and novice psychographers—mediums who communicate with the deceased via automatic writing in a trance state—were studied. Experienced psychographers were found to have more complex responses in their automatic writing than novice mediums. Additionally, it was found that the experienced mediums had decreased blood flow to certain parts of the brain, compared to the control group.

Specifically, there was less blood flow to the following areas: left culmen, left hippocampus, left inferior occipital gyrus, left anterior cingulate, right superior temporal gyrus, and right precentral gyrus. There was a scientifically measurable blood flow shift occurring when mediums connected with departed loved ones. It cannot be argued that "nothing was happening," or that this person was just "thinking of the deceased loved one and guessing." There was a demonstrable shift in blood flow, which means something different was occurring during psychography. **That something was intuition.**

In a similar study, the famous medium Theresa Caputo was studied on television doing mediumship readings. Quantitative studies were done to demonstrate brain activity. The studies done at rest with EEG were very different from those done when Caputo was doing a reading. When doing a reading, Caputo demonstrated less frontal lobe activity and more temporal lobe activity. Again, this shows us that something is happening during readings which is different than "normal." This difference, studied numerous times shows there is a definite neurological shift occurring when intuition is being used.

These findings show us the difference between a brain using intuition versus a "thinking and planning" brain. There are specific parts of our brains meant for intuition, and the parts we use for intuition, like any muscle, can be woken up and strengthened.

Gut

Our gut is often called our "second brain." The reason for this term is because the gut is lined and innervated with millions of nerve endings, and the neural tissue also has millions of neurotransmitters (like the ones in the brain) that do more than digestion.

The gut is technically called the enteric nervous system and consists of over one hundred million neurons. The gut is considered a part of the nervous system because of all the neurons that reside there. These sheaths of neurons are embedded in the walls of the gut, esophagus, the small and large intestines and go all the way to the anus. It is commonly termed "from the gums to the bum." The number of neurons in the gut is actually more than the number of nerve cells in the spinal cord or peripheral nervous system. This huge number of neurons allow us to "feel" our gut.

One of the main functions of this part of our body is to digest food—metabolize, digest, absorb, and process. What a job! The gut digests independently from the brain, meaning it doesn't need the brain to cue it to start digesting. It works independently. However, the gut speaks to the brain with a large amount of emotional information. It has been found that the vagus nerve (the primary visceral nerve in our bodies) carries information from the gut to the brain (not the other way around).

We've all had gut feelings before, butterflies in our stomach. That is an example of an interoceptive sensation due to the large number of neurons in our gut. Interoception is the ability of our body to sense physiological signals that come from within our body. For example, heart rate, temperature, hunger, and pain are interoceptive signals. Interoception and intuition go hand in hand. Our gut can pick up on these signals and use them to tell us something: eat, don't do that, do this, you are nervous. These interoceptive signals are transferred to the brain via the vagus nerve, and studies have shown that the signals going up the vagus nerve have been linked to our mood and certain types of fear and anxiety.

Fear and anxiety then send signals to our body, triggering our sympathetic nervous system. The sympathetic nervous system is responsible for what is most commonly known as our "fight or flight" response. When we perceive something stressful our blood pressure, heart rate, and respiratory rates go up—thanks to our sympathetic nervous system. When this activates, we get a sense of mental confusion and brain fog as well as decreased digestive function. Medical science used to think that once the sympathetic nervous system was activated, there was no going back until we were out of danger. It was thought that there was no way to deactivate the sympathetic nervous system and activate the parasympathetic system—the part of our nervous system activated when we are in a safe setting. This old belief was changed when Dr. Benson did revolutionary work in the 1970s and showed us that we could activate the parasympathetic nervous system with conscious activation of breath, meaning that when we are in danger we can turn off our "flight or fight" reaction.

Conscious focus on our breath stimulates the vagus nerve and the parasympathetic system, allowing us to transition our bodies from fear and danger to ease and safety. The vagus nerve is a key asset to supporting intuition because it activates the parasympathetic system which then decreases blood flow, respiratory rate, and increases calm and mental clarity. The calmer, more focused, more balanced we are emotionally and mentally the deeper our connection with our intuition. We can start to see that our second brain is key in the emotional and intuitive realms.

Heart

Similar to the gut, the heart is lined with a network of intricate nerve fibers. Scientific research shows us that the heart generates a powerful and measurable electromagnetic field. This electromagnetic field of our heart interacts with the field of the hearts of others around us. It is strong and has been measured at distances of hundreds of meters. Isn't that fascinating?

In a study out of the HeartMath Institute, 26 participants were shown a series of 45 pictures—30 of these pictures were neutral and 15 were emotionally arousing. All participants were hooked up to an electrocardiogram which would show heart accelerations and decelerations. They were also hooked up to an electroencephalogram to measure the heartbeats' electrical strength on the surface of the skin. The interesting finding was that the heart was responding to emotional arousing stimuli prior to the stimuli being shown. It was as if the heart anticipated the emotional stimuli coming up. What was even more fascinating is that the heart responded faster than the brain! What this HeartMath study shows is that both the heart and brain receive and respond to external cues prior to seeing them. Both the heart and brain are intuitive. And in this case, the heart received information faster than the brain. From this, it was concluded that the heart and brain were both intuitive processors and likely linked to the other body systems that play a critical role in intuition.

Pineal Gland and DMT

The heart, gut, and brain are key players in intuition, but we also have other chemical processes taking place in our bodies that support our intuitive abilities. N-Dimethyltryptamine (DMT) is a hormone we produce naturally in our bodies, and this natural hormone we produce doesn't induce a psychedelic response. DMT aids in our sleep and dream states, and it is said that we experience a surge of DMT at the time of death. This explains the intensity some people have with near-death experiences.

Scientists have had difficulty studying DMT and argue amongst themselves about the clinical effects, benefits, and uses of DMT. Despite this internal squabble, there has been significant research on animals that shows that DMT is secreted by the pineal gland (which also secretes melatonin—a hormone that helps us sleep). Recent research shows that the mammalian brain produces DMT in many different areas including the visual cortex. The pineal gland, where DMT is produced, corresponds to the spiritual third eye that many religions speak of as the seat of the soul and the gateway between normal consciousness and Divine consciousness. Coincidence? Maybe, maybe not.

As science and our studies of DMT are refined we may see a causal link between concussions and surges in DMT. Both of us have had remarkably similar experiences with concussions in our own histories and throughout the decades have heard similar stories from many other practicing intuitives, this may circle back to the link between concussions and DMT or it may be just mean that intuitives are also klutzes.

We can enhance our own levels of DMT, and consequently, support our intuitive abilities through a few simple practices. When we enhance the DMT in our bodies, our intuition is more likely to be present. This isn't the only avenue to enhancing our intuition, but enhancing our DMT is like adding oxygen to our intuitive fire. The fire needs oxygen to burn, but with too much or too little oxygen, the intuitive fire won't ignite or burn efficiently. We can use these practices when we feel a wobble with our guidance especially in difficult uncertain times such as this COVID-19 pandemic or other worldly chaos. Focusing on these natural ways to boost our DMT may help us steady our boat when there are choppy waters.

Dark Room. Entering a contemplative state in a dark room can increase the secretion of DMT. The dark room helps to increase the production of serotonin and melatonin which are precursors to DMT. An easy way to do this is to use black out curtains when you sleep.

Meditation. A regular meditation practice has been scientifically shown to increase our production of DMT.

Binaural Beats. Listening to binaural beats—sound transmitted to both ears—has been shown to increase the production of precursors to DMT as well.

Breath Work and Yoga. Many teachings believe that slowing down our breathing can increase DMT production. Kundalini yoga offers pranayama breathing techniques which support DMT secretion.

CHAPTER 5

What Intuition Isn't

"Intellect is rational; instinct is primal.
Intuition is within and held in the heart."

Intuition is *not* positive thinking. Positive thinking is affirming something in the direction of our desire—like a goal. It is like painting over our reality with a wash of color in hopes we can achieve our desired result. And while affirmations and positive thinking do make living this life better, they are not intuition. Intuition isn't painting over reality. It is tuning into it. Intuition is receiving—actually receiving—guidance about a situation or person. Intuition is the guidance that says stop, don't go that way, go this way, get out, or stay away.

Intuition is also not imagination. Imagination is a powerful tool of visualization that will support us on our paths, but it is not intuition. The benefit of utilizing imagination is that it allows us to open the channels of communication within our mind; it dissipates the angst of our fears so that we can be open to receiving our intuition.

CHAPTER 6

Who's Intuitive?

"EVERYONE."

Every single person has intuition. If you are breathing, you have the gift of intuition. And guess what? An intuitive isn't someone wielding a wizard cloak (though they can if they want). An intuitive looks like you and me and that guy over there and that woman over here. Intuition is a part of all of us.

- Intuition is the doctor in the emergency room using his knowledge and intuition to diagnose someone.
- Intuition is the woman walking home late at night who feels like someone is following her and moves to a lighted path surrounded with people.
- Intuition is the girl on the playground knowing that something feels off, runs to find the rest of her friends, and learns that one of them is hurt.
- Intuition is the woman in the delivery room knowing that she will need extra blood on hand for the birth of her child.
- Intuition is knowing when the person across from us is telling the truth.
- Intuition is the boy sitting in a parking lot with his friends knowing he needs to get home right away and arriving home just in time to take his sister to the hospital.
- Intuition is the young person picking out the ideal clothes for their interview.
- Intuition is you; it's me. It's us.

CHAPTER 7

Claim Your Superpower

"A serene mind easily hears intuition over fear."

We like using the term superpower because it relates to a superior power, which is the perfect description of intuition. Intuition is a natural and exceptional talent everyone has, but it has been buried away, forced to lay dormant under layers of our cultural and societal conditioning. Intuition, our natural gift, is unique for each person, but our ability to access it is similar for all of us.

When we start using our intuition and accessing it deliberately, we must look beyond our cultural consciousness. What exactly does cultural consciousness mean? It means in order to connect with our intuition we have to start somewhere other than where we've been and what we know. We need to look beyond our life "training" and conditioning. We need to acknowledge the beliefs and fears instilled in us by our environment, family, and caregivers, and then, we must suspend those beliefs and judgments (our thinking mind) momentarily to remember that our inner truth is buried under all of these societal trainings, beliefs, and expectations. We must not forget our truth, even if it gets buried: we are perfect, complete, and whole, lacking nothing.

Suspending our past isn't asking ourselves to stop believing in what we believe; we're asking ourselves to pause for just a moment to look behind the curtain of our lives and consider that we assumed we knew what was behind it because someone told us. But what if there is something more to our lives and actions than what we were told and what we've imagined or considered? What if there is an entire world behind that curtain that we couldn't see—that is, until now.

Consider that we all have patterns that have been ingrained in us since childhood. These patterns manifest as neural pathways in our brain and often present themselves in our lives as subconscious habits. Neural pathways are the electrical highways of our brain, and every thought, habit, emotion, and feeling strengthens their prominence in our lives. With practice, we can redirect old pathways or create new neural pathways that reinforce new habits and experiences of success. They are why we wake up one day in our mid 40s and realize that we have the same lives as our parents. We have similar patterns and mannerisms as our parents did, and say things we always swore we would never say. To understand why neural pathways make us like our parents and how we can rewire them to have a more fulfilling life, let's take a look at our brain structures.

Our human brain is schematically (not literally) composed of three different parts: the reptilian brain, the mammalian brain, and the cortex. These three sections of the human brain actually work together and are a development in our evolution. As the words imply, we have evolved as a species from the reptilian brain to the basic mammalian brain to the human brain. As a human, we still have all three brain parts.

The reptilian brain fits with its name. This was the original brain found in reptiles. This is the "housekeeping" part of the brain, and its main functions include muscle control, balance, heartbeat, feeding, reproduction, breathing, and digestion. It is the most basic part and controls the functions necessary for life.

Next, we have the mammalian brain, which is also called the limbic brain. This part of the brain is evolved and can be seen in animals like cats, dogs, mice, and horses. The limbic system/limbic brain is responsible for our emotions. Our emotions are needed for survival and safety. The limbic system developed in order to regulate emotions associated with feeding, reproduction, and attachment. Basically, the limbic system looks at the external world and sees things as agreeable (pleasure/good) or disagreeable (pain/avoidance/bad). In order to survive, we enhance the pleasurable and decrease the pain because it makes life tolerable.

Third is the neocortex of the brain, which developed in primates and humans. Its main function is the development of human language, abstract thought, imagination, and consciousness. This part of the brain is responsible for planning and calculation. It can do multiple tasks and is thought to be the "higher brain."

These three parts of the brain do not work independently, but are interconnected and influence each other. This is how it works: the mammalian brain (limbic system) is the home to the amygdala. The amygdala is a little organ the size of an almond. This organ scans the environment around us and looks for anything that feels unsafe. If this is triggered, our reptilian brain tells our body to do one of three things: 1) the fight response or 2) the flight response or 3) the freeze response.

The brain parts work together and impact how we interact with the world. Maybe you can relate to having a physiological or emotional reaction within your body that does not match the event that is happening. This is common because our brain can't decipher between real and unreal dangers. Our mammalian brain can trigger our reptilian brain at times that aren't actually dangerous. For example, our ancestors may have been triggered by a saber-toothed tiger while today our perceived threat may be our work email. Either way, if we consider something a threat, we are triggered, explaining why we can get worked up over seemingly small things. A common expression I hear from my clients is "I went from 0 to 100, and I don't know why." This is something they often say in retrospect to a stressful situation.

Think about it for a minute. Have you ever experienced looking back at a situation and wondering why you reacted the way you did? Do you find your reaction is a recurring pattern? Wondering why you repeatedly catch yourself saying things like, "That person drives like an idiot" in response to every driver on the road? The list of examples is endless, the point here is to see we have thoughts, perceptions, and emotional responses that may not be in line with what is actually happening.

The key to understanding our lives behind the curtain is uncovering our unique patterning. This is what the "work" is really about. The beauty of humans is that we have the neocortex part of our brain (the most developed, human part of our brains), and within that cortex, lies our consciousness. Consciousness means we have the choice to respond mindfully rather than relying on our reptilian brain to react obliviously to each situation. Much of personal development is recognizing our patterns and exercising our mindful choices, allowing us to heal.

Let's look at an example from my own life. Many women from my Indian culture were taught that men were superior and were to be respected and adored. There is even a day in the Hindu faith called *Karwa Chauth*. On this day, married women fast and pray for the long life of their husbands and the happiness of their family. Unmarried women also fast in the hope of finding a good husband. At night, after sighting the moon, the women can eat their first morsel of food from the hands of their husband. As beautiful and romantic as this sounds (and the history is held in the Hindu scriptures), it can create a pattern of beliefs that trigger me emotionally, tapping into the limbic (emotional) part of my brain. I had always felt that my husband's happiness was my responsibility. This is one of those "unconscious patterns" that I only started to realize after being in adult relationships. I would do classic things like give up my interests and default to what my partner wanted to do. I would feel guilty if I was doing something and he was sitting at home by himself. I would feel excessively responsible for his happiness level during the day. I felt this in my chest and heart on a physical level. Physically, my chest would cave in and I would shut down like I was going from 0 to 100 within seconds.

As you can see in these examples, nothing was disastrous. No one was getting killed.

There was no violence, and yet my physiology responded like there was something life-threatening running at me! This is what our body does when we have experienced an amygdala (emotional) trigger. The mammalian brain wants to protect us when it perceives death or danger, even though there isn't anything dangerous, physically.

We all have reactions like this. These are classic examples of being triggered. And yet, when we look at how I was raised (fasting for years of my life before getting married for the well-being of my future husband), we can see how and why my amygdala patterns are so deeply ingrained.

Uncovering this patterning and shining a light on it is the only way to heal it. First, we have to witness it, and then, we have to choose differently.

That is the choice we have, and we can exercise it daily. Does this sound like work? Yes! I always remind myself (and my clients) that it is work, but being sick, getting divorced, and fighting with our partners and kids repetitively are also work. It is work to deliberately choose how we want our lives to be and show up as that person each and every day. It is easy to let our lives happen to us, rather than for us, and reap the consequences later rather than now. Whether the work is done now or later, there will be work. Do the work now and skip out on the sickness later. Having a life you love is worth it, I promise.

Given the physiology of humans, expecting ourselves to not react to triggers is impossible. We have a mammalian brain that is "wired" to do this. The key is to pause once our response has occurred and see what it is telling us about ourselves. How is your brain patterned? What do you hold onto as a fear that is not serving you anymore? Are you willing to uncover your patterns and expose them so they can be re-routed?

Let's look at another classic example of how we act unconsciously. Imagine a room full of executives in a staff meeting trying to brainstorm a solution. It is a female-dominated company. The gathering is being led by one of the female executive staff, and the room is full of women and a handful of men. Ideas get passed around and a male staff person suggests one, but his input is discounted or ignored. About five minutes later, a female colleague mentions an identical solution to which she is met with praise and acknowledgment. The female is met with applause, and the male is ignored. This is a clear example of a gender bias that affects the decision making in this situation. Classically, the boss's unconscious patterns that are stored in her amygdala are that women are "like me" and safe; men are "not like me" and potentially unsafe. As a result, the unconscious fear-based pattern shows up when she overlooks the idea provided by the man. It is not necessarily consciously biased but rather an unconscious pattern. It is based out of fear and what she may perceive as normal. This is classic patterning that both women and men have in their amygdala as a way of keeping themselves safe and making sure they make the right decisions.

We all have unconscious patterning. We are raised with the beliefs of our ancestors. Each generation passes down their version of wisdom, values, beliefs, fears, and neural pathways, which we accept and assume are the truth. We may push against them, depart from our ancestor's customs or ideology, or even declare we will be anything but them, but they are in our DNA. Even adopted children carry the cellular memory of their birth mother's fears.

With these beliefs and daily external distractions (phones and computer screens), there is simply no way for the recessive "gene" of intuition to get through regularly or for us to notice it without practice. And since we can't hear our intuition, we are constantly asking Google or external sources questions, when our intuition would be a better resource. In a time when screens and technology have replaced personal interactions, it is essential that we start to notice, listen, and follow our intuition.

In order for us to grow past our childhood patterns and hear our intuition, we first need to become aware of the patterns we have. Awareness is the first step to growth. For example, when sheltering in place for extended amounts of time—like we're doing currently for the COVID-19 pandemic—regardless if you're alone or with family, you will see your old conditioning from your childhood patterns rear their heads. If we aren't aware, we will continue fueling these old neural pathways and these patterns that don't support our new expanded vision for our lives. As we become aware, we can steadily start to create the life we want.

A word of caution: we are the creators and stabilizers of our lives. To claim our intuitive superpower, we will need to see and witness our own beliefs about ourselves and our intuition. Often, people are drawn to using their intuition in their lives, yet they push the idea to the side because they were taught that only double-talking frauds use this type of hocus-pocus to trick people. To access our intuition, we must address our patterning along with these limiting and false beliefs. If we do not, we will not be able to access our superpowers.

CHAPTER 8

In The Beginning Was The Vibe

"If you knew your potential to feel good, you would ask no one to be different so that you can feel good. You would free yourself of all of that cumbersome impossibility of needing to control the world, or control your mate, or control your child. You are the only one who creates your reality. For no one else can think for you, no one else can do it. It is only you, every bit of it you."

- ABRAHAM / ESTHER HICKS

When I think of the word "vibration," I immediately think of the lyrics from a Beach Boys song. We would all love to be in that good, summer happy vibe that we fall into when we hear that song. Wouldn't life be interesting if we could create that feeling without hearing the song? Or, just bring that sensation on cue?

As energy workers and lightworkers, we are here to help the planet. We are here to bring balance, healing, and love. We are here to help people and be of service to the Divine within.

In order to do that, we are asked to continuously work on ourselves. It is through our own inner work and expansion that we can truly be a conduit of the Divine energy. In our own daily life, we are exposed to contrast and challenges, and it is through working with our emotions and consciousness that we can clear our own channels to be that conduit. For example, if I harbor anger towards men and I am working with a client who feels the same, then I will be unable to be of service to them. Because I'm in that wound, I will access my intuition through the censor of my angry energy field and give distorted or unclear information. In order to allow a message of Divine Guidance and be of service to my client, it's essential to heal my own story. In order to be able to give messages of love, from Spirit, I have to be willing to look at my own beliefs and energy, and practice forgiveness and atonement while working through my own stories.

Diving into our energy, beliefs, and stories is a vital part of taking on the path of practicing as an intuitive coach. It is not always the easy part, as we have to be willing to dance with those 60,000 thoughts we have every day and acknowledge which ones aren't serving us! The payoff for this energy work is profound though. Greater happiness, inner peace, and contentment are just a few of the wins!

Emotions and Mind vs Intuitive Voice

Understanding our energy, vibe, and emotions is paramount to having a happy life.

Having a greater awareness of our emotions and patterns helps us connect to our intuition. When our heads are spinning in fear, it is challenging, if not impossible, to sense our intuitive voice. On the other hand, when we are relaxed, easy going, and in our flow, we can have greater knowing, more insight, and greater connection to our intuitive voice. To really understand energy, we need to dive into a deeper understanding of our emotions, mind's voice, and intuitive voice.

We have two distinct voices inside of us at all times that affect our emotional vibe. The two voices are our mind's voice and our intuitive voice. The mind's voice is the one that thinks all of the time. Most of us can relate to a mind's voice that is chatty, busy, and overwhelming. In general, the mind's voice can be critical and judgmental. You want to make a distinction between the mind's voice—think of it like a chatterbox squirrel that repeats our worries, fears, and judgments—versus our intuitive voice which is the receiver of thoughts from the Divine.

The difference is simple: the mind cycles over and over again whereas intuitive thoughts from the Divine come in with love—seemingly out of nowhere—to help, reassure, and guide us. When we refer to our intuitive voice in this section, we are referring to those Divine thoughts we receive from our intuition, not our squirrelly mind's voice.

The intuitive voice is distinct from our mind's voice. Our intuitive voice is the non-physical voice that is within us, around us, and bigger than us as well. It is a part of us and a part of all that is non-physical. The intuitive voice only loves us, and it sits in a constant place of love, appreciation, joy, and empowerment.

The intuitive voice is always present, looking at every situation through the lens of empowerment, and it speaks to us through our gut feelings. As humans, our minds are either aligned or unaligned with our intuitive voice. As children, this alignment is obvious. Kids only want to be in the moment and have fun. As a result, they are continuously joyful. They do not hold onto grudges, guilt, or anger. Their primary focus is on feeling alive and joyful.

Consider visualizing the two voices as knobs on a radio dial. One knob is labeled mind's voice and the other is labeled intuitive voice. For the majority of adults, the mind's voice is turned up louder than their intuitive voice. In this work, we will raise the volume of our intuitive voice. Kids show us that our intuitive voice is originally loud and strong and that we just need to go back to that. Kids' intuitive voices are louder than their mind's voice. In the average child, the mind's voice starts to get stronger and louder than the intuitive voice between ages four and nine, depending on the child and their family. When the mind's voice gets louder, it judges. It makes someone feel more right or wrong than another person and it wants to put people or things down. As we get older, the mind's voice gets stronger than our intuitive voice, and we start to stay fixated on what the mind wants to say. But if we listen only to the chatter of our mind's voice, we can start to spiral into false beliefs of ourselves as it chatters away in our heads.

To truly be empowered, we need to start to wake up our intuitive voice and quiet the mind's voice. The intuitive voice inside of us never leaves us or gives up on us, and it is always available to us. The intuitive voice is always present in the now. It is not five seconds ahead, or five minutes behind. It is in the moment at hand. The easiest way to begin to wake it up is through meditation. Meditation quiets the mind and has us focus on our intuitive voice, our true gut feeling. Being still and quiet with yourself is a powerful tool you have to raise the volume of your intuitive voice. It keeps us in the present moment which is where our intuitive voice lives. Our mind's voice dwells on the past or future. When we slip into our mind's voice, coming back to our meditation practice and breath will bring us back to the present moment. This process helps us see the mind as distinct and separate from our intuition.

So how do these two voices relate to our emotions? (consciously or not)

It may sound silly that we are talking about emotions, because we all have emotions and we are quite familiar with them. We feel them all day and everyday whether we feel anger, sadness, resentment, joy, freedom, empowerment, our emotions are present. But what exactly is an emotion?

In this context, emotions are energy in motion, and they represent the gap in between our mind's voice and our intuitive voice. For example, when we feel anger at the car that cuts us off in traffic, the emotion of anger is telling us one thing. It tells us that the focus of our mind on the perceived wrongdoing of the car is different from what our intuitive voice is trying to tell us. The gap between these two voices is why we are experiencing anger. On the other hand, when we feel joy, that emotion tells us that in this moment, our mind is focused and aligned with how our intuition is viewing the topic. For example, when we are excited with our child, our mind and intuitive voices are overlapping in the same thought. As a result, we experience joy. When we are able to step back and observe our emotions, we are able to pick up on important messages that we are receiving from our intuition. That leads us into momentum.

Momentum

Momentum is the speed energy moves from point A to B; it is like the energetic byway through the creation process. While momentum has a use in the sciences, for this context, we use it to define the moment-to-moment creation of our emotions. Momentum is the speed and direction at which one thought becomes a second thought and that thought becomes a third thought and so on. It is the speed and weight by which our energy of emotion moves from creation to thoughts and into material form. A negative thought you think once in a while takes you in a negative direction but with very little impact. It's no big deal since the regularity of the thought is so low. But if you think about it constantly and with great emotion and attention to specifics, you create a speeding bullet with a lot of negative momentum.

Positive emotional states generate positive momentum. The better we feel and the more we focus on our positive feelings, the stronger our positive momentum becomes. Once we understand this, we understand it is important to embrace the concept of momentum. Momentum is everything.

For example, when you've just landed that perfect new client who's thrilled to work with you and happy to pay you well, your thoughts generate huge amounts of positive momentum.

You can get as specific as you'd like about your elation, and it will keep attracting more of the same. The same can also happen with negative momentum. Whether the momentum is positive or negative, it attracts more of the same.

Esther Hicks is a leader within the new-thought community. She channels Abraham, a non-physical entity, to teach the Law of Attraction, a Universal Law that we will discuss more in depth later. Together, Abraham and Esther's work on attraction is quite well known, and they have a plethora of books and videos about it. They do a great job describing the occurrence of momentum through the following analogy:

There are logs burning in the fire. If a spark from the fire lands on your sweater and you flick it off quickly, no damage is done. But if you don't notice the spark and you allow it to burn, your sweater is ruined. If you've permitted this particular negative spark to keep burning, forget about finding a-better-feeling thought "right this red-hot minute," as Abraham would say. Your spark has become a raging inferno. Your first negative thought has created a downward spiral momentum. We want to understand the words general and specific thoughts. General thoughts are like thoughts that occur from the airplane viewpoint versus specific thoughts are thoughts that occur from looking under a microscope. For example, a general thought is something like this: it is cold outside. Specific thoughts are more like this: it is minus 40 degrees, with a wind factor of 45 km/hour out of the east dropping the temperature to minus 50 with the windchill and there is more snow in the forecast. Can you feel the difference? Specific thoughts actually speed momentum up and general thoughts slow momentum down. The best thing to do when you get stuck in a downward spiral of negative thoughts is to find a distraction.

Distractions serve to break our momentum (and stop the "raging inferno"), and they can be found in many things: watching a movie, taking a nap, going for a walk in a place of natural beauty, and the list goes on. You can also take charge of your upset mind and say: stop it!

Esther Hicks's favorite distraction is saying "I don't have to think about this now." Interestingly, the truth is, you really don't. Reminding yourself of this truth halts the downward spiral and allows you to come back to the present moment. In doing that, you slow your negative momentum. Now, you may be able to find a better-feeling thought and step onto a different track. If not, reconsider a nap, or one of your other healthy distractions.

Learning to manage your momentum requires you to become more conscious of what your thoughts create in any given moment. If you catch a negative emotional spark early, it's easily realigned. Observing your momentum and learning to break momentum are valuable tools as we continue to learn about intuition. As we said earlier, our emotions can impact how well we can hear our intuition.

Abraham Hicks also teaches us about the vortex and the five steps of manifestation. Everything is energy and we are creators. If you think about it, we are manifesting all day and every day. Nothing happens to us. We are the center of our own Universe, so we are creating what is happening around us all the time. The only way to truly heal is to dive into a deep understanding of ourselves, our thoughts, our emotions and our vibration. The easiest way to understand our vibration is by seeing what is in physical form in our life. At each moment we emit a vibration and we also are creating. The Vortex is Abraham's term for alignment to Source energy. (Or whatever you call Universe, God, All That Is, etc.) Being in the vortex means you're at one with who you really are, you're feeling fabulous, you feel light, you feel flow in the moment and you are in what is called vibrational alignment to your desires.

Five Steps of Manifestation

Step 1. This happens all day long, every day to everyone through experiencing contrast (what we do not want). There is nothing to "do" to activate this step because it happens for us naturally through our awareness that something we don't want is occurring. The purpose of this contrast is to give us incredible clarity of what we DO want.

"Step 1 is contrast helps you to define what you want.
Wanting is born out of it. Clarity of desire."- Abraham

Step 2. In this step, the Universe becomes what we have asked for through our vibrational broadcast and alignment. Source provides what you desire in vibration, (think atoms, subatomic particles swirling around) not yet in physical form. To have what we desire it must move from vibration and subatomic particles into the physical, which is what happens in Steps 3-5.

"Step 2 is Source begins right away,
actualizing around what you're asking for." - Abraham

Step 3. This is where it gets interesting because this step is about allowing. We use our mind and emotions to create a vibration and resonance in our body that is open, easy, flowing, and free. When we are in contrast (Step 1), we are in a different vibration than what we are desiring to have or experience. Allowing is the state of ease, openness and flow. In this state, you are a vibrational and energetic match to your desires.

"You, in a moment, find yourself a vibrational match to what the Vortex is. So there's no gap between your vibration and the vibration of the [Vortex]." - Abraham*

Step 4. Step 4 is simply a mastery of the allowing we begin when we activate Step 3. Step 4 is where we purposely practice creating a momentum or steady state of allowing. It requires conscious and deliberate focus. The more we practice this mastery the easier it is to manage the contrast we experience in Step 1.

"This step is practicing [Step 3] more consistently. By acknowledging that the condition hasn't changed yet but that your alignment has."- Abraham

Step 5. We know contrast happens all the time. In Step 4 we create momentum with the state of allowing. Despite creating this allowing and alignment, we want to remember contrast will always occur, showing us what we truly want. Step 5 is the mastery of allowing, knowing there will be contrast and not allowing it to take us out of our momentum. Here we hold our alignment with ease.

So, while practicing Step 4, we are in alignment, feeling good and living life, then "wham!"—contrast occurs. Because we are not in the wobbly place of Step 1, we understand and are aware there is a ripple in the pond of our vibrational setting and it doesn't activate us into stress or panic because we know we can move through it. This knowing that this will pass strengthens your vibration and heightens your attraction.

Quantum Physics and Vibration

Now that we are aware of our emotions and how they operate, we can take a look at how they affect us on a day-to-day basis. I discovered early in my career as an intuitive that understanding energy is paramount to this work. An understanding of energy allows us to be "in the driver's seat" of our life, where it becomes obvious how important it is to be conscious of our thoughts as a significant aspect of creative energy and momentum.
Everything is made up of atoms, including us, and at a microscopic level, all these atoms are continuously moving and vibrating, even though our eyes can't see it. According to quantum physics, we then emit this atomic vibration as our personal energy. The speed at which our atoms move is

determined by our thoughts, which determine our frequency. Imagine seeing your body not as solid but as millions of cells moving. When we can see our whole body as vibrational, then we can see that all day, every day, in every moment, we are emitting a vibrational frequency based on our thoughts.

Through this vibration, we create. Whatever we vibrate or resonate with (sometimes unconsciously), we attract more of in our life. Maybe you've experienced waking up feeling angry in the morning, only to have your entire day become a pileup of angry experiences, like a snowball rolling down the mountain getting bigger the further it goes. If you are new to this work and practice, simply try this: View yourself as a vibrational magnet. Watch what comes to you, and if you are honest with yourself, you will see that what you are attracting is what is inside of you as well.

The reason most of us are unaware of this anger pileup is simply because we are unaware of our vibration and the emotions that are creating it. It is "normal" to diminish how we feel or even ignore it completely. Many of us come from families which were emotionally unaware. Much of this intuitive work is to start to uncover and wake up our emotional sensitivity to be aware of our emotions. Emotional awareness is the essential key to manifesting. Once we are aware of our patterning and how we feel, we really can start to shift our entire life.

As you go through your day, notice how you feel moment by moment. You may recognize the ease to live with or through dampened emotions, feeling flat or frustrated most of the time. When we realize our ability to create in this world, we start to purposely create an emotional vibration set point for longer than we have in the past, and that's when things start to change around us.

For most of us this is a new concept, and as soon as we start, we are completely astonished at our own ability to have what we really want in our lives and in the world. We take ownership of the power within us. We start to understand why things happen, and more importantly, we understand how we can shift things and create our lives. It takes time, but with patience and regular, daily practice, we see that we are the center of our life. As opposed to thinking that things happen to us, we acknowledge the truth that things we have and experience are brought about through our vibrational match. We begin to realize we create everything in our lives, and when we own this ability to deliberately create, that is when life gets more interesting.

When my client Meredith began working with me, she had end-stage breast cancer. Despite surgery and chemotherapy, it had metastasized to her bones and skin. The skin manifestation is rare in breast cancer and continued to spread daily. Meredith had not given up hope, but she lived her life with chronic anxiety, all the while not knowing why she was anxious. She didn't sleep well, yet was in a supportive, loving relationship. She was doing everything else "right." She was a vegan, exercised regularly, took a lot of supplements, but intuitively, she knew that there was a link between her mind and her cancer. Knowing this, she still could not make the connection that associated her cancer to her state of mind. She started to understand the power of her thoughts, momentum, and vibration. While studying with me, she asked, "So if I am able to switch my vibration to love, are you saying that I can heal?" I explained to her that this was the theory of this practice. Meredith is a determined woman, and she said to me, "That is it! I'm going to start vibrating a positive vibration of love."

She chose a period of a few weeks when she did not have to go to the doctor or have blood work done. With her intention and focus set, she began meditating daily and setting her vibration first thing in the morning. She didn't work and was able to walk on the beach and journal daily. Every time her vibration dropped, she would take a nap or do an activity to purposely break her momentum. She started listening to her intuitive voice and realized that it was loud and powerful. This was all new to her and she found such peace in her inner voice. Twenty-one days from the day she began to deliberately set her vibration and listen to her intuitive voice, her skin discoloration disappeared. It went away completely! When she went to the doctor, the oncologist said, "This is a miracle. Your cancer has gone into remission."

As we shift our thoughts and vibration and tune into our intuition, we decrease the chronic stress we live in, impacting our body in miraculous ways.

We create positive energy around us, and our health can shift dramatically. This positive energy is created by our emotions, momentum, and vibrational frequency. Meredith shifted her thoughts, vibration, and energy, and her cancer went into remission. The energy we give off in the world is a direct indicator of what we will attract, and it is directly impacted by our thoughts.

The energy pattern we create is directly responsible for what we experience, and in turn, it impacts our intuition. Meredith's story is a perfect example of what is possible, but it is in no means a standard. As we dive into this work we become more aware of our physical body, we know our bodies the best, and when we combine that knowledge with advice from our doctor, we can create an incredible healing regimen that works best for us. We believe working with all medicines—east, west, body, mind, and soul—are important. Meredith's unique experience shows us what is possible, but in no way do we advocate dismissing western medicine and skipping a trip to the doctor.

CHAPTER 9

Tuning In Has Its Perks

"A woman knows by intuition, or instinct what is best for herself."
- MARILYN MONROE

Over 2+ decades as a professional intuitive and mystic, I've worked with people from all walks of life and have seen the benefits of using intuition firsthand. The most interesting to me are my C-suite clients—my CEOs, CFOs, CIOs, mostly men. Once they begin this work, they have incredible success in their businesses and lives. Once given the permission to believe in this energy, unknown and seemingly bigger than themselves, they allow themselves to actually experience it firsthand, and it is as if they are set free—like a three-year-old in Disneyland. A whole new world opens up for them. Before they know it, their business has tripled in revenues, their relationships with their partners and family are more meaningful, and life is richer than they ever imagined.

One of my favorite stories to share is about Joe Kudla. We met at a fourth of July party in Laguna Beach, and we started chatting. Before we knew it, we were in a deep conversation about intuition. Soon, a group crowded around, and I began to "read" Joe and a couple of his friends. Through my intuition, I heard loud and clear that I was supposed to support, coach, and cheer him on toward his goals. So, I told him I didn't want any of his money. If he was interested, I would be an intuitive success coach and sounding board in building and redirecting his business. He immediately said "yes" and we began to meet regularly.

One of the biggest pieces of guidance I received for Joe and his company was that his company wasn't in the "right" form. Some changes needed to happen for him and his business. He needed to dig deep and look at his business connections, intentions, and what he truly wanted.

He trusted, he listened, and he went inward. He did all the heavy lifting while I held the space and kept sharing the guidance I received. Over the next three years, Joe turned his business into one of the big hitters in his industry despite not having extensive experience in it. His performance apparel is now carried in major stores as well as having its own brick-and-mortar home. Joe trusted his guidance and he surrounded himself with people who were aligned with his goal: to make comfortable, good looking activewear that reflects the Cali vibe and ease. And that he did. He turned it into a multi-million dollar "athleisure" brand by using his instincts and natural Divine connections.

Another example of using intuition in the "regular" business world is my client Bob Milburn. As one of my C-level clients working with one of the largest broker-dealers in the United States, he was referred to me by his wife. In the beginning, he questioned the need to discuss his beliefs and family life. "We are focusing on my business. Why do I need to talk about my family?" he asked. (It was a very logical question.) I explained to him that our life is holographic, meaning whatever is going on in our family or social relationships is going to show up in our career and business. We have been trained to compartmentalize everything—and everyone. We ask others what their Zodiac sign is, what their Enneagram is, or what their Human Design is in order to understand them, sometimes putting them in a box. Everyone in perfect little boxes, it makes us feel safe and quite separate, frankly. In reality, everything is connected affecting all areas of our lives. Life isn't a series of boxes; it is interconnected and beautifully interwoven. It is holographic.

Once Bob took on this new and different perspective of his life—family, career, health, relationships, and wealth—his life shifted dramatically. He began to see how his agitation about personal situations impacted his productivity in his business. By working on trusting his intuition, his confidence grew. He expanded his career and has since opened up his own thriving consulting business.

Using our intuitive talents helps us to have clarity and connection to our purpose and what we want in life. It lets us cut through the minutiae of drama and tells us when something is just not "right." Using our intuition our creativity, expands our self-knowledge, and creates ease in making decisions. With intuition, many things become clear:

- You know when you can trust someone.
- You find answers within yourself versus outside of yourself.
- You lose the fear of saying yes to your dreams.
- You have the courage to say no and mean it.
- You expand your self-esteem.
- You trust your choices more.
- You gain practical information about anything.
- You empower yourself to live the life you've always wanted.
- You reinforce your boundaries so you don't give too much of yourself away.
- You amp up your productivity.
- You add quality to your life.

So often, we are riddled with confusion, doubt, fear, and anxiety, we don't have to look far to see all of it prevalently lodged deep within our society. It has even been said that 95 percent of our health ailments are stress related, and one of the biggest components of stress is anxiety. Anxiety originates from our mind running on perpetual fear of the future, fear of our choices, anxiety about the unknown and past decisions. Eckhart Tolle defines stress as *"the desire for life to be different, wanting whatever the moment is to be something else, a form of insanity because it can only be what it is."* Anxiety requires acceptance, not resignation. It requires acknowledging where we are and accepting it as it is rather than wishing the present was something other than what it is.

What if you could trust your decisions? Another study was done in 2006 on intuitive decision-making for large purchases (like a car or house). These results were compared to logical decision-making. What researchers found was when studying all of the logical and technical material about a car purchase spurred a decision based solely on logic, the purchaser was only satisfied with the car 25 percent of the time. This is in contrast to the 60 percent who were pleased with their purchase after making a decision using intuitive decision-making, a phrase coined to describe a quick, instinctive decision. This study showed that those who went with their intuition and purchased the car that "felt" right to them were more satisfied in the long run. While knowing the mile-per-gallon efficiency and safety rating of a car is important, as the buyer we know intuitively which car we want in our lives. When we go with that intuitive choice, we choose the car that is best for us.

Waking up our intuition has huge benefits and certainty of our decisions is one of them. One of the most common things people say to me about waking up their intuition is that there is a feeling of "knowing," a sense of ease. Our intuition, our superpower, connects us with something much bigger than ourselves. Having access to our superpower can feel comforting, it allows our feeling of inner connection to soar. That inner connection is everything! I don't believe that we are meant to come to this planet to be alone and struggle. Waking up our intuition can bring us solace and a sense of comfort knowing that it is always with us, guiding us to what is best for ourselves.

How does this transition into our lives and health? The body's natural state is wellness. Our health is a byproduct of our mind. Hence, the expression mind-body. The mind-body complex is an entity of its own, and through this work, we can see that they are connected. What we think affects our body, and what we do affects our mind. We all can identify with our minds and the struggles it gives us, creating stress and anxiety. The body's physical symptoms are a reflection of the human mind's agitation. And yet we also have a spiritual mind—a superpower connection, our intuition. If we accessed our spiritual mind more, would we see our anxiety and stress states decrease, getting rid of the physical body's agitation? The body's natural state is wellness.

Divi has had the benefit of working with a lot of people on their health issues, given her background as a doctor. She's seen the physical connection between intuition and health so often she could write a book about it. Once, Divi worked with a woman who was struggling with anxiety, hated her job, and felt trapped. She was 42 years old and wanted a baby, but was struggling with infertility. She had a long history of over-exercise, eating disorders, and body dysmorphia. When her anxiety peaked, she'd started having panic attacks which left her curled up in a fetal position on the bathroom floor.

The woman studied with Divi and I extensively, and started to understand her mind, energy, momentum, and thoughts. She began to see her anxiety was directly linked to ignoring her intuition. As she woke up her natural innate superpower, she realized her anxiety was a way to avoid listening to her own inner voice. Her speed in life and overexercise were ways to control her life because she had lost touch with her inner-knowing. After studying with us for nine months, she got pregnant naturally after years of infertility. Now, she lives with her beautiful baby, using her superpower to listen and raise her child with love. Waking up our intuition not only benefits us but also the communities and people around us. Living our lives aligned with our intuition can have major impacts on many facets of our lives.

CHAPTER 10

Who's Who?

"Follow your instincts. That's where true wisdom manifests itself."

- OPRAH

Though we all have the superpower of intuition, there are different levels of practicing it. At the foundation of our being, we are all psychic, which at its core is the ability to be intuitive. A psychic is nothing more than you and me at this very moment. All humans are intuitive and therefore psychic. From there, people can develop a deeper level of intuition through training and practice.

Psychic

Everyone is psychic. It is part of our innate being, like breathing. And while we all have the ability to access our intuition, it does require a level of awareness and consistent practice. Psychics don't have a specific look or smell. Yes, the word may summon the smells of patchouli, visions of crystal balls and retro 60s hippie clothes dripping with esoteric symbols, but the stereotype is inaccurate. Psychic looks like life, nature, and this moment. It is exactly who we are in this second. There is a big qualifying difference between a psychic and an intuitive. An intuitive is trained and a psychic isn't. A psychic is shooting from the hip, relaying information through their personal filter and their own wounds. An intuitive learns to set aside their own judgment, allowing the true Divine Guidance to speak through them.

Intuitive

An intuitive is a psychic who has received training and extensive practice. They have trained and honed their skills. As professional intuitives, we use our intuition and skills to be of service to others, through coaching and doing readings, for others as well as for ourselves.

I have seen many gifted intuitives who are fantastic at tapping into their intuition to do readings for other people, yet in their own lives, they haven't taken accountability for their own life situations. So many of my successful clients have told me they didn't trust the "new age" dogma because they watched intuitives share their Guidance, only to not listen to it themselves. For example, one intuitive would say, "Don't smoke. It's not good for your energy and creates congestion," only to walk outside after the session for a cigarette break. This presents a big incongruence between the words they spoke and their way of being, and the impact is the message falls short and isn't received because of the inauthenticity.

In this line of work, walking the talk is essential. That is the biggest difference between an intuitive and a mystic. An intuitive, like all of us, has access to Divine information and has been trained, a mystic not only has access to this information and training as an intuitive does but they also "walk the talk."

Mediumship

All mediums are psychic, but not all psychics are mediums.

Mediums are trained intuitives who plug their antenna into the radio station of deceased loved ones and hold the channel for longer time frames. Holding this specific vibration longer allows them to get detailed characteristics, quirks, and personality of the deceased.

The powerful magic that happens through mediumship is the healing of unresolved issues with deceased loved ones. Be it anger, shame, hurt, or resentment, this is where healing conversations can happen. Receiving direction or guidance through mediumship isn't the same as receiving it from the Divine. When we connect with deceased loved ones, we must remember they haven't become saints because they've transitioned. They hold their same personality traits as they did when they existed in the physical world. They have more insights and a higher perspective because they have transitioned, but they still have their human quirks and personalities. If your Aunt Clara was staunchly against drinking alcohol when she was alive, her guidance today would be the same as if she was in the physical: Stay away from that hooch!

When I went to my first intuition workshop, the teacher kept using "Uncle Fred" as an example of a deceased loved one all throughout the day. I was moved, and my path was validated, since I had an Uncle Fred who'd recently died. Everything she said during the workshop was my uncle's personality, 100 percent. I knew it was him reaching out to me through her to show me that this connection and work were real.

While mediumship is a powerful healing tool, it isn't the purest form of the intuitive channels. The reason I say this is because, as we mention above, our deceased loved ones retain their personalities so there is still condition and judgment present. When you tap into your Divine Guidance that is the highest channel as it doesn't hold human aspects; there is no judgment, only 100 percent love and complete neutrality. Utilizing mediumship to help yourself or others through anger, unresolved issues, or upset is definitely a fast track to healing and moving on, but let us be very clear here: while this level of communication is powerful in healing, it still holds condition, duality, and fear. Only tuning into our Divine Guidance will bring 100 percent unconditional love and Divine direction.

If you want to connect with your deceased Uncle Bill because he was a fantastic golfer and you want some tips to up your game, definitely use mediumship. If you want help with your money situation and your grandmother was an epic money manager, definitely connect with her. If your father deserted you early in your life and you never had the relationship you wanted, use mediumship to heal and see the reason your soul chose this lesson, this relationship. If you were adopted and your biological parents chose not to be in your life, you can heal that and so much more through mediumship. If you lost a child, regardless of age (even from miscarriage or abortion), you can connect with that soul through mediumship.

Mediumship is a powerful tool when used properly and with respect. This is why we see some sacred texts that say practicing or partaking in mediumship is strictly forbidden. I'd like to shine a little light on this piece of information. What these texts are alluding to is the danger of *only* following the guidance of deceased loved ones. To put deceased loved ones on a pedestal higher than our Divine intuition can be harmful. It's a good idea to remember that we each have a part in this tapestry of life. This is why relying solely on your deceased loved ones for guidance isn't the highest connection.

Our deceased loved ones are always keeping tabs on us, even if we were abandoned, adopted, or abused. They are here. Consider this thought: if you have children, wouldn't you want to see their children and their children's children? Energetically supporting our lineage is what our deceased loved ones want, and that's why so much healing happens through mediumship. The release of the vibrations of anger, hurt, and disappointment allows for more light and power to come into our bodies and energize us, our legacy, and our lineage.

Even though your deceased loved ones are with you, it doesn't mean they are watching you in the shower or in times of intimacy. What I have been shown through this work is our deceased loved ones see us as energy, as our light body (our personal energy field and structure), not as our physical body.

In short, an intuitive can choose to be a medium or not through extensive training connecting to the deceased. However, you do not have to use mediumship to become intuitive.

Mystic

A mystic lives with their intuition all of the time, knowing when to turn its volume up or down. They are always sensing—always listening and looking because they use this as a constant connection, a powerful communication that allows them to contribute to others and the world. As a mystic, there is a deeper, more subtle state of life than what "appears" in day-to-day living. They know unity is the primary focus both internally and externally as they seek the truth about themselves and their relationship to others. A mystic is a person who believes in the empowerment of the spirit within them and others, who knows that magic and miracles are possible and present in everyday life because they experience them regularly. These are people who practice their intuition, walk the talk, and know that everyone is a part of the whole. A mystic doesn't feel they need to prove their abilities or perform parlor tricks with their gifts and talents. They know intuition is a naturally given ability we all have. This goes beyond specific religious ideology or dogmas because they know there is a kernel of truth in every religious tradition—something that lies beyond the surface.

Now that you understand these subtle but significant differences between the types of intuitives, it's important to remember these as you move forward on this voyage of intuition so you can choose HOW you will work with your Divine Guidance as you move forward. So, how do you get started practicing intuition? The first step in accessing your intuition is understanding and developing your primary channel. Knowing your key access point, you can begin to notice, practice, and activate your skills more directly.

PART 2

Intuition

Tools, Tips, and Treasures

"When I stepped into my intuition, the first thing I realized was I had been using it my whole life without knowing. This new awareness led me to a deeper connection with myself, the world, and the sacred."

- LYNNETTE BROWN

CHAPTER 1

You Are Here

"Everyone has unique development and experience of their intuition."

For us to say there is only one way to cultivate and expand intuition would be erroneous and quite disturbing, given that this natural ability is as simple as taking a breath and as complex as synthesizing oxygen into strong bodies, muscles, and energy.

There will be times when you may stand at a fork in the road—a fork that asks you to choose to believe in your intuition or not. You may ask yourself, "Do I believe? Do I trust this intuition thing?" or "Do I not? Is it just a bunch of poppycock?" When and if you reach this fork, I want you to know that in my 30-plus years on this spiritual path, I have found that in all situations, trusting my intuition has kept my head above water, but I had to be willing to trust it enough to look like an idiot at times. Since using intuition looks different for everyone, we have to be willing to stand out to use it and ultimately do what's best for ourselves.

If you find yourself wondering if you dare share your gifts, I always like to look to the teachers who have walked before me and learn from them. For example, Mahatma Gandhi sums it up in his nonviolent philosophy in "*Freedom's Battle.*" He says every movement goes through four stages: "First they ignore you; then they abuse you; then they crack down on you and then you win." The *satyagraha*, a Sanskrit word for "holding onto truth," shows us that we must follow our Divine Guidance, our Truth, even if others don't agree. We must, like the word implies, hold onto our individual truth. We must persist in accessing our truth and not let others stop us. While everyone's experience and development of intuition are unique, there are certain patterns that can get in our way when we try to access our intuition: a couple of big ones are isolation and fear.

One of the patterns that seems to repeat itself consistently with intuitives is the feeling of isolation. Ninety-nine percent of all intuitives I have known, taught, shared the stage with, worked with, or coached expressed this experience of feeling completely alone—even with family and friends surrounding them. Unknowingly, this can get in the way of using our intuition or alter the messages that are coming through. Feeling alone even around family and friends? If this sounds familiar, don't make any assumptions quite yet. This awareness will come in handy when you are receiving intuitive messages, but this is also a clue about how your intuitive skills developed.

The message here is to stop focusing on the thought: "My family doesn't understand me." The truth is, our families aren't meant to understand us. They are meant to give us a foundation to build our intuition. They give us the challenges and relationships that help us develop our superpower.

Many intuitives refrain from choosing a side in situations. Often, they do this because of their deep feeling of loneliness. Choosing a side will only separate them further from others. Instead, some intuitives, subconsciously, tune in to what others expect or want so they can "give" what is wanted. They are sensitive and don't want to be the odd man out. Because of that, they learn to be people pleasers to avoid conflict early on in their lives. By doing this, they feel wanted, desired, and included, and their loneliness is abated in the short-term. This deep-rooted loneliness gets in the way of intuitives developing their intuition because they fear standing out. Rather than using their superpower, they'd rather fit in with others to abate their loneliness. Further down the road, their loneliness could get in the way of sharing an authentic, intuitive message from the Divine, especially if they are always trying to please people. The message could come out distorted especially if their sole intention is to please someone. Recognizing our loneliness now and understanding what it is trying to tell us is important when understanding and developing our intuition.

Personally, I developed my intuition as a survival mechanism when I was young. It started as a strategy to make sure I didn't get kicked to the curb like my father did. One day, I came home and he was gone, as if he had vanished into thin air. At five years old, I understood that to stay safe at home I needed to play the role of being a good girl. I needed to do the "right" stuff, and I needed to obey my mom so that what happened to my dad wouldn't happen to me.

This made me a hypervigilant child, attuning myself to anything that would be considered "out of place" or "wrong." I spent my time constantly scanning each moment for signs that I would be the next to walk the plank and be cast aside.

Fear was how my intuition developed. On some level, I believed it was the only thing that would keep me safe. I needed to know what was coming so I could prepare for the worst. It took me decades to unpack my hypervigilance, and I have been able to turn that into, as my friends jokingly say, "my relentlessness." We all have this talent, but we've forgotten how to turn it on and use it in our lives. Our experiences as children happened the way they did so that our intuition could develop.

Imagine the events in your life that brought you here. It could be something you resented for most of your life, or something that you didn't think was important. Everything in your life has happened so that it would bring you here. Everything has helped you develop your intuition. Now, let's learn how to tune into it.

CHAPTER 2

Let's Be Clair

"With that strange knowing that comes over me, like a clairvoyance, I know that I am sure of myself and my enormous and alarmingly timeless love for you; which will always be."

- SYLVIA PLATH

Intuition is an energy of heightened awareness that comes through our bodies. It comes through in four main forms, and we call these the four clairs: clairvoyance, clairaudience, claircognizance, and clairsentience. Everyone has all four of these abilities available to them, no one is left out. However, generally, in the beginning, one of the four clairs is a little stronger than the rest. We call this your dominant channel because it's receiving information despite all the contrast and noise blocking out the rest. All of this is a mouthful, right? Let's break it down so it's clear.

Clairvoyance

Clairvoyance is Divine seeing. It is the one clair that everyone seems to know thanks to Hollywood's scary movies. The movies depict clairvoyance as a creepy capability that leads nowhere except to horrifying experiences. Trust us, clairvoyance is not that!

Clairvoyance, like every channel, comes through differently for everyone. Take our thoughts for example: we don't all think or process information the same, and we definitely don't see things the same. Please don't let the idea of individuality turn you off because you're thinking, "My intuitive way won't be right." Nothing is further from the truth. We let you know this up front so that you avoid judging your skills.

Clairvoyance can be received in multiple ways, some of which you may not considered. Being psychic doesn't look a certain way, and you may even be surprised to learn that you've already been using it without knowing it.

Has this ever happened to you?

- You had a vivid dream which later came true.
- You "lost" your keys or wallet. Then, a picture of the place where you left the item flashed into your mind.
- As you were driving, you saw a mental image of the car ahead of you turning left. Two minutes later, the car turned left exactly as you'd visualized it.
- You suddenly saw an image of a person in your mind's eye. Later that day, they called, texted, or reached out.

If one or any of these have happened to you, you were accessing your clairvoyance. These experiences are quite normal, but we rarely attribute them to clairvoyance.

Over the decades we've been teaching intuition and energy work, we always have so many people screaming, "That's what I want! I want to see!" But, when it comes down to receiving and actually "seeing," they become frightened and shut down. The first thing we want to share about clairvoyance is that there is nothing to fear. If you follow our directions deliberately, you will open up your channel with ease and in a manner that is comfortable for you.

The information that comes forth through our intuition is not meant to scare us; it is truly a way for us to stay connected to our purpose and path. It also is the best way for us to stay safe. Yes, that's what we said: safe! Would you prefer to walk down a dark alley with or without a flashlight? Intuition is your flashlight. Clairvoyance is your beacon of light in the dark. It is guiding you, and even though the flashlight can't dissipate all of the shadows, it allows you to see further than you could without it.

The chakra associated with clairvoyance is the third eye located between the eyebrows. If you aren't familiar with chakras, put simply, they are energy centers, vortexes in your body that receive and broadcast energy. And the energy center for clairvoyance is located between the eyebrows in a place known as the third eye.

Because of all the Hollywood hype, we want to show you some of the natural ways clairvoyance manifests. Receiving information through clairvoyance isn't always seeing something solid outside of you, as is so often depicted in movies. Though that is one way it reveals itself, it is not the **only** way. This Divine Guidance is also delivered through dreams, daydreaming (not to be confused with imagining or visualizing), mental pictures, signs (literally and figuratively), mental movies, pictures in nature (clouds and trees that look like something), colors, and even orbs that show up in photos.

Allowing your clairvoyance to open up requires trust and belief, as does all intuition. Without that trust and belief, it would be a crapshoot. Sometimes it will be spot on, and other times it will be completely off. Building belief in yourself will grow as you play with your intuition and discover how helpful it can be.

Clarisentience

Clarisentience is receiving divine information through one's feelings and senses. An example of this is when you walk into a new place and get the "sense" you don't want to be there, or when something happens and you feel "goosebumps." Clairsentience is about feeling, and its channel of broadcast—or where it comes through—is the heart chakra. Interestingly enough, while we all have this clair, so many of us ignore it and chalk it up to coincidence. Clairsentience is one of the most overlooked clairs because everyone feels, and because we all feel, we often disregard the messages that come with those "feelings."

It can also show up like pressure changes in the room as well as actual physical feelings and sensations. It is like walking into a room and having the "sense" of what's going on even though you have never been in the room, or maybe, you don't know the people who are there. As we've already discussed, we are trained to disregard our feelings and senses, but they can impact us negatively if we continue to ignore them. These impacts can manifest as gaining weight, depression, anxiety, physical pain, and emotional outbursts, to name just a few.

Clairsentience also comes in the form of smells and tastes as well. When I first experienced it I thought someone was smoking outside my office, when the message was about my client's smoking habit. If you find yourself smelling flowers or another fragrance that isn't in your surroundings, that is your clairsentience.

The good news about clairsentience is once you are aware of it, things become much easier. So much about clairsentience is trusting your senses. An example of this is when someone says, "I'm not sure why I chose to do or say that. I just trusted my instincts." Clairsentience is the ultimate guide if we can allow ourselves to be aware of it.

Clairaudience

Clairaudience is receiving intuition through hearing. Yes, hearing! Before you jump to conclusions about being locked away due to "hearing" voices, consider this: we all receive clairaudience, but we don't associate it with intuition. We disregard it and toss it aside.

Intuition through hearing—located at the ear chakras—comes in multiple forms, some of which can be confusing. One of the ways it shows up is through ringing in your ears. This ringing is not tinnitus, which is constant. This ringing is a download of information which may happen for a few minutes, not all day. The difficulty with this is that the download isn't audible as such, which requires trust, yet again, to understand that it is okay to not know what message we are hearing.

Other ways you receive clairaudience is through overhearing a conversation, one that you are not a part of, and the information you "overhear" answers questions that you have been pondering. And if you are hearing the same thing repetitively, whether it's a song lyric, a statement, or a quote, they are all forms of clairaudience. The guidance you hear may be right next to your ear as if it is whispering, or it could even be in your own mind.

Any guidance that comes forward through your hearing that answers a question or directs you in some way is clairaudience. Most people will disregard hearing that song or jingle every time they turn around, but in truth, it is their intuition.

People who use clairaudience as their dominant clair are usually very direct and to the point, and they may sound disconnected. A big detriment to clairaudience has been our increased use of headphones. Our culture is tuning out, walking around with ear buds crammed in our ears, unaware of what's going on around us, which is okay in small doses. Using earbuds for more than three hours consecutively can impact your clairaudience sensitivity. We recommend giving your ears an opportunity to hear what is around you daily. It's amazing what you can hear when you listen through your clairaudience.

Claircognizance

Claircognizance is receiving intuition through thought. There is a very subtle difference between "thinking" and receiving thought blocks, claircognizance is NOT thinking. The energy center for claircognizance is the crown chakra. With claircognizance, you receive information about something you didn't have any previous knowledge about (and you don't know how you know it).

While all the clairs can seem tricky in the beginning, this is one that gave me a bit of a challenge. I struggled because I believed, when I started, that my thoughts and everything I thought was mine. This may sound strange, but consider that we have 60,000-80,000 thoughts per day and 2,500-3,300 thoughts per hour. According to the National Science Foundation, 80 percent of these thoughts are negative, so it is easy to jump to the conclusion that our thoughts are ours. But what about the idea you had for an invention that someone else invents? If intuition is energy, doesn't it stand to reason that some of that energy is through our thoughts?

The claircognizant person is a deep and clear thinker who receives information through their thoughts and ideas. These thoughts or concepts just suddenly appear like a download on a computer. Of course, this can create a lot of frustration because we may not understand how we got it. Claircognizance brings new ideas, solutions, and understanding. The challenge with this clair is being aware of the ego (or lower self). It will want to weave an extravagant story about the information to explain it—oftentimes it is a negative story, too. With claircognizance, we are often called "know it alls" because we look for meaning in everything, which puts trust at the heart of this matter, as it is in all the clairs—but with claircognizance, trust is even more important. When this is your dominant clair, you may have a tendency to want to be a hermit in your office or home. Because of this, it is essential for claircognizants to get out in the world and be social.

CHAPTER 3

X Marks The Spot

"The privilege of a lifetime is to become who you truly are."
- CARL JUNG

Are you wondering what your main or dominant clair is? In beginning to discover your main channel, try this: watch a movie or imagine a movie in your mind. What is the main element of the movie for you? Is it the sounds of the movie? Is it the setting, colors, and textures? Is it the feelings you have for the characters or the situation the movie is set in? Is it what you know may happen or the dialogue? Knowing which aspect of the movie you notice the most, start paying attention to it and see which messages or signs come through for you in that form.

What if while doing this exercise you can't let go of your logical, analytical, left-brain thinking? We don't expect you to completely let go of your logical mind; we are simply asking to add the creative and intuitive aspects of your right-brain mind. The way we do this is by first acknowledging our fears. Ask yourself, "What am I afraid of when I consider using my intuition?" Allow those fears to come forward—maybe they're our childhood nightmares, or even remnants from those scary movies we watched. And as you look at those fears, ask yourself, am I going to let this stop me? If not, let's explore your dominant clair. Below is a quiz that will help you get a stronger sense of your dominant channel.

Identifying Your Dominant Clair

We've created this easy quiz to help you determine your primary channel of intuition. Primary doesn't mean that the other clairs aren't there; it just means this clair is the strongest and therefore the easiest for you to access. Remember, it is about ease and fun.

Dominant Clair Quiz

After each scenario or question, circle the response that is your first instinct—the one with the strongest pull—even if each answer applies to you. Choose the first and strongest response so you can determine your dominant clair.

1. When watching a movie, what jumps out at you the most?

a. How the characters are interacting and responding to each other
b. The plot or story line, figuring it out
c. The cinematography, the costume design, the setting
d. The soundtrack, dialects of the characters, languages

2. When you are in the mood for fun, what is your favorite choice?

a. Dancing, exercising, walking in nature
b. Going to an inspirational event or lecture
c. Taking in a movie or art gallery
d. Going to a concert to see your favorite band

3. When you are asked a difficult question, how do you respond?

a. From an emotional feeling level, trusting your gut
b. Know what to say right off the top of your head
c. Look at the question and see the possible answers
d. Ask for guidance and listen

4. After taking an amazing vacation, how do you remember your trip?

a. How it felt
b. What you learned about your visit
c. All the sites, people, and landscape
d. All the sounds from the waves of the ocean to the dialect of the locals

5. When meeting new people, what is the first thing you notice about them?

a. How you feel about them
b. Know right away if you click with them
c. Their style of clothes, height, color of their eyes, hair
d. Interested in hearing about who they are, the tone of their voice

6. When you are under a deadline at work, how do you manage your project?

a. The team agrees on what is needed and you work with your team to achieve it
b. You know what needs to be done and you do it
c. You envision the results your boss wants and you go for it
d. By listening to your inner voice, you move forward to complete the project

7. When you have a new idea, what do you do?

a. Get a sense of it
b. Know it's beneficial
c. Visualize it consistently until it's crystal clear
d. Consult or ask experts

8. When someone is not telling you the truth, how do you respond?

a. You feel jittery and notice something feels off
b. You know the truth regardless of what is being said
c. You look to see what shows up and see if it resonates with you
d. Notice what you are hearing and then choose

9. Which of these four colors are you drawn to?

a. Green
b. Purple
c. Blue
d. Pink

10. When someone around you isn't feeling well, what do you do?

a. You can feel their discomfort, and you try to comfort them
b. You know what they need to do to feel better and you tell them
c. You can see the area of their body where the discomfort lies
d. You listen to your guidance on how to support them.

Now total up how many you have in each category.

How many A's did you circle?
How many B's did you circle?
How many C's did you circle?
How many D's did you circle?

Now you have a sense of your dominant clair:

All A responses are = Clairsentience
All B responses are = Claircognizance
All C responses are = Clairvoyance
All D responses = Clairaudience

Congratulations on determining your dominant clair! While one clair is typically prominent, you may have a couple that outscored the rest. Have no fear! We all have the ability to use all four clairs, and this quiz was only meant to determine which one is dominant. If you had two or three dominant clairs, keep that in mind as you start to tune into your intuition.

CHAPTER 4

Navigating Truth

"Everything will line up perfectly when knowing and living the truth becomes more important than looking good."
- ALAN COHEN

Now that you know how your intuition is showing up in your life. How do you know if you are doing it right? How do you know that what you're hearing is truly your Divine Guidance and not something you're making up or your ego?

When clients first start working with their intuition, one of the first things they ask is, "How will I know if I'm doing it right?" My answer may shock you, so I'll say it slowly. **You can't get it wrong!** Yes, you read that right, my friend. If your heart and intentions are in the right place, you will always get an intuitive "hit" that makes a difference. A hit is any knowledge or information you receive from your intuition. A hit isn't any information that comes through; it's the information that resonates with your client that hits the bullseye and is undeniably accurate and precise.

There is something important to note about intuition: wherever your focus is, that's the level of intuitive communication you will receive. In other words, if your focus is on how everyone is out to get you, all of the guidance you receive will be from the perspective of a victim.

When you sit down to do a reading for someone else, it is a special connection and relationship, one that my colleagues and I take very seriously. It's not just the person in front of you who is being read in that session. You, the intuitive guide, are also being read. If the intuitive guide isn't walking the talk, doesn't take care of themselves, or is focused on a split vibration, the clarity of their intuitive message won't be on the deepest possible level. When that happens, you have what we call a "dark reading". A dark reading is what happens when an intuitive's readings are filtered through the spiritual colander of fear. Because of this the guidance that comes through is foggy, lacking clarity, amplifying shadow aspects. In these types of readings recipients may experience heaviness, confusion, uncertainty or a general imbalanced energy feeling. So, you see the importance of self-care and walking the talk.

I want to be very clear here, folks. We aren't saying that all intuitive readings are going to be sunshine and unicorns. Uh, no, that's not how it works. A real intuitive will tell you the truth in a way that your personality can hear, digest, and be open to receiving. They won't shame you or judge you for mistakes. They'll show you how each of those steps (or life events) were necessary in understanding yourself, your connection to your intuition and the Universe. The work in understanding your path isn't gravy, it's challenging and many times uncomfortable. That discomfort is not the same as the heavy confusion a dark reading dishes out.

The best intuitives treat each session like communion with the Divine. They feel blessed and honored to be the vessel of communication, and they treat it with respect.

So, here's the scoop on how to know what is Divine Guidance and what is false, ego-driven guidance:

Divine Guidance is Soft and Easy

It may be a quiet whisper in your ear that says, "Check your tires" as you are getting ready for work. Then as you drive to the office, you notice a gas station sign that says, "Free Air." You've never seemed to notice that sign before today, even though you drive this way to work all the time. As you are walking into your office, you hear a coworker talking about an accident on the freeway caused by a big truck having a blowout. This is where our logical mind would say these are all coincidences, but they aren't. It is the Universe reaching out to communicate: "Check your tires!!" Eventually, if we are listening, we give into the subtle nudges and actually check our tires to find out that we were moments from a blowout because of a nail. Good thing we stopped and checked, right?

False Guidance is Harsh and Critical

False guidance has the big harsh voice of ego. False guidance says, "Don't do that! How could you?" False guidance is the voice of judgment, edgy and cold, often yelling to get your attention. You know you are dabbling in false guidance when you are feeling exhausted, disconnected, torn, and lacking clarity or inspiration. False guidance can seem tricky in the beginning because it can sound like the harsh voice we use when we speak to ourselves.

The most frequent question I get asked is, "How do I know the difference between true and false guidance? My answer is this: by noticing how it feels. This is why our awareness is so important. Our consciousness of energy is what directs us into knowing when our guidance is true and when it is false or from the ego. When I first started deliberately working with my intuition, it was handy to have a little guide.

"Divine Guidance is soft and easy.
Divine Guidance is repetitive and consistent."

On the next page, there is a list that helped me when I first started working with my intuition, and hopefully, it will help make your maiden voyage through the sea of intuition a little easier.

The Truth Detector Test

Divine Guidance	False Guidance
• Repetitive	• Switches subjects impulsively
• Calm tone	• Immature tone
• Strong	• Sneaky
• Sounds familiar	• Out of sync with your needs
• Empowers you	• Diminishes you
• Feels loving	• Feels draining and exhaustive
• Direct and to the point	• Wordy and full of criticism
• Sounds supportive/motivational	• Uses harsh critical words
• Assures that you can do it	• Tears down your confidence
• Usually uses "you"	• Uses "I" constantly
• Can come on suddenly	• Comes slowly in response to worry
• Safe/feels protective	• Scary

So now you have a sense of what your dominant clair is as well as what true Divine Guidance looks and feels like, let's start unlocking your gift. Are you ready?

CHAPTER 5

Ready, Set, Go

"Once we give up searching for approval we often find it easier to earn respect."
- GLORIA STEINEM

Now that you know your dominant clair and how to tell the difference between false and true guidance, let's start using your Divine Guidance. The best way to start using it is to tune in and get information for yourself.

Below we give you suggestions on how to prepare yourself and your environment along with some easy steps to begin tuning in with the most success, especially in the beginning. One thing I have witnessed repeatedly in my years of study and practice with intuition, it can be more difficult to allow Divine Guidance in for ourselves than it is for us to receive messages for others. This is because of our beautiful mind, our ego doesn't want us to alter from our programming, "don't change the channel we're surviving just fine" it screams. The preparations and setting the stage, so to speak, are as important as your process to get there.

Receiving Guidance for Yourself

1. **Create Sacred Space.** What is sacred space? Sacred space is a place where you can leave the chaos of the rest of the world behind and go inward with reverence and respect. This isn't the same kind of "place" as a physical location. Sacred space is created from within and the more you return to it, the more your energy builds. If you are doing a personal reading, it can enhance your abilities in the beginning to use the same physical location as your sacred space. You may not know this, but locations hold energy. That is why people make pilgrimages all over the world to locations of spiritual significance. These locations

hold energy of past experiences. As a practicing intuitive, remember to be present to regularly clearing clutter and bottled emotions out of your sacred space.

2. **Ground Yourself.** Make sure you are completely clear and present. Grounding is an essential exercise to help you feel rooted and connected. It involves doing things that ground or electrically reconnect us to the earth.

    - **Sit (or stand) in a quiet place.** You can do this outside in nature if you would like, but it's not a requirement.

    - **Visualize.** Imagine roots streaming from the bottoms of your feet, continuing to grow downward, connecting the soles of your feet deep into the core of the earth. Breathe in through your mouth and out through your nose. Visualize all the toxins, anxiety, and stress flowing through these roots and dissolving into Mother Earth. Visualize green healing energy coming back up these roots through the soles of your feet, running up your legs to your heart, moving up into your chest, down each arm, then up through your throat, head, and through your crown chakra, filling you with healing, grounding energy.

    - **Be Present With Yourself.** Feel the sensations in your body. Breathe deeply to become present with yourself and your surroundings. Checking in with your breath is an effective way to make sure you remain grounded. Connecting to your body through breath enables you to ground yourself and be present to any Divine Guidance, signs or symbols that may come through. Once you've prepared yourself and your surroundings, you are ready to start tapping into intuition for yourself.

3. **Ask The Question.** This may sound a bit ridiculous, but hear us out. The clarity of what you are truly wanting to know is essential. Questions you desire to receive Divine Guidance about need to be specific and about something that matters to you. Case in point is compound questions, like "Will I get this job and have incredible success?" Compound questions can be difficult for a beginning intuitive. As you advance in your abilities, you will be able to direct your intuition more deeply, in the beginning, it is difficult to separate the answers you receive for each part of the question at once. A simple question would be "Will I get this job offer?" And perhaps, the follow up question will be "Will I have great success?" When the questions are separated, it makes it easier to get a hit for each one.

4. **Listen.** Using our intuition to receive Divine Guidance for ourselves is a helpful tool, and it's important to be clear on what you are seeking to know. This requires us to be as free of judgment and full of compassion as possible for ourselves. Once you've asked the question listen actively to connect on a deeper level. Listen to hear, see, know, feel, and understand. Active listening is done from the heart without judgment.

5. **Receive** The Divine Guidance. Allow any messages to come through. Don't try to force them, simply sit with what is coming forward for you. The most important thing I learned during my intuitive training is to be ready to receive guidance NOW. What I mean by that is to ask the question, take a breath, and start receiving without censoring the information. If you are utilizing automatic writing to receive your guidance, relay the question and start writing with a clear mind and intention to receive the answers to your question. Automatic writing is a practice of sitting with a pen in hand freeing your mind and allowing the Divine energy to move your hand, leaving you with a written message. If you are sharing guidance with another person, simply start sharing anything you are receiving.

6. **Don't Censor Yourself.** Don't think about or rationalize what you receive. Censoring is a short path to stunting your intuition. If you start to panic or doubt because you aren't getting anything, remember this: IT IS IMPOSSIBLE TO GET NOTHING! Everything, every single thing you see, feel, think, sense and hear, is part of the Divine Guidance you are receiving. This is why it is important to hold your sacred space. Everything matters: the pressure in the room shifting, the bird flying past your window, the movie clip you remember out of nowhere, or the song that pops into your head are all a part of your intuitive guidance. When you realize your intention is to be connected to the Divine, your "need" to get it right is overruled by your soul's desire to connect and experience it. After you receive the message, translate your intuitive symbols and vocabulary for yourself. Take care to make note of everything you receive, whether it be through feeling, hearing, sensing or knowing.

7. **Notice Symbols and Signs.** The Universe is always speaking to us; we are usually the ones who aren't listening. Often, it is a repetitive symbol that will get our attention and relay a message. As you continue to build your intuition, you will start to receive shorthand messages which will speed up your reception of Divine messages. In the beginning, we suggest that you create your own Symbol Legend. Symbols are shorthand from the Divine that help us understand blocks of information rather than using words. They are shortcuts to intuitive access points for us to use. They have personal meanings connected to them. For example, some folks may see yellow roses and think of friendship or devotion. For me, yellow roses have multiple meanings. First, they represent the state of my birth, Texas, and they also represent the first flowers I ever received from a boyfriend, my first love. So, in a reading, if I saw yellow roses, that symbol shorthand would lead me to Texas-sized first love—whereas for someone else, it could mean something entirely different. Your own Symbol Legend could be something as simple as a list in your journal or a Pinterest Board. Using a Symbol Legend deepens your

connections with the symbology in your life. And, it is important to note, only YOU can interpret or decipher your symbols and wording.

8. **Collect Your Hits.** Wait! We're not saying to get violent. The hits we are referring to are you hitting the mark, the bullseye with your reading. What does that look like when you're doing a reading for yourself? It feels like the truth, a sense of knowing in your gut, and possibly having an emotional response. You've hit the mark!

9. **Energy Healing Process.** After receiving your Divine Guidance, you may also have a sense to integrate the message with a healing exercise. It can be anything from brief meditation, breath work, or an energy clearing exercise, or a walk in nature.

10. **Message of Love.** Every message of Divine Guidance includes a message of love, especially when we are tuning in personally. This can look like an array of messages such as: you are loved, everything is going to be okay. It could be the wave of ease you feel. Without a doubt the message of love is always given even when we may not be open to receiving it.

11. **Completion.** As you continue to build your skills, you will find your intuitive connection will "pull" back or ease off as the connection comes to an end. In my experience, I believe our Divine Support Team knows when we've received our Divine Guidance, they will hang in there as long as it takes for us to "get it". Thank goodness especially if you're hardheaded like me, it's reassuring to know the Divine Guidance never leaves, it will continue to repeat, over and over, like an LP skipping.

12. **Thank Your Divine Support Team.** After feeling the energy ease, make sure to thank your Divine Support Team and ancestors for their support. The acknowledgment of that energy and support builds our awareness and connection.

Essentials To Support Your Intuitive Connection

Own Your Uniqueness

The most powerful step you can take on your path to intuition is acknowledging and claiming your uniqueness. Owning this is essential. If you have difficulty with this, simply look at your fingers. Each and every one of us has completely different fingerprints, like snowflakes, no two are the same. When we acknowledge ourselves and our abilities, we can more quickly get down to business. The whole point of having this ability is to use it despite being different. We must embrace our uniqueness.

Practice

The best way to build your intuition is to use it! Yes, you heard us right practice, practice, practice. This may sound repetitive, but it's worth repeating...PRACTICE, PRACTICE, PRACTICE.

Because practice is the only way to build this connection, we want to provide you with some ways to do this without feeling like you have to sit down with your friend and tell her what her deceased Aunt Clara says. No, you don't have to come out of the intuitive closet quite yet. There are ways to practice your intuition privately so that you can build your confidence by witnessing your actual skills for yourself.

Have Fun and Play

I always tell my students, "Remember there is nothing serious going on here." We take things so seriously as adults, and the object is to play with our intuition the way we did as children, daydreaming, telling stories, being open to allowing our Divine Guidance to come through.

Breathe

Breath is a powerful source, and it is a natural relaxer for your mind. Divine Guidance flows with and through each and every breath.

Trust

To expand your intuition, there has to be trust between you and your talent, an understanding so to speak. How do you believe and trust? You're going to get sick of hearing us say this, but the answer to your question is "Practice, practice, practice." The more you practice the more you are able to witness your intuitive "hits." The more your confidence expands, the more you begin to trust this connection that is within you. And the more you trust, the bigger your intuitive abilities become. The way I learned to believe in my abilities was by noticing what I was receiving and then trusting and following it.

Translating Your Intuitive Information

Notice what you are receiving and translate the message. Depending on the clair, you may have to do some detective work as to what the signs, symbols, or feelings mean.

As we mentioned before, automatic writing is an excellent way to translate the Divine information you receive through your clairs. This is a great tool to utilize in building your abilities as it allows you to tap into and receive higher conscious connections.

And what about sharing your new ability with another?

Your translation of your intuition will be perfect if you trust it. And it's important to note that I took sharing my intuitive messages way too far in the beginning, so please learn from my, shall I say, relentlessness. When I first started feeling confident about my abilities, I "thought" it was my job to go around and tell the world about it, even if no one asked or wanted to know. I overstepped boundaries with strangers because their deceased loved ones would not leave me alone until I did. I had to learn, as you will in practicing this work, that it is important to maintain your own boundaries, to choose when you practice your intuition and when you don't.

It's a good practice to not just whip it out on a whim and use it on an unsuspecting bystander. Just as J.K. Rowling says, *"The moment you are old enough to take the wheel, the responsibility lies with you."* To be responsible in working with your intuition means making sure the person you are sharing with is, in fact, interested in hearing it from you.

When we run around using our intuition to show others we are accurate and have something important to say, that's false guidance, folks. As you can see by my experience, I got caught up in my ego, and I lost sight of the sacredness of this information and the impact on those I randomly shared it with. Yes, you are a great intuitive. Yes, you have an incredible ability to build, and sculpt, and yes, it is best to share **only** with those who are ready and desire to hear what you have to say. If they don't have the desire to hear or receive it, they will miss the message and blessing. This is a part of the gift of this work. A person has to be ready to receive it, and we can't push or force them to hear it. Always remember why you are doing this work. It isn't to prove yourself or show someone how much you know. It is to be of benefit to others.

I have seen more than my fair share of intuitives who burn out because without realizing it they become attached to what others said or thought. They were always subconsciously looking for validation from others, and they were always looking for someone to say, "Hey, you're good!" That, my friends, isn't the purpose of these sacred connections. If you use these steps to work with your intuition, you will be an amazing benefit and contribution to others without falling into the gaps in between.

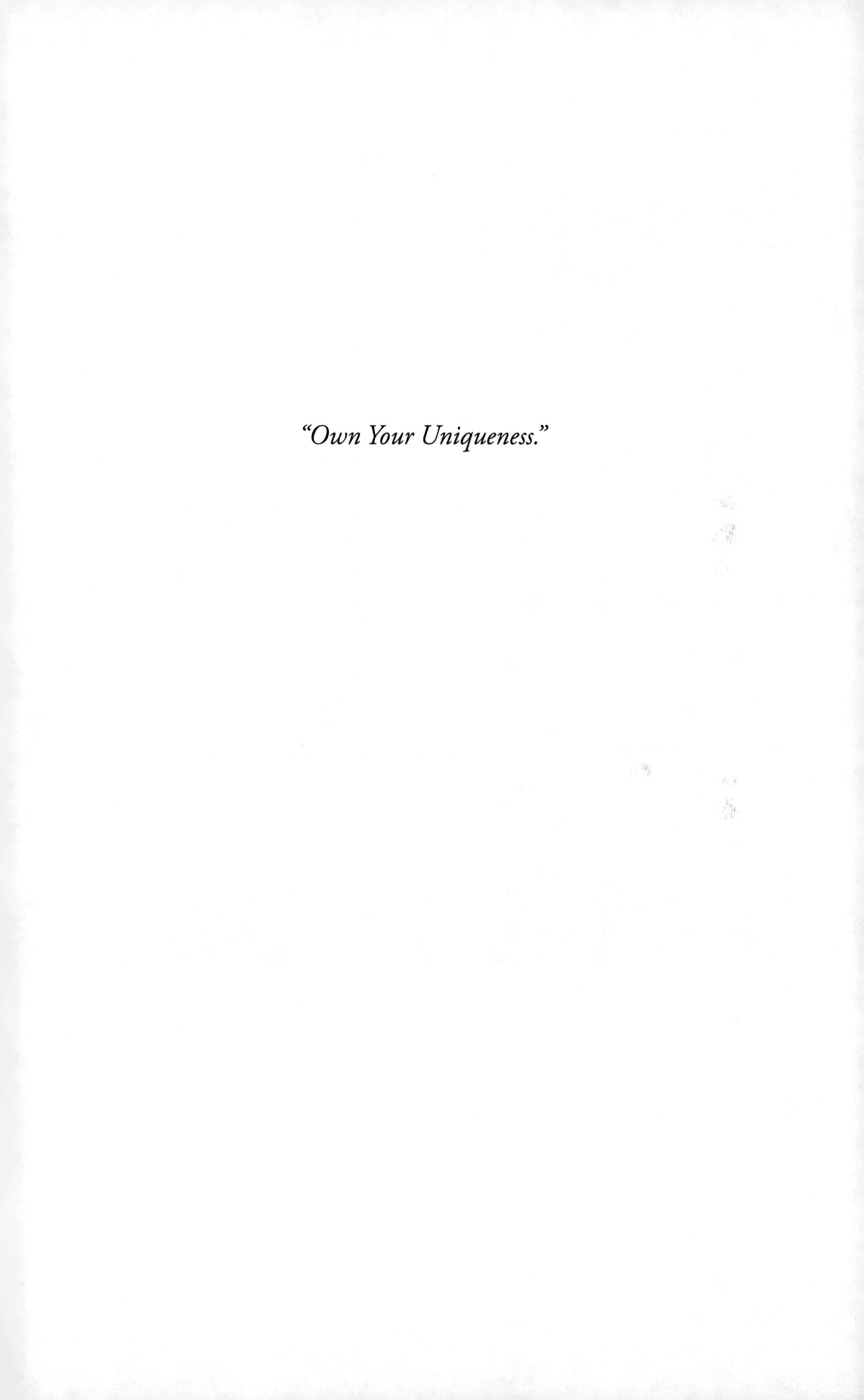

"Own Your Uniqueness."

CHAPTER 6

Stay Sharp

"Knowing yourself is the beginning of all wisdom."
- ARISTOTLE

Throughout this book we have placed strategies, exercises, processes, and suggestions to support building your intuitive connection because the best intuitives are continually strengthening their connections, talents and abilities. How do we do that? Through living intentionally, deliberately directing our focus and energy towards our service as a Divine instrument and being exactly that. Sounds like a bunch of hocus pocus? Well this is where we separate the psychics from the intuitives, remember? We are using the definition of a psychic as someone who doesn't live the work, but merely dishes out a "Do as I say, not as I do" type of message. It is essential as an intuitive to continue to work on yourself, to be open to learning new things, and having new experiences. You wouldn't get a new car and never change the oil, would you? Same goes with this powerful energy connection of intuition; your clarity and precision will hinge on how well you maintain your foundation. Here are the foundational tools and cornerstones to keeping your lines of intuition wide open.

These tools are great to play with in order to strengthen, not only your connection to your Divine Guidance, but also to your confidence that the Divine truly exists. Sometimes when we've just begun to live with our intuitive switch flipped on, our doubts can outweigh our belief. That's where these tools come in handy. They can validate the Divine Guidance you are receiving as well as give you a jump start into a reading, for yourself or another. And we would be remiss if we didn't caution you about becoming overly dependent of tools, because relying solely on exterior tools can impede the growth and development of your own intuitive channels. Sure, casting runes and laying out a card spread is a good place to start and/or confirm the Divine Guidance we receive, but seeing them as our access point to the Divine is where we get into trouble. We begin to believe it is the cards that have the power, instead of us. We are the ones that have the Divine within us, which flows through the tools not the other way around. We are the Divine vessels who have a gifted access. Our advice is to use the tools with respect and remember where the true access point is...you.

These days there is a wide array of divination tools, skills, and practices. We are only going to address those we have used along our journey—not to decrease the importance of any other, but because we can only speak from our experiences with these tools and how they support our confidence in trusting our intuition.

Meditation and Mindfulness

Meditation and mindfulness are key components to building intuition. This is important for us to understand as many of us assume that by taking a course or using pendulums regularly, we will wake up our intuition and be accurate. While these things may help, a strong foundation for our intuitive skills is connected to our ability to know and connect with ourselves. Mindfulness is simply defined as the process of focusing our awareness on the present moment while acknowledging and accepting our feelings, thoughts, and bodily sensations without judgment or attachment.

Meditation is a key practice that helps increase mindfulness. This is a practice that we can use all day, every day! This is paramount to intuition. When we are the observer of our thoughts and feelings without attachment or judgment, we can not only get to know ourselves but also, more importantly, understand our Divine connection and communication abilities. Our awareness of who and what we are—and honestly, understanding our energy and what we are creating in our lives—is a big part of our gift. Through regular meditation and mindfulness, we can shift our perspective and heal. This is a key piece of living a life with greater joy, connection, and love.

Chakra Clearing Exercises and Inner Child Meditations are examples of processes for developing our energy and intuitive gifts. These exercises along with other helpful processes can be found in the Divine Prescriptions section of this book.

Belief

The words "I am" are the most powerful words we will ever use in our life. The words when combined are a declaration to the world. The "I am" is said to call forth the great eternal and everlasting flow of life.

We often use these words half-heartedly and jokingly to degrade ourselves. We say statements like: "I am fat. I am exhausted. I am not good enough. I am never going to make it" and so on. These statements don't serve us—not only in thought but also from a breath and word perspective. Every word we utter with our breath, as the Native Americans say, is a prayer to the Universe. These statements are not aligned with our Higher Selves, and they feel heavy, exhausting, and hard.

Read the following statements and notice how they impact your emotional, mental and physical body: "I am good enough. I am Divine. I am connected. I am peace. I am free. I am love." Coming from a place of love instead of fear, creates a different energy, a different vibration, and thereby a drastically different experience.

The same is true for our intuition and Divine Guidance. When I first studied intuition, one of the statements I was told to repeat to myself was, "I am powerfully clairvoyant." I would say it to myself with a chuckle. At the time, I hadn't opened up to my clairvoyance and definitely did not think I was powerful! And yet, I would repeat it, and after a while, the chuckle disappeared.

Start using statements such as: "I am intuitive. I am capable. I am powerful. I am enough. I am a recipient of Divine messages." As you start to use these statements in your regular life, you will increase your intuition and be surprised by the nudges and guidance you receive.

Trust

Why don't we trust our intuition? Young children are powerfully intuitive and have a knowing that is clear. Like little lie detectors, they know when something is awry, when something isn't right. They know when their parents are struggling long before their parent shows or speaks about it. They naturally gravitate toward like-minded kids on the playground and move between friends with a sense of trust and natural discernment.

And yet, our world teaches children to not trust themselves. They are taught to put their faith in their parents and teachers—people who seemingly look wiser and can make decisions for them. This, of course, is valuable when learning lessons like not crossing the street when the light is red. But when they are told, "You don't know how you feel" or "You don't know because you're young," they immediately start to develop a gap between themselves and their intuition—the little guiding voice inside all of us. The more they are told to listen to adults and not themselves, the easier it is to lose a sense of who they truly are and what they know. As soon as that happens, they start looking externally for answers that are within them, and they lose faith in their intuitive nudges and their Divine connection.

As we grow older, societies and school systems teach us to use the logical, reasoning part of our minds. We are taught to rationalize and convince ourselves to validate our decisions. This creates a strong muscle for the left side of our brain. When we exclude creative arts, music and play from education and instead favor science, math and logical studies we are again, emphasizing, and strengthening only the left, logical side of our brain.

Yet, we have a whole other side of our brain. The right side, creative, intuitive, and sensitive, is a whole half of us, and we are rarely taught to use it. We are taught that creative arts won't lead us anywhere. The weakening of the creative side continues, and when we do get intuitive nudges, we are asked to prove them with logic, and they are often dismissed as childhood dreaming or fantasizing.

A misunderstanding of intuition in our world labels many of us as ridiculous, laughable, and even "crazy" for knowing things that turn out to be true. Many children see things and have experiences with the unseen realm only to be told they are seeing or imagining things, and they are told to stop this type of behavior. Given this, it's not surprising that we don't instinctually trust our intuition.

Gratitude

Gratitude is another foundational piece of intuition. When we are receiving information for ourselves or our clients, it is a gift that brings forth a deep sense of gratitude. These intuitive hits are valuable, life-altering, and can create immense joy and healing.

Gratitude is defined as thankfulness or gratefulness, which is a feeling of appreciation felt or shown by the recipient of a kind deed. One of the greatest things we can do on this intuitive journey is have gratitude for our intuitive gifts. Gratefully acknowledging our messages, our Divine Guidance, our service to others, is how we truly give thanks for what we have.

The beauty of gratitude is that whatever we put our focus on gets bigger. So as we focus on our gift through the lens of gratitude, we increase it—we make it bigger. The more we do this, the more we are fueling the momentum to receive more.

Forgiveness

Forgiveness is an incredibly powerful and essential tool of intuition. It builds our happiness and sustains our growth. When we hold onto anger, resentment, pain, and hurt, we allow these emotions to grow within us and harden inside of us. This can eventually hurt us more than the person whose actions angered us in the first place. There's a saying that describes this point quite well: "Unforgiveness is like taking poison and expecting the other person to die". We think holding grudges and unforgiveness protects us from the situation happening again, but unfortunately it does the exact opposite. It builds the energy to have it happen again.

Acknowledging our emotions and letting them free is pertinent to our health. Forgiveness is part of the process of letting these emotions go. Forgiveness is the key to our locked prison cell. I always think of Nelson Mandela, the world's most famous prisoner, who showed us the power of forgiveness. It takes strength and courage to forgive. Nelson Mandela said, "Forgiveness liberates the soul; it removes fear. That's why it is such a powerful weapon." He is a model of what can be accomplished through forgiveness and nonviolence. Consider the resentment you may be holding, whether it be from childhood or yesterday. It is to your own benefit to acknowledge it and let it go. There are meditations and processes to work with forgiveness in the Divine Prescriptions section, if you want support in letting things go.

Detachment

In psychology, detachment refers to the inability to connect. We are not speaking about that type of detachment. The detachment we are speaking about is not being or having a dependent connection with a person, object or accomplishment.

How do you know if you're attached? When we have feelings of attachment, we feel like we won't be complete without having this object, or experience; and that can show up through feelings of worry, fear, jealousy, pride, sadness, vanity, or entitlement. Detachment asks us to remember that nothing owns us nor do we own anything. We may have possessions, but we are the creators of all of our experiences.

We are not owned by anyone or anything. We are completely free; we just may not believe it. The biggest hurdle in detachment is embracing uncertainty, which is something we aren't always masters at accomplishing.

The detachment we want to encourage is not being attached to outcomes and what others think or say. Deepak Chopra calls it the great paradox of life: in order to receive, we have to relinquish our bond to having it. The interesting thing about this paradox is that detachment allows for deep involvement. We are like a character in a movie, completely enthralled in the happenings, yet unlike the character, we can step outside of our emotions and fixations. Ron Rathbun, spiritual author, speaks to the heart of the matter, "True detachment isn't a separation from life but the absolute freedom within your mind to explore living."

Pendulums

Dowsing, the practice of using pendulums, dates back as far as 6000 BC and still today remains one of the simplest divination tools to use.

A pendulum is something weighted on a string or chain, traditionally used to locate hidden water, minerals and other things buried underground. Responding to energy, converting it back and forth the pendulum detects the energy and physically moves the weighted object. Acting as a receiver and transmitter, it is easy to gain spiritual and material insight with a pendulum. This simple tool is powerful access to quick, straight forward and sometimes surprising answers.

You can purchase some beautiful pendulums from artisans and even make your own. I always love watching workshop participants learning about pendulums getting excited by making their own. We create a rudimentary pendulum by putting a regular ordinary washer from the local hardware store at the end of a piece of string and watching how this simple primitive tool surprises and delights them. Who knew such rudimental objects would work? Our ancestors.

Oracle or Tarot Cards

These can be as ornate or as simple as an ordinary deck of cards. The system of tarot is a language and journey of its own. If you are called to investigate it, know you are working with ancient wisdom dating back centuries. Oracle cards are not based on a specific system they are as unique and original as their authors.

Runes

There is some speculation as to how far back runes date. Some say the 1st century, regardless of their date of origin, they are considered to have a magical quality about them, each rune a unique Divine being representing the codes of life and wisdom. There are documented rune inscriptions found on ancient artifacts leaving experts to believe they were used for the purpose of healing and protection.

"Our world teaches children to not trust themselves."

CHAPTER 7

Rules of The Cosmos

"All that we are is the result of what we have thought.
The mind is everything. What we think we become."
- BUDDHA

Universal Laws (UL) not only help us understand the world and how it works, but they also give us an important framework to build our lives around. Most importantly, they give us stable footing in times when our life has more wobble than sure-footedness. Understanding and living the ULs gives intuitives the essential grounding they need to do this work daily, especially as a profession.

Having the ULs in our back pocket keeps us from feeling ungrounded, alone, and segregated. Living the ULs gives practicing intuitives the freedom to unhook from the need of validation about what they see, feel, or know. Living as a professional intuitive, we cross paths with those who are confronting or at best skeptical of our work. ULs support us in understanding those people as well as ourselves so we don't feel the need to convince or prove our abilities to anyone.

The other outstanding benefit of the ULs is that they are the best way to market our businesses. It supports us in building the perfect practice with ideal clients (without all the constant hype you see out on Facebook and other social media platforms). No longer is it essential to post 12 times a day to make sure our audience knows we're out there. No more used car salesman tactics. (Sorry, but it's true.)

ULs are directives that show us how to create magic, or as they called it in the early days of Egypt, alchemy. Does this sound far-fetched? For that precise reason, these principles have been passed down for over 5,000 years in secret only to those who were ready to hear and receive this wisdom.

The cornerstone of the ULs are the Hermetic Principles, created by Hermes Trismegistus, a man the earliest Egyptians called the "scribe of the gods." His teachings and the Hermetic Principles gave insight into the relationship between the physical and spiritual planes. Because of the persecution of free thinkers back in those times, these, like many other sacred texts, were passed down verbally and in secrecy. Even today, the word hermetic means protectively sealed.

In 1908, Yogi Publication Society published *The Kybalion*, a book written by three initiates of Hermetic philosophy. It is said that they created it with the purpose to share how we can all tap into a consciousness that allows us to see our Universe existing in complete and perfect unity.

How the additional ULs came into being is not exactly explained as far as origins, but much like *The Kybalion*—whose authors used a *nom de plume* to avoid suffering persecution—we can assume these Laws surfaced through understanding our consciousness, reality, and the Universe. These principles are in no way quick fixes; they are deeply rooted spiritual principles that require dedication. Since the seven Hermetic Principles are the heart of the ULs, we'll start by diving into those first.

Hermetic Principle 1: The Principle of Mentalism

"The ALL is mind; The Universe is mental." - The Kybalion

Interestingly enough, in *The Kybalion*, the scribes spend four chapters preparing the foundation and context for this first Principle. This shows us how important this first Principle is and why we must acknowledge it: at its core, it states that we live in a mental Universe. This Principle teaches us that the Universe is a mental creation, and in our mind is where we live.

Everything we see and experience in our physical world begins in the invisible, "mental" realm. We create our own Universe with our thoughts and imagination. Mental creation is a way to change or redirect our lives and experiences.

Every aspect of life, energy, material, and matter are thoughts of a living Mind. Everything shares a common connection because everything exists in the Mind of "The ALL that is." Some say the very nature of consciousness can be explained through this Principle due to the expansion of our ability to change thoughts and transform our outer experience. Consider this for just a moment, everything—every little thing, including us, energy, matter, nature, everything, is of the Mind. And not only are they of the Mind, but all of this, everything is reliant upon the Mind to exist.

This Principle helped me understand on a daily basis that I create my world and my experiences. The best way I can personally illustrate this Hermetic Principle to you is through this somewhat embarrassing example. Most of my life, I've been "afraid" of the cops. If a police car pulls up beside me when I'm driving, my heart races, my palms sweat. I'm driving the speed limit too, folks. I'm obeying the law, but I still get nervous. There's no rational reason for my physical responses. Because of my continued mental state of fearing the police, I've had crazy experiences.

Once, I had a Detective show up at our front door, gun on his hip, and another time, I had a "swat-like" experience on our little street when officers chased down a shoplifter who decided to climb one of our massive trees. Both of these experiences can be explained away logically. The detective was investigating a theft in our town and the onslaught of cop cars swarming my street was about a shoplifter, not me. Still, the experience of trauma of those two happenings was very real to me, and it didn't happen to anyone else. My partner wasn't home and even our neighbors didn't see the swarming police vehicles. It was as if both situations were orchestrated for me, by me, because my mental state created my reality. That is Mentalism in action.

Mentalism helps me to see the meanings I associate with everything; both "yay" and "boo" meanings. I feel empowered in knowing it is within me and in my power to create mental alchemy—magic—to change my thoughts to reflect a more empowering state. This is the power to see a divorce as an opportunity, and losing a job as an opportunity. This is a true game changer. If you believe it, you can do it, and that is the true power of this Law.

When sharing this Principle with my students I always like to use the example of optical illusion art. When you first look at this art what do you see?

A tree? Or a woman's face? The ability to see first one image, shift perspectives, and see the other one is possible through the Principle of Mentalism. Our reality of this picture changes as we see the different images. It proves everything we experience begins in our inner worlds, in our minds, in the mental universe. *The Kybalion* says without understanding this, mastery is impossible. No matter how many doors you knock on, access to the temple will not be given. Access to the temple in those days referred to sacred or hallowed ground—in some cases, the temple of heaven. Even without religious or spiritual connotations a temple is a holy place or sanctuary. This is why the principle of Mentalism is FIRST. Without it, we don't understand our ability to harness it to use the Universal Laws—without it we believe we are victims to circumstance and situations are only one-sided. When really, there are multiple perspectives we could take.

Hermetic Principle 2: The Principle of Correspondence

"As above, so below; as below, so above." - The Kybalion

There are three planes of existence—physical, mental, and spiritual. These planes of existence are merged together, and because of this, what happens on one plane of existence impacts another, like a ripple effect. This Principle was known to be very important to the ancients because through it they could see what was hidden from their view. With this Principle, we can understand any paradoxes of nature or the Universe. The truth this Principle teaches is that there is always a "congruence" between life and the unknown. This shows us there is agreement between the physical, mental, and spiritual realms, showing us there is no separation. We are all one.

The "above" is the heavens, the macrocosm, or the Divine, while the "below" refers to the earth, the physical plane, the microcosm, the human soul. Just as "without" is outer reality, the realm we would call the physical "real" world, where we work, play, eat, pay bills. And "within" points to what Jung called our "inner world," where our ego and personality live. Hermetic philosophy teaches that all things are connected to each other. This is why something from one area of our life can be the cause of the effect we are experiencing in another area. We don't think it is related, but it is.

The Principle of Correspondence shows us how we can understand heaven and earth, our loved ones, and our enemies. With this Principle, we can be certain in uncertainty—as we are now with this global pandemic. The ancient Greeks understood this when they said, "Know thyself, and thou shalt know the Universe and God." Just as there is a direct correspondence between the way you think, the way you feel, who you are in your inner world, and who you are in the outer world, the same is true for our Universe and world. When we create energy with our emotions, feelings, thoughts, desires, and impulses, we send out energetic broadcasts that seek out the corresponding energy. That same energy that equals our broadcast of our emotions, thoughts, feelings bounces straight back to us.

In ancient times, the human body was regarded as a microcosm of the world's macrocosm. In the alchemist's cabinet, there were always 7 metals relating to the 7 planets. This belief that everything is connected to everything, this "as above so below," explains the basis of astrology, the heavens representing "above," relating to the individual's planets time of birth which gives insight into their personality, likes, destiny, lessons. Our ancestors understood the link between the planets and each of us individually, energetically. There are places beyond our knowing and when we are able to use the Principle of Correspondence we can understand what would otherwise be unknowable. Furthermore, this Principle supports us in manifestation.

Consider how geometry allows an astrophysicist to measure the distance and movement of planets from a chair in an observatory, intellectually calculating and transforming the unknown into the known. The micro is in the macro, and the macro is in the micro. The ocean is the wave and the wave is the ocean, but they are inherently separate.

As intuitives, we know that intuition helps us connect with the planes of the unknown and unseen, which reinforces the Principle of Correspondence. As intuitives, we understand the difference between everyday happenings and getting a hit of Divine Guidance. This is the same reason why when we resist and block our intuition, it will show up in our physicality as allergies, headaches, fatigue, and lethargy.

The power behind this Principle is not only that it allows us to see into the unknown, but it also shows us our repetitive patterns in our daily lives, how they are interconnected and impacting us mentally, physically and spiritually. When we want to take on personal change—when we truly step into doing our inner work to become more conscious—it really does lead to greater happiness and a connection with our life purpose and Divine direction.

Because our world is based completely on the material aspect of things it is a big stretch to consider the idea of working with the subtle side of things—the stuff we can't see, measure or touch—yet it will bring about a changed reality if we dare to take that stretch. It may take you experiencing the true magic of this Hermetic Principle before you can believe it.

This Principle is one that I love because it feels safe. It shows how everything in this closed system called the Universe is working in harmony, across heaven and earth, oceans and land, neighborhoods and our bodies. So, if something is happening that we don't like, we must take ownership that it is reflecting something within us, something we created through Mentalism, through thought. The Principle of Correspondence shows us what we are broadcasting with absolute certainty because it says it will be undeniably matched.

Hermetic Principle 3: The Principle of Vibration

"Nothing rests; everything moves; everything vibrates." - The Kybalion

The idea of this Hermetic Principle is that everything is in motion. Everything is vibrating—you, the chair you're sitting on, the tree outside, even the music you may be listening to as you are reading this book. Not too long ago, this idea was considered ridiculous, but science validated what Hermetics have known for thousands of years. You might have heard it in your high school chemistry class: everything is made up of atoms, which are in a constant state of motion. It's the atoms' speed that determines if things appear solid, gas or liquid. Everything vibrates! From atoms to the oceans to the world and the multiple universes, everything, every single thing, is in some sort of vibratory motion. I read somewhere recently that "we live in an ocean of motion" this speaks 100 percent to this Principle. But, don't take on the adage "seeing is believing" because you don't always see vibration; the chair you're sitting on right now is vibrating, but it looks solid, doesn't it? Trippy, right?

The beauty behind this Principle is that it shows us the different manifestations of matter, energy, mind, and spirit. There isn't anything that this Principle doesn't include. The master Hermetic students used this Principle to manage their own mental vibrations as well as those of others. Hermeticists believe thoughts have their own rate of vibration, and can be controlled like tuning an instrument, to get the results desired in life. Interesting, right? Isn't that something you would like to be able to do? It is said, "He who understands the Principle of Vibration has grasped the scepter of power."

But what does that look like in our world, today? A great example of the Principle of Vibration is a dog whistle. A whistle that makes an ultrasonic sound only dogs can hear. Humans can't hear anything coming out of the dog whistle, we can't see the vibration coming from it, either but our pups sure do! So, you see, when it comes to the Principle of Vibration seeing isn't always believing. We can't always see the vibration with our human eyes, but it exists.

To work with the Principle of Vibration regularly, we recommend using the exercises in our Divine Prescriptions section to align your vibration so there's agreement between what you want and your vibration. Then you can build upon this with the other Principles and Laws to enhance your manifestation. I want to be clear here, this Principle isn't about visualization—it's about being present to the actual vibration you are broadcasting, and when necessary, adjusting it to be in alignment with what you desire. This isn't just walking around thinking about what you want, expecting it to show up. All of the Laws and Principles work together, they cannot be separated. If what you want isn't showing up, this could be why. Just simply thinking about what you want isn't going to bring it into material form, you and your vibration must be in alignment with it.

Hermetic Principle 4: The Principle of Polarity

"Everything is dual; everything has poles; everything has its opposite pair; like and unlike are the same; opposites are identical in nature, but different in degree; extremes meet; all truths are but half-truths; all paradoxes may be reconciled." - The Kybalion

This Principle states that everything has two sides, much like Abraham's teachings through Esther Hicks: for every yin, there is a yang. In *The Kybalion*, it says "Thesis and antithesis are identical in nature, but different in degree," meaning opposites are the same, but different by degree. They are really two extremes of the same thing, like hot and cold. While they are complete opposites, they are truly the same thing: temperature. The only delta between the two opposites are the degrees.

We cannot arbitrarily say where heat stops and cold begins because there is no absolute heat or absolute cold; they are varying degrees of the same thing. The same concept applies to light and dark. They are two different ends of the same stick, but where does light begin and darkness end? The beauty behind the Principle of Polarity is that it explains all these paradoxes. The power of this Principle is the ability to transmute from one pole to the other. It is said that the "Art of Polarization" is a phase of "mental alchemy" that has been known and practiced by the ancients. By utilizing this Principle, we hold in our hands (and our minds) the ability to shift and change anything from one pole to the other.

When I work with UL of Polarity, I am reminded of Joseph Campbell's words: "You yourself are participating in the evil, or you are not alive. Whatever you do is evil for somebody. This is one of the ironies of the whole creation." It's a hard pill that we learn to swallow as we grow up. No circumstance or event is completely tragic or 100 percent beautiful. It is impossible to have one without the other. Because I am a bit hard-headed (as my mom would say) I needed to understand this UL on a deeper level—how it was connected to the other ULs, and why it was important to understand the varying degrees of polarity.

Many years ago, I had this heavy emotional breakup with a man I deeply loved. The situation doesn't matter, but what is relevant is that I saw the situation as being terribly tragic. I experienced all of the intense emotions that went along with it, (anger, abandonment, fear, sadness, doubt). I stewed in it until I had this thought: How can I use the ULs to help me in this situation? I had tried using the Law of Attraction but it was falling flat, all I was attracting was more heavy emotion. Intuitively, I was drawn to the UL of Polarity—how is this UL going to help?

I sat with my journal and started looking at the polarity throughout the relationship and into the break-up. I began to understand nothing was one sided, and everything has its opposite.

Yes, he was gone from my life, which felt hard and sad, but what was the polar opposite of that? I felt myself asking, What about this breakup can I be happy about? Seriously?

At that moment, I thought, uh, absolutely nothing…Then, I started breathing into that thought: What could be on the opposite side of this pain? Suddenly, I felt a surge of awareness; it felt like a cool breeze brushing over my body. I realized this person wasn't a trusting person and because of that, I was constantly feeling the need to explain myself, my work, and my actions. Big stressor for an intuitive! I realized I hadn't felt free to truly be my authentic self without being judged for my age, intuition business, weight, fitness level, and more. In that moment, there was a break in the heaviness, and I felt lighter. I saw and felt the polarity of my sadness was freedom. As much as my heart hurt, I was now looking at a newfound freedom.

I continued to look at each emotion I was feeling and its polar opposite this way, and each time I did, it brought me back to my center, so to speak. It lifted the heaviness. It didn't "take away" the energy called sadness; it was like I exchanged it for the energy called freedom. We'll talk more about that exchange later on as it involves the UL of Perpetual Transmutation which will be a fun ride. Buckle your seatbelts for that one.

By using UL of Polarity, I was able to ease my pain and sadness. I didn't need to spend weeks rolling around in the heaviness and drama the way I used to. I could see my freedom sitting at the other end of the tunnel. This was a healthy way to move through heartbreak—not spiritually bypassing it—just allowing a new perspective to reflect on the whole experience, both the "yays" and the "boos."

Another time to use the UL of Polarity in our daily lives is when we are feeling off center—not feeling as optimal as we would like. We can take a moment and look at the polar opposite of what we are experiencing, feeling, thinking, and then see what action would need to happen to experience the opposite. For example, are you feeling lonely and don't like it? The polar opposite feeling is feeling loved and in community with others. An action you could take would be to take steps to connect with or be around others.

The next time you find yourself feeling wobbly, consider the polar opposite of what you're feeling, even if it is just for a moment. You may be surprised what you experience.

Hermetic Principle 5: The Principle of Rhythm

"Everything flows, out and in; everything has its tides; all things rise and fall; the pendulum—swing manifests in everything; the measure of the swing to the right is the measure of the swing to the left; rhythm compensates."
- The Kybalion

This Principle states that everything manifested has a measured motion—a pendulum like movement, ebb and flow between two poles. Newton scientifically showed that for every action there is an equal and opposite reaction. The importance of this Principle is how it relates to our mental states and our ability to move through them, knowing that they will ebb and flow. When we learn how to use this Principle consciously versus being used by it, we attain mastery over it all.

When it came to using the Principle of Rhythm in my life, I thought long and hard. Because this Principle says that everything goes through cycles, that every little thing has a rhythm and pattern, I wondered how that could help me, personally. Sure, it was great to notice the cycles of nature—Summer, Fall, Winter, Spring—but how does that support me in business? Those cycles were valuable when I was choosing a vacation or what to wear hiking, but I didn't quite understand how they would affect my personal and inner world. I was always working hard, but it wasn't until I learned to trust the phases in my own life that I really embraced this Principle.

Interestingly enough, I have found this Principle to be a valuable tool in my toolbox, especially in building my business. Let me illustrate how this Principle works through my client Bob Milburn, entrepreneur and consulting business owner. In the beginning, as with any business, there is a "revving of the engines," a momentum that needs to happen. New clients or gigs seemed too distant, even impossible, in the beginning, causing him to doubt his destination.

"You yourself are participating in the evil,

or you are not alive. Whatever you do is evil for somebody.

This is one of the ironies of the whole creation."

- JOSEPH CAMPBELL

The Principle of Rhythm helped him to see that keeping his focus on his destination, let him spend his energy on making connections and contributing to his community. It's as if understanding there is a rhythm releases the pressure of forcing something to happen.

Bob arrived at his destination and tripled his income "without really trying." He knew that "hard" times now, beget "easier" times later due to the natural cycles and rhythms of the world. It gave him the confidence to not give up on himself or his dream. Thanks Bob for being an epic example of dancing in your rhythms!

Hermetic Principle 6: The Principle of Cause and Effect

"Every cause has its effect; every effect has its cause; everything happens according to Law; Chance is but a name for Law not recognized; There are many planes of causation, but nothing escapes the Law." - The Kybalion

This Principle shows us that nothing happens without a cause and effect. Nothing is left up to chance. In mastering this Principle, we learn that we can be the "cause" of events, showing us yet again that we are the creators of our life, our thoughts and our moods.

This may sound strange to you, but this UL soothes me. I know, I know, soothing sounds strange. I told you it was going to sound strange, at first. This one soothes me mostly because once I understood there are no accidents or coincidences, and that everything has a cause, I felt a sense of relief. I felt a power I hadn't known before. All of my circumstances, experiences, and conditions were all an effect, and I was the cause, not anyone else.

Now there's a double edge sword with this Principle, and that is it requires—yes, I said requires—us to own the truth that the choices we make really do create our experiences. What we plant we will harvest. What we reap we will sow. Acknowledging this truth is easy to do when everything is going our way—yes, I created this success, look how fun; it gets a little dicey when things are not going the way we would prefer. That's when we get out the old projector and start making everyone BUT ourselves accountable for our experiences. We think it's simply bad luck, nope, sorry folks, that's not true. That's a lie we've grown comfortable believing. There's no such thing as bad luck. With this Principle, I had to step up and take full accountability for everything: the bogus boyfriends, the snarky sales person, the bad breakup, the speeding ticket as well as all the good stuff. The French philosopher Voltaire said that words like luck, chance and coincidence were invented to express the known effects of the unknown causes.

It may sound strange, or maybe it doesn't sound so strange anymore, but acknowledging this Principle and beginning to see it in action in my life made a big difference in my career. Here's how.

In the beginning of my professional career as an intuitive, I felt responsible for my clients. When I say, responsible I don't mean in the way of being authentic and shooting straight with Divine Guidance. I mean that when they would have something difficult happen to them, I would actually feel it. Because of being an empath with such strong clairsentience, I could feel their fear, their anxiety, and I made it mean that I should have done something to prevent this difficulty. Perhaps I could've saved them. As I grew to understand and be with this Principle, I had an epiphany: my clients (and my kids, for that matter) were encountering the conditions brought on by the effect of which they were the cause.

Stick with me here. The trauma or difficult situation they were having was the cause of their thoughts, words, and actions, which come into form through these Principles. This realization gave me an incredible amount of freedom. I was able to set aside my concerns in order to coach and support them through it. That freedom allowed me to expand my business, and my income. My little business grew; my clientele doubled, and I knew it was because I was the cause. It wasn't because I signed on to a new marketing program or posted on social media 1000 times a day. It was because I was keeping my focus, thoughts, and actions directed at what I wanted to experience.

To further accelerate the growth in my career, I looked at all the successful people in my field as well as others I respected in other fields. I then took note of their lifestyles—not just the private jets, but the way they lived their lives. I read that Oprah and Richard Branson both got up before the sun every morning, so I tried that. I paid attention to the books they read, and read them. I noticed how they spent their money, what they studied, what their values were, and how they spent their time. All of this showed me how they got to where they did, and I knew because of the Hermetic Principle of Cause and Effect that if I, too, took on the same conscious strategies, I would have the same effect. Always growing, I'm not yet an Oprah or Sir Richard Branson, but if I'm truthful with you, I feel like I'm right there with them.

We are currently living in the impact of the Principle of Cause and Effect as I write this. Our world is facing a pandemic of COVID-19, and around the globe we are experiencing the effect of it. Our entire world—how we interact and do business—has seemingly completely turned on its axis. And while we have yet to uncover the outcome of this particular experience, I'm completely positive of one of the reasons for this situation, and that is to bring another level of awareness and consciousness to us all, despite being separated by oceans. We are all impacted; we are one in this cause that is bringing our world together. As one, together, we are focused on the same thing: health and well-being.

Hermetic Principle 7: The Principle of Gender

"Gender is in everything; everything has its masculine and feminine principles; gender manifests on all planes." - *The Kybalion*

This Principle states that everything and everyone contains both masculine and feminine energies. This aspect is evident throughout creation in the conversation of opposite sexes, not only in humans, but also in plants, minerals, electrons, and magnetic poles. Feminine and masculine energies are the activators of each other, joining together in creation.

Gender association is an ongoing conversation in our world today, and looking at this Hermetic Principle, it took me a bit to see how I access it in my daily life. My biggest understanding of gender, in the beginning, came from the physical association and anatomy—either you're a girl or a boy. Very shortsighted, right?

I started understanding more about the physical manifestation of this Hermetic Principle watching my son, a child psychiatrist, support his clients through discovering their gender identification. Knowing this Principle made it easier for me to understand how someone could associate more with one energy in their body compared to another, regardless of the outward expression of their body. Diving in deeper, I knew there was more to understand. More specifically, what was the importance of everything having both feminine and masculine aspects?

Masculine energy is seen as the outward movement into the world, whereas feminine energy is the receptive energy. Hermetists believe the "me" is a mixture of your habits, moods, and physical body—the feminine energy. The "I" is the being within who can move the "me" into action—a masculine energy. Both energies together are an amazing creative force. The "me" receives ideas, the "I" puts it into movement. This is why it's important for us to be balanced in giving and receiving. It benefits our bodies and our intuitive connection. This principle of gender relates to our mental states as well.

Let's look at this more closely. I had a client who was a survivor of a messy divorce and basically stopped trusting men. Raised by a single mother, she was very strong in her masculine, could take care of herself, didn't need or want a man. It made sense considering she was living 100 percent in her masculine. The reasons she came to see me was because she was having serious stress, headaches, and increased anxiety, and the final straw was when she blew up at her children. She knew she needed to change something especially after her doctor said it was all stress related. After sitting with her for our first session, it was quite clear she was a woman on a mission—a doer. If you wanted anything done, give it to her, the busiest woman on the planet. Yet, this clearly wasn't working for her or her body.

I spoke to her about balancing the masculine and feminine energies in her body, in her life. Of course, it was as if I was speaking alien. I was able to point out that her energy (her power source) was slowly going out, dimming. She was not allowing herself to receive—feminine energy—anything back. She was heading for a massive burnout and already experiencing the beginning "symptoms." I had hit a nerve.

She began to look for areas in her life where she felt safe to receive, whether it was from her "ride or die" girlfriends, or from herself, and when she found them, I had her write about the experience of having a sister (friend) who would "be there" for her.

She began to see where she had completely cut off her feminine (receptive) side. She even commented that some of her friends were shocked by how quickly she'd shifted. They said she'd softened and seemed more at ease, simply by being more receptive. As she began to bring more of the feminine into her life she began to feel not only more balanced but also more harmony within herself. She didn't feel the need to go out and FIGHT the world, or her sons for that matter. The simple process of noticing if we are out of balance in our giving and/or receiving, it will shift our entire energy.

How do we know we are out of balance? When we are too far over on the masculine side of things we can step into chaos, reckless abandon, where we forget the most important thing: WHY we are taking the action. When we are tilting the scales too far in the feminine direction, we may be too deeply grounded (not in a good way) in external circumstances, usually resulting in little or no accomplishments. Without the feminine (receiving), the masculine (action) will act without order or reason. While the feminine going solo will result in ultimate stagnation, no movement. With the feminine and masculine in harmony there is action with thoughtfulness, which brings SUCCESS!

As we complete our journey through the Hermetic Principles and begin our trip into the Universal Laws (ULs), it is important to remember all of these Principles and Laws work in harmony together. Despite their unknown origin story the ULs are considered extensions of the Hermetic Principles. Again, all of these cosmic laws work together, without separation, to show us how the Universe works and how we can thrive within it. Buckle your seatbelts, this is going to be good.

Universal Law of Attraction

This Law states that like attracts like. Meaning that what you are focused on is drawn to you.

If you are focused on not having enough money, you will bring exactly that into your experience: not enough money.

Esther and Jerry Hicks explain this Law well in their book, *Ask and It Is Given*. With this book, Esther and Jerry Hicks have created one of the best channeled works of our time. They are New York Times best-selling authors and largely responsible for the current popularity and accessibility of Law of Attraction. Explaining the Law of Attraction, Esther writes:

You understand this principle when you turn on your radio and deliberately tune your receiver to match a signal from a broadcasting tower. You do not expect to hear music that is being broadcast on the radio frequency of 101 FM to be received on your tuner when it is set at 98.6 FM. You understand that radio vibrational frequencies must match, and the Law of Attraction agrees.

Emotions of fear, grief, anger, and anxiety emit a different resonance or vibrational output than those emotions of love, joy, and gratitude—one is 98.6 FM frequency and the other is the 101 FM frequency. To further explain this Law, we can say that our thoughts are broadcasting a vibrational frequency and they seek out energy in this world that is a match. This is why we say every thought counts, even the ones we aren't aware of. Putting our attention on something brings it into our experience, but no need to worry. Thankfully we don't instantly manifest things. So we have an opportunity to turn around all the disempowering thoughts and amplify the ones that bring freedom, clarity and power. When we are noticing a lack and we want to turn it around, ask yourself this: "What is it that I truly want?" Curiosity dissipates doubt and fear.

While living in Laguna Beach, we were experiencing some big fires. I had just moved to California from Texas so it was my first experience with California's wildfires. I had a big event, 300+ people coming into Laguna Beach from all over the country in the middle of one of the largest fires up to that time. The sky was eerie, a red tint giving way to these white flakes that my brain insisted were snowflakes, but in reality, were ash. Laguna was fast turning into what resembled Mordor from Lord of the Rings.

In California, we had first responders jumping into action with courage and conviction in a way that took my breath away. I hadn't witnessed anything like that since September 11th. I was so moved by all these firefighters, career and volunteers both side by side, fighting back the destructive flames. I decided I would do a mini ceremony to honor our firefighters. I got a yellow candle and blessed it by putting it to my heart and pouring love into it, and then I drew down the side of it a heart and this note: "For all the Cali firefighters, their families and all who support them" then I drew a peace sign and lit it.

I placed the candle in a safe container and left it on my granite kitchen counter—all by itself. Hours later, while at the hair salon, I got a notification that the firefighters had been called to my home. I called the Laguna Beach police and they told me it was a false alarm, the house and everything in it was safe.

When I returned home I walked into my kitchen and there was a note on my countertop beside the extinguished candle. The note was from the fire chief telling me they had entered my home and that he had no idea why they were called to my home, but they found nothing out of order. The note continued to say that since they were here they'd took it upon themselves to blow out my candle, and to please be careful leaving an unwatched flame burning.

It hit me like a ton of bricks: my intention infused into this candle, to send support and love to firefighters, is what called them to my home. And as per usual, being the heroes they are, they made sure I was safe and sound.

Universal Law of Resonance

The Law of Resonance is the UL that determines how anything and everything is brought into our physical world. This Law made a lot of sense to me right off the bat; it was the deciding factor as to WHAT I attracted into my life. But, in the beginning, I collapsed this Law with the UL of

Attraction. I thought that the UL of Attraction was what determined what I experienced in my life. It wasn't until I began studying and looking for ways to see this Law at work that I truly understood the power of it. This is how we manifest. This Law determines precisely what it is that you will attract into your life based on the resonance or frequency of the energy that you are broadcasting. This Law is the real manifesting mechanism that we use to create. It's how we can easily match our vibration to the vibration of the things we desire, causing them to appear in our life experience.

The Law of Resonance is the Law which determines precisely what is attracted based on our resonance or energy frequency that we are broadcasting. It determines the type and quality of the frequency projected which the Law of Attraction then uses to determine precisely *what* is attracted. Resonance is the outgoing frequency you project based on the quality of awareness. It determines what will be attracted, just like the outgoing broadcast from a radio determines which radio station is picked up. The UL of Resonance is the Law that determines the different vibrational patterns we create through our thoughts, beliefs, and emotions. These patterns are then projected through us, magnetizing energies that resonate at the same level of our broadcast. This determines and creates what we experience in our physical reality. When one object is vibrating, it forces the second object into vibrational motion. The result is a larger vibration.

A client who began working with me wanted to build his current business. We had discussed the creation process, and how we are all accountable for what we experience as well as multiple Universal Laws. One of the practices I have my 1:1 coaching clients do is to build a master manifestation list. This is a list of everything you want to experience in every area of your life. To create one for his business, he and his partner wrote down everything they wanted to experience with this company. They wanted to grow the business by 20 percent. They wanted it to be easy and apparent. They wrote their complete list, and when they were finished, I'm sure a part of their business minds wondered how in the heck this was going to happen; but that's not where they focused. My client recalls saying, "I don't know how this will come about, but somehow, someway this is going to happen."

Fast forward two months and everything plus some happened. A competitor gave their company a million dollars' worth of business. Yes, you read this correctly, a competitor, not a known ally, dropped in their laps a revenue of a million dollars. Something like that doesn't happen every day, folks. The form was different then they anticipated and they moved well beyond the 20 percent increase. In fact, within two weeks of doing the master manifestation list they found an additional 10 percent in another new stream of income. So not only did they grow their business but they went beyond what they had written down.

This happened because of the essence—the energy of how they approached their list. They knew, in their bones, one way or another, this was going to happen. Their resonance didn't falter. Their focus was a specialized tracking beam that locked on and didn't let go!

To understand the concept of resonance, it may be helpful to look at an experiment done with two tuning forks. There are two tuning forks that have the same natural frequency (rate of vibration) and each one is mounted onto "sound boxes" located just a few feet away from each other. The first tuning fork is struck, and it starts to vibrate actively, disturbing the air molecules around it and creating sound waves that produce a ringing sound. A moment later, the second tuning fork starts to actively vibrate and begins making the same sound, even though it hasn't been physically struck. The second tuning fork starts producing sound because its natural frequency matches the natural frequency of the first tuning fork (the one that was struck).

The second tuning fork starts ringing, and there's a very loud sound, two tuning forks ringing in unison. It's as if the vibration of the first tuning fork awakened the second. Because the two tuning forks have the same natural frequency, both forks become aware of the other's presence, even though they weren't before. The two tuning forks were always there, just a few feet away from each other. Still they didn't recognize that the other was there because they weren't actively vibrating at the same frequency. They were undetectable to each other until the ringing began. But as soon as they both started actively vibrating at the same frequency, they became "visible" to each other. It is as if they could experience each other in a physical sense only because this resonance occurred.

Consider that you are a tuning fork. Your body vibrates at a rate specific to the thoughts, sensations, and emotions that you hold at any one time. The experience you desire is the second tuning fork, with its own unique frequency. In the beginning, your desired experiences are invisible to you because you aren't actively resonating at the same frequency, but once you start resonating, you and your desired result are visible to one another, making it easy to attract. Your resonance is the outgoing frequency that you project. It works just like a radio that harmonizes with the frequency emitted from a radio tower. The quality of your awareness determines your outbound resonance; your consciousness is a magnet. Your quality of consciousness determines the quality or vibrational intensity of the energy you broadcast, which in turn, determines what is attracted to you.

It is important to understand that resonance **only starts** when the frequency of the two systems (the receiving and the emitting) are very close, or identical in frequency. Their ability to **harmonize determines what the Law of Attraction will draw to you**. In other words, you can't expect to send out a frequency of fear and get something that you love. A vibrational output of what is "loved" or "desired" can only resonate and draw to you a harmonious frequency resulting in a physical manifestation of the thing loved and desired.

Another way we can interpret the UL of Resonance is that it shows us how everything in the Universe is linked and communicates, acting as a whole. The way we all connect is through vibrations and resonance. This UL of Resonance expands on the Hermetic Principle of Vibration stating that within vibration there is also frequency and resonance.

Many people collapse the Law of Attraction and the Law of Resonance into one. These two Laws, like all the Laws, work together in harmony, but they aren't the same. Their origin story is they work in unison, collectively; no Law can be separate or severed from the others.

The Law of Attraction and The Law of Resonance

The Law of Attraction has a role in the manifestation process, but it doesn't work alone, none of the Laws do. The UL of Resonance is the *real* mechanism by which we manifest things. It's how we match our vibration to the vibration of the things we desire, causing them to appear in our lives. Understanding how resonance works in the manifestation process, shows us what we need to do in order to be successful in manifesting. So often we focus merely on raising our vibration, which is helpful, as we've seen; but all the ULs and Hermetic Principles work together, without separation, showing us that vibration is only a part of the process.

An important aspect of the tuning fork example is to notice that the second tuning fork didn't analyze whether it was a good idea to resonate with the first fork. It didn't say, "Oh, this is a bad thing or a good thing." It just responded to what it was receiving—the frequency from the first tuning fork.

The Universe is exactly the same, completely impersonal. It responds to what we send it without overthinking about it. This resonance is called sympathetic resonance. This sympathetic resonance is valuable to witness because it impacts all of us, it is why every empath and intuitive takes on the weight of the world—sometimes literally. This is why it's so important to be aware of this UL.

Our life force will respond and adjust to every energy that it is exposed to. If the momentum of the energy is stronger than the inner life force or our awareness, then our bodies are forced to adjust in a way where we feel a consequence.

If the energy is not aligned with our physical body, the consequence of that impact can range from mildly unpleasant to painful. This is why it is important to be aware of UL of Resonance. When we are unfocused and unpracticed, the energies can weaken our emotional and physical bodies.

Our energy field and physical body act like the tuning forks which will resonate to an internal or external stimulus. The stimulus can be anything—a person, place or thing—that carries a fundamental frequency and energetic signature. When we encounter someone that our energetic field harmonizes with, we actually feel the sensation of our vibrations matching. It's a wonderful feeling of attraction and deep connection. It feels like the most natural thing in the world. That's the feeling of resonance. UL Resonance is all around us, but somehow, we don't always recognize it because it isn't as obvious as the rattling of window panes.

This power of matching our frequency to the things we desire can only happen when we're willing to give up the idea that we have to willfully attract things into our life, the myth that **struggle** or work are required to have what we desire. Believing that you must work to attract something into your life is "efforting" (as Abraham calls it). In fact, looking at it this way is what keeps you from successful manifestations. This is why you feel you don't achieve resonance with your desires because you're also holding onto the idea that you must "attract" things into your life.

Attraction is what is so, there is no doing. When we focus on our resonance instead, there is a more accurate matching between us and our desire. If you're *trying* to attract something into your life, it stands to reason that you believe you don't already have it. The thing or experience you desire is somewhere separate from you, and you're attempting to draw it closer to you, into your life, through sheer effort. This creates more wobble because the way the Universe works is that if you perceive, feel, or believe you don't have something (because you think of it as being "over there" and not here), and that you must attract it toward you, that "separation" or "lack" is exactly what you'll get more of. You will literally manifest more of the "lack" of whatever you want.

Remember the tuning forks? They were recognizing each other, coming into resonance with each other. Recognize is the key word here. In order for two things to start actively vibrating at the same rate (coming into resonance), one must first recognize the other on a vibrational level. But the truth of the manifestation process is that you can only have or experience something once you perceive, feel, and believe that you already have it. This is where resonance comes in. This can only happen when the first tuning fork is "struck." (We are the tuning fork being struck when we acknowledge our desire and know we have the essence of it.) Only then, after they have "recognized" each other, will they start actively vibrating at the same rate. When they start actively vibrating at the same rate, they become visible and audible to one another, and they can experience being in each other's presence.

Universal Law of Reciprocity

UL of Reciprocity was another hair I felt I had to split when it came to the Universal Laws. Like the UL of Resonance, UL of Reciprocity plays a big part in all the Laws—how they relate and are in perfect harmony—working together all of the time without fail or bias, completely impersonal. This Universal Law, for me, takes things even deeper; this Law speaks to how all the Laws interact, without fail, always mutually dependent and connected but it also speaks to how manifestation happens. The Universe responds to our vibes, thoughts, actions and energy through UL of Reciprocity, the engine of creation.

This UL is the glue that keeps all the Laws working together. It states that all Laws must reciprocate and cooperate in harmony with each other for the mutual benefit of all. The more time I spent with this Universal Law I became incredibly aware of where I give my time, energy, and presence. I questioned where I wasn't giving and if that was a subconscious choice or conscious one. As I dove into that awareness, the more it made me think about Gandhi, and how he said if you want peace in the world, you must first be it. To me, this is the UL of Reciprocity. If I am peace, I will receive peace.

There are so many personal stories I could share around this UL revealing itself in my life, and the one similarity that runs through each of them is an understanding that we cannot have anything we are not—to have that loving partner who adores us, we must first adore ourselves. I find so much healing happens in this little incognito Law. So many people say this Law is a "freebie." Folks, in my experience nothing is further from the truth. This UL gives us a hint (wink, wink) to how we are to be in our world to get what we want, not just for our personal experience but for everyone on a global level as well.

The power of this Law is that it shows us why we can't completely manifest by using only one or two ULs (i.e. Law of Attraction and Vibration). Manifesting change into our lives requires using all of the ULs together, not just one or two. Using only one or two Laws is like trying to operate a car using only the engine and the brakes. For the car to work well, you also need the transmission, tires, and steering wheel.

It's interesting that we don't hear as much about the UL of Reciprocity as we do about the UL of Attraction (LOA). Perhaps this is because so many people collapse the two. LOA makes sure that *something* is attracted. It's the UL of Reciprocity that determines *how much* that something is.

UL of Reciprocity assures that what we receive is based on what we put out there, without fail. This is why the quality of the energy we broadcast is so important. What we put out comes back to us. This adage is true, yet sometimes we forget the quality or essence of the "what" is determined by our thoughts. This is why the quality of your broadcast is so powerful.

As you observe your physical outcomes and attach emotions to them, regardless of whether you may perceive them—good or bad—you are planting them as seeds into the infinite field of your potential and possibility. You can't plant corn and expect to get rice.

Regardless of our current experience, this is an exciting realization to arrive at because once we become consciously aware of these processes—how and why things work this way—we come to the realization that it is us who are creating our outcome through the quality of our emotional and thought based broadcast. We always have the choice to change those broadcasts and plant new seeds when we choose.

Let's look at the Law of Reciprocity (LOR) in a strictly physical sense. Some would simplify the LOR as "You scratch my back, I'll scratch yours," but this is inaccurate and limiting. When we fully "allow" the LOR to work, it bypasses the outcomes that are limited by fear, and opens us up to the infinite nature of potential. In other words, when you do something, always do it with deliberate focus and intention to contribute and you will receive an outcome based on the level of value that you gave. Although this Law is unwavering and predictable, when you focus only on a specific outcome, you are limiting the scope of possibility. When you can only see a person—including yourself—in a certain way then they can only be the way you see them. This is the LOR at work.

An outcome is delivered 100 percent of the time without fail with the LOR. That outcome is a direct reflection of what was given. Any other outcome is absolutely impossible and would violate every law of nature. This is why people who keep saying, "I believe in the LOA, but where's my money?" don't get the outcomes they are looking for. They are projecting the broadcast of their fear (of not having money) rather than truly giving. So the UL of Reciprocity gives them just exactly that, not having money.

Universal Law of Action

The UL of Action states that "No matter what we feel or know, no matter what our potential gifts or talents, only action brings them to life." This Law reflects the importance of action steps as a way of bringing consciousness into physical form.

This Universal Law for me is a tricky one. Because it speaks to action, most people collapse it to mean *doing*. So when I'm dancing with this Law, I remember the words of Ernest Hemingway, "Never mistake motion for action." The spirit behind this UL is that bringing anything into matter, physical form, requires an action. Action can look like many things, from visualization to literal physical action. Our movement toward our desire stirs the pot, so to speak, of those subatomic particle vibrations. This is the beginning of connecting and building our dreams in the physical form. Often times, people use the Law of Attraction as a way to keep themselves from stepping into action. They think they only need to sit on the sofa and think about what they want. Which is true to a certain extent, but the difference here is in the time of the manifestation. If you were to truly just sit on the sofa directing your mind to thoughts of having this thing you wanted, you would be moved and inspired into action. It is not enough to believe or know something in our mind; action is what brings it into existence. Our talents and gifts are lifeless until they are put into material expression through the physical steps we take. There is a fine line between Divine inspired action and getting things done. This is why the UL of Action comes into play and is an important step in manifesting our desires.

I read somewhere that the difference between an apprentice and a master is that an apprentice is always doing—so much so, that he ends up with "do-do" all over his face. A master, on the other hand, is focused on being, and in that being, actions unfold naturally. I learned that the most important thing is to step up with ready willingness to serve and then to follow through. I also learned that no matter how tired I think I am, if I step up and show up, the energy needed to complete a given goal is there for me. We can realize that we don't have to try to control everything; you don't have to "do" it all yourself. When you are in the flow, inspired actions become a graceful dance with the Divine. I now trust the Universe, the Divine I AM, the giver of all to provide the energies and opportunities, and I trust myself to take action appropriately.

Over my 20+ years of professional intuitive practice, I have seen so many clients alternating between being too depressed to act on anything and being so manic that they jump through millions of hoops of random actions that don't provide the outcome they desired. This is why it's important to focus on all the ULs, not just the Law of Action. It's not enough to take action. It is best if it is action integrated with all of the Laws, otherwise the action can be unfocused or misdirected. The Law of Action requires you to take a proactive role in creating your life. It isn't about leaving the other Principles and Laws behind. The Law of Action is a foundational step, and when interwoven with the other Laws, you move with intentional purpose.

When something feels forced, take a step back, reassess, but don't stay there. Set a time limit, a container for your reevaluation. Then, tune in and act accordingly. Action is where so many get tripped up on living the ULs because our culture is so focused on the outward expression of how things look. If you look busy, then you must be important, valuable, and worthy. If you look like you're struggling, others will think you are brave and courageous. These actions bring us manifestation of various results depending on our specifically chosen broadcast.

This Law teaches us how to act with purpose. It shows us that every action and step we take is with purpose. Each action also creates energy, action converts energy into motion, which is a necessary step in the manifestation process. Action means directing your energy and taking the inspired steps toward your desired outcome, your inspired goal. We want to extinguish old beliefs around what action is. It isn't being busy, rushing around, or struggling in motion. It is intentional action. We can't sit still with our idea for too long. When we sit in idleness after receiving that spark of inspiration from the Divine I AM within us, what happens is an equaled lack of motion, which means our dreams stay dormant and unrealized. Elizabeth Gilbert's shares in her book *Big Magic* what happens next. That Divine inspiration, that bubble of creation, becomes magnetized to energy and momentum which allows it to come into form. In other words, if you sit dormant, that idea seeks another avenue of creation. That's why when you have an idea and take no action and later you see someone "stole" your idea: "Hey, that's what I thought of." Divine inspiration will always find an outlet, and you are the amazing vessel it comes through. When you sit there immobile, the energy will move on to another. The Divine will always find an outlet for its expression.

So why do we stop? Why do we sit there frozen, convinced we don't know how or what to do next? Sometimes it's because we feel scared to take a risk or make a change. Taking action is important, but making sure that action is intentional is key. That's why we like to recommend using success habits, which are any actions that empower or direct your energy to expand and deepen. Some examples include journaling, meditation, exercise, and reaching out to friends to connect. We ask everyone to choose 3-5 to track weekly so they can understand why their alignment varies from week to week. When we show up for our success habits, we are consistently building our broadcast, creating movement in the direction of our goal, and it also shows us on paper that we've shown up for ourselves.

Other times you may start an action, but then give up before it has a chance to come into being. Maybe because we want everything "now," or we get discouraged when we don't see any immediate evidence or results. This is where some people stop. They give up thinking the ULs "don't work" and down they spiral. But, this is where we can utilize our intuitive connection to shift an old perspective. Any action is Divine, even if it is an action that you regret. It is still a lesson, an experience that heightened your awareness.

Taking action takes belief, faith, discipline, mental power, and persistent dedication. It is a commitment that requires energy, endurance, and focus.

Universal Law of Perpetual Transmutation

This UL gave me a solid foundation. Let me share what I mean. When I began to study the ULs deeply, asking tough questions—how does this relate to me, my life and the world?—I found this Law to be particularly exciting. How can a UL be exciting you might ask? Well, let me just say it this way: understanding that everything can be transmuted, changed, and shifted is powerful. The sheer thought of this mental model gave me a sense of my own personal power that I hadn't realized was possible. You see, when we can acknowledge that every situation, feeling, thought we have can be "moved" or transmuted into something new, power is placed in our laps.

The Law of Perpetual Transmutation states that energy is forever moving in and out of form. It cannot be created nor destroyed. Basically, this UL is about something we know already: the only constant is change. Universal energy is all around and within us changing states, and we have the power and capability to tap in and utilize it.

You cannot "create" energy, as it already exists in a quantum field of oneness. Energy can only be passed on from one to the other—neither created nor destroyed. Energy is transmutable.

Perpetual transmutation means that energy can transfer into matter and then back again into its pure state of energy, indefinitely. This means that energy, including us, cannot die, but instead simply changes form.

My biggest teachers in this Law have been my granddaughters, Layla, 12, and Keira, 7. Spending time with them shows me the ease of allowing personal "transmutation" to happen. Perhaps you've witnessed the same in your kiddos, or when you've been around toddlers? When they are extremely upset about something? They put their entire body into the process, their face grows red, tears run down their cheeks, crying desperately because their world is not as they want; five minutes later they are as happy as can be, as if the upset never happened. In those brief circumstances they are showing us how the UL of Transmutation works. They feel it, and their innate nature (their Divine nature) allows there to be a movement, a shifting from the horrid to the happy. Energy is ever transient—malleable and easily directed. Like they say: out of the mouth of babes...truer than we ever knew. By seeing the ease of allowing the shift of emotion in children, we know it's possible, even for us adults, despite it being a foreign path: it is possible and the rewards are epic. Imagine yourself not jumping on the bandwagon of anger, but instead allowing it to morph and move to reveal your happiness. Sounds impossible, doesn't it? Magic is possible to those who believe. The question here is, how much do you want to feel good? Or is it more dramatic and fun to feel like a victim of lack?

"Without birth and death, and without the perpetual transmutation of all forms of life, the world would be static, rhythm-less, undancing, mummified." - Alan Watts

Consider water, whose chemical makeup is H_2O, two hydrogen atoms and one oxygen atom. When we slow down the water's vibration it transmutes into ice. When we speed up the vibration, the water's form transmutes into steam. The water's energy isn't being destroyed or created; it is simply moving into different forms: liquid water, ice, and steam.

Any situation is always shifting, moving, changing. Everything—every person, place, or thing—is constantly adjusting, changing form, shifting conditions, moving into another nature.

Energy is evenly present in all places at all times. It is in a constant state of transmission and transmutation. Everything vibrates, and it changes as it moves from one vibratory state to another—from a higher frequency to a lower frequency and then back to a higher frequency. All energy is moving into form and out of form and into form and out of form. Energy is either creating or disintegrating; nothing ever dies—it only transforms.

We are energy, and our brain acts like an electromagnetic switching station, which converts light rays into signals we understand. Our thoughts are energy that transform and manifest our lives. The more attention given an idea (especially when we add emotion to it), the faster it will change form. This is why our emotions are so powerful. They fuel our trajectory, the direction of our momentum.

By using our mind and connecting with our intuition, we tap into a higher consciousness and create the image we want to bring into the physical realm.

Again, the universal truth of this Law is that energy can be actively transmuted.

In *The Science Of Getting Rich*, Wallace D. Wattles, an American new thought author, speaks to how energy from the formless realm is constantly flowing into the material world and taking form. Constantly flowing, this energy is limitless and inexhaustible. As old forms are exhausted, they give way for new forms to emerge. The Law of Perpetual Transmutation gives us the understanding that everything seen and unseen is constantly changing. We can harness this energy and transform it into whatever form we desire. Do you realize this means all those so-called mistakes from the past are disintegrating and becoming a part of something new, the new you? Bringing this awareness into your body, you will see if you spend time looking at the past, judging yourself, your choices, your experiences, you are recreating and signaling the same things to come into form again. You are the one directing those recurrences in your experience because you refuse to let that energy disembark and dis-integrate into a new form.

Everything is always changing—growing or dying. We can work to ease up our resistance to not only change but also welcome the unknown. If we're living the ULs, we know the future because we create it, now and now and now and now. Our current results are nothing more than the side effects of our historic thoughts. Read that again.

In order to change our results, we must change the way we think. There is a direct relation between the quality of our thinking and the quality of our results. Whatever thought we impress upon our mind will move into physical form. It does not matter if this is a positive or negative thought. The subconscious mind must accept whatever thought energy is impressed upon it. When we realize that any thought held in our mind must move into physical form, we have direct control over the thoughts we think. Therefore, we have direct control over the results we get. In reality, there is nothing that we can actually lose, since in terms of energy, everything is and always will be. Nothing is destroyed.

Everything that exists is energy manifested in different forms. Therefore, there are only changes, transformations, movement, transfers, flow, and exchanges occurring all the time, no losses. Whatever we believe, we create. Money flows in our lives, coming and going, but it is never lost. Knowing this, we wouldn't view death as a loss but as a metamorphosis. That is, the beginning of a new life. No longer having a job does not mean losing a job but rather changing the type of work we do. For example, no clients may mean it's time to work on a book. No longer having a partner doesn't mean losing them, but rather a shift of the depth, condition, and energy of the relationship.

The entire universe is made up of energy, and all of it is moving at varying speeds. All energy fields are connected. From the physical body that we can touch, see, and feel, to the sun's rays, we are all connected.

Universal Law of Oneness

This UL of Oneness states that everything affects everything else. All is inter-related. All we say, do, and think affects everyone and everything. This Law states that everything that exists is connected with everything else, because we all originate from the exact same source. We are all inter-linked. John Lennon simplified oneness in his song *Imagine*. Everything that exists, seen and unseen, is connected to each other and inseparable from one another. What we think, say, do, and believe will have a corresponding effect on others and the world around us.

When we work with this UL, we realize that what we think of each other (as we learned in the Hermetic Principle of Correspondence) is a reflection of not only how we think of ourselves but also how they think of us (since the energy gets shared). As we think of the Divine in others, they will in turn think of the Divine in us. This is where our thoughts, feelings, and actions weave into each aspect of our lives. Hence the saying, "We reap what we sow." This is yet another beautiful example of the weaving of the ULs together. They are all interrelated and connected. There is not one without the others.

Everything consists of energy. Your subatomic particles aren't fixed. In fact, particles may be flowing into and out of you now from the sky, the floor, your best friend, and your loved one. In other words, **there is no separation**. We are lead to embrace that we are continuously creating our experiences. We are accountable regardless if we are "awake," woke, or enlightened. Even if someone has no awareness of these ULs, they are still activating them. Oneness is also known as unity or universal consciousness, the unified field, God, or even love.

In Taoism, Divine oneness is known as the concept of "Tao." The "unified field" in physics is a term for what ancients have known to be as pure consciousness. The eternal essence of oneness in its purest sense denotes that it is timeless and universal. Oneness is truth. Its opposing force is the illusion of duality and separation. Mystical traditions teach that mind and matter are not separate, and you can place your mind over matter.

"You are not separate from the whole. You are one with the sun, the earth, the air. You don't have a life. You are life." - Eckhart Tolle

This is where being of service and being collaborative with others puts us in Divine alignment. The UL of Oneness is one of the ways we can explore a sense of oneness as well as begin to truly embody and appreciate the Divine love, power, and wisdom we have to share, focus, and direct into creation. The UL of Oneness states that everything that exists emanates from one, the same Source.

But how exactly are we all connected? Well, at the most basic level, the elements which make up our bodies, and every object in our physical world, originates from the nuclear fusion reactions at the core of distant stars. When these stars reach the end of their lives, they detonate in massive supernova explosions and send their raw materials hurtling through space at the speed of light. These raw materials deposit on different planets and give those planets the building blocks for life. From this perspective, we can say we are all the direct descendants of stardust; on a molecular frame of reference, everything and everyone within the Universe is comprised of the same building blocks. This interconnectedness means that the world does not consist of separate things. Mind and matter are not separate from each other nor are we human beings separate from each other, or from the world around us, or from nature, or from seemingly non-living matter. Consider how you belong to the greater web of life.

Let's look at an example: What can we do with one brick? Perhaps use it as a doorstop, or maybe a paper weight. Its uses are small when used alone. But if you have over a billion bricks, think of all the potential possibilities. They can be used to build walls, buildings, houses, driveways, and schools.

Together they can build what one brick could not. So, during those times when we are feeling small, when the desire ahead is bigger than we think we are—like that lonely brick—remember we have the whole to draw upon. We are not alone, ever.

That single brick couldn't build a house by itself, but it is extremely important, as a part of the whole. That solo brick becomes support for the other bricks and equally needs the support of the rest of the bricks to become important and valuable as well. Those who work alone and are unclear on their "why," thinking they don't need others to support them, resemble the single brick. They are useful, but they are not attaining their Divine potential. Whereas someone acting out of service for others and supporting and being supported by one another can achieve their true potential. The service we are talking about here is being of service to the Divine I AM within you. What does that mean? It means listening and following our Divine Guidance. It does not mean that we are here to act how others want us to or in a way that makes others feel better about themselves. We are here to have our journeys, our adventures, while remembering our Divine power, love, wisdom, and interconnectedness with the world around us. The word "Universe" itself reveals this fact. *Uni* is Latin for "one." Universe comes from the Latin word *universus* which translates into "combined into one."

Universal Law of Relativity

This is another powerful Law to dance with. I like looking at it that way—dancing and exploring the energy and feeling of these Laws and how they connect with the energy that is around us, all day and every day. When I sunk my teeth into this UL, it was a savory flavor that has fueled me each and every moment of my life ever since.

In 1905, Albert Einstein's theory of Relativity used the principles of physics to deduce that there is no fixed frame of reference in the Universe. Everything is moving relative to everything else. You have been living this theory your whole life, comparing and walking through thresholds of initiation—learning, expanding—and experiencing the meaning you have placed on your experiences.

This Law states that each person will receive a series of problems (initiation tests or lessons) for the purpose of strengthening their soul experience within them. Each of these experiences, tests, and lessons are meant to be a challenge. The goal is to remain connected to our hearts when proceeding to step into the solution, resolution, and understanding. We must walk through the gateways of obstacles, challenges, and hindrances in order to both experience and master our path. This is all a part of our human and soul's journey of growth and development. It is the difficulties in life that test our character and inner fortitude. Enduring a series of trials and tribulations allows us to cultivate strength, endurance, and wisdom.

This Law also teaches us to compare our problems to others' problems, which puts them into their proper perspective. No matter how bad we perceive our situation to be, there is always someone who is in a worse position. It's all relative.

After writing a book with Doreen Virtue, we went on tour with the publishing house, Hay House. I attended a party for the authors and had an incredible interaction with Wayne Dyer (a well-known spiritual thought leader) that changed everything for me. I was "accidentally" perched next to him in the cozy setting—a VIP suite—where I got to literally rub elbows with some incredible teachers and authors. He looked at me with his bright blue eyes and said, "Hey kiddo, what's your deal?" Seriously, he was so down to earth, and I was arrogant enough to feel comfortable in the space of a wise man like him. I smiled and began talking at 90 miles an hour. Being the quintessential Divine Masculine, he listened intently, and we began a conversation about Universal Laws and how their application is essential to truly knowing them.

We talked about the UL of Relativity and how prayer helped him to activate it. He said that prayer allowed him to see the situation he was praying about from a different angle, the Divine angle. Still, when I share this story, I feel him beside me, chuckling. As I sat there, speechless on my little perch beside him taking in his words, he nodded and winked at me—Yeah, you get it.

Honestly, at the time, I wasn't sure I "got" it. After our chat, I spent time focusing on what he shared with me. I wondered how could I change everything simply by the way I look at it. I would lie on my bed, put my head over the edge, and look at everything upside down. It was my way to begin to look at things differently—until the blood rushed to my head.

With the Universal Law of Relativity, I learned that it was me who was accepting the stories of disempowerment. I began to research different ways to expand my connection to my power and as I did I began to hit the roadblocks of my stories of being enough. Putting this UL to work, I stopped looking at my perceived failures as mistakes, and instead, I looked at them as roadside railings to keep me going the direction that best fulfills my Divine potential.

I was also able to change how I saw not only my life choices but also the choices of others, which obliterates the victim conversation. As I write this, I can hear Wayne Dyer's voice in my head saying, "If you change the way you look at things, the things you look at change." Which to me is the true expression of this Law.

Both the spiritual and metaphysical aspects of this Law tell us that everything in our physical world is only made real by its relationship or comparison to something else. Light only exists because we compare it to darkness. Good can only exist because we compare it to bad. Hot can only exist because we compare it to cold. In fact, everything in our life, ***just is,*** until we compare it to something else. **Nothing in life has any meaning, except for the meaning that we give it.**

It is all about how you look at your situation and what thoughts and perspective you choose to focus on within the situation. When you focus on good thoughts and energies, more good things will come to you. Likewise, if you focus on how difficult your situation is, you will attract more of the same. This is where we start melding with the Law of Attraction, right? You see that all the Laws are relative to one another. What if the "reality" of a situation is difficult to see or accept? From a spiritual point of view, we can remove barriers of labeling and accept everything as it is.

"In form, you are and will always be inferior to some, superior to others. In essence, you are neither inferior nor superior to anyone. True self-esteem and true humility arise out of that realization. In the eyes of the ego, self-esteem and humility are contradictory. In truth, they are one and the same."
- Eckhart Tolle

We want to make a special note here: we aren't meant to suffer, to have epic pain, before stepping into our freedom. That's not what this is about. This UL shows us that we can expect and understand contrasts (times that are opposite in nature to other phases or experiences in our lives). Contrasts reveal themselves as lessons. They are here with a purpose to guide us to master our life purpose, not to send us into a death spiral.

On Suffering

In many spiritual and religious dogmas, it is believed that to suffer and to struggle is to be noble. It is thought that we are held in greater respect if we have walked through fire or sacrificed ourselves for the benefit of another, constantly and consistently. Do we want to live this as a truth? Do we really believe that to be worthy means to suffer every second of our life? When I sit with my intuition and this thought, it doesn't feel good.

We are not meant to suffer as humans, as children of the Divine. We are meant to live life fully with love, and while suffering will occur in our lives through contrasting experiences, it is not a place to reside. Suffering is not meant to be a place where we dwell. It is not where we make our home. What I mean by that is that, yes, we will experience suffering, but we do not have to perpetuate this suffering to be worthy. We can move through it and create the best outcome with what we have. Yes, contrasting moments will happen in our life. In fact, contrasting moments and suffering are the fuel that brings clarity. Sometimes, struggle arises as we compare ourselves to others. Maybe, we want the opinions of others to validate our path. Or maybe we seek validation through the number of social media followers we have. As we do this, we create inner suffering, because that external validation will not always exist. We must move past the suffering and create this inner validation for ourselves. The danger exists in dwelling on our suffering and never moving past it.

When we recognize that we are a part of this interconnected Universe of love and connection, we realize that we are not alone. We are not against the world. There is no one trying to hurt us. It is us who is in a beautiful interwoven partnership with the energy that creates and connects everything. The Divine exists in our computers, inside of the pages we are reading, inside of our apple, our tea, our home. The Divine is in everything. We are not separate from it and it is not separate from us. Keeping this in mind about suffering, as we look at the four Noble Truths of Buddhism, we see the truth that there is a way out of suffering, and that the way out is within ourselves:

The Four Noble Truths

Noble Truth One. Life always involves suffering. This suffering may be obvious or it may be subtle. Even when things feel good, most of us have an undercurrent of anxiety or uncertainty within us.

Noble Truth Two. The cause of suffering is our never-ending cravings. We crave and suffer because we have learned and developed a mistaken thought: we are separate from Spirit. We live in this separateness of "I" and this is a cycle that is painful. It is a cycle that keeps our ego intact and ensures ongoing pain.

Noble Truth Three. The great news is that there is an end to this suffering! It is just a matter of us parting the clouds to see the sunshine above. This awakened consciousness lies within ourselves, and it has always been here.

Noble Truth Four. We can rise to enlightenment and freedom. We can take the path of the Buddha by living ethically and incorporating a regular meditation practice. Through this, we can wake up and step out of our struggle and suffering.

From a higher standpoint, this Law shows us that how we view an experience can be changed or adjusted. It is all a matter of perception and perspective. Understanding all of this helps us endure and solve problems with more grace. When we look at it from the viewpoint of relativity, we can keep everything in perspective.

As we step deeper into living the ULs, we can work with the Law of Relativity as we choose to live consciously versus living on auto-pilot. In that consciousness, we step forward being accountable and aware of everything we say, especially as it "relates" to our perspective and goals. This is where we can witness our judgment. When we slow down and see the UL of Relativity at work, we can acknowledge what meanings we have attached to things.

What helps me to stop and slow down and get a hold of judging someone else, is this UL of Relativity. The challenge is to utilize a judgment from a Divine perspective. We use judgment as a fast way to sort through options to make choices without thinking. The distance of a car—is it safe to make the turn or should I wait? That requires judgment. Where it can get sticky is when we start using it as a measure that is fixed, or anchored so that everything is compared to it. This UL builds our conscious awareness of comparison and shows us how we give meanings to things. *Remember, every single decision a person makes is relative to some other decision.*

The Law of Relativity states that all things are relative, good or bad, big or small, rich or poor. It is all relative. So, be diligent in what you compare yourself to. Be grateful for those things that bring you joy. Be grateful for what you have because not everyone has it. Be grateful for who you are because there is no one else like you.

This UL is one of my favorites, mostly because it gives me solace. In those times when things are bumpy, I'm reminded that the Divine within me lives these Principles with ease, and my personality—my ego—can be quieted when I realize this UL can help me assess the meanings I tie to things. I AM the creator because everything in this physical world is made real by my comparisons and my relationships to them. The people we cross paths with, regardless of the interaction, are here to guide us to expansion, expanding our capacity to love.

Many people use this Law against themselves in a self-defeating way, and that's a big reason why there is such a huge percentage of our world suffering from an inferiority complex. And this is probably why low self-esteem is so predominant in our world. Many are unconsciously using this Law to sabotage their self-image, skills, and talents.

The main work I've had to do on myself is establishing a wealth consciousness. Being raised by a single mom who worked two jobs, I witnessed my mom unconsciously using this Law in a self-defeating way. Despite wanting abundance and wealth, she focused on the struggle and the "not having" aspect in every situation. Her focus on this was so prevalent in her life that it became a habit. This is an example where habit is the obstacle we need to walk through (as in the habit of self-sabotage). But the good news is, this default habit can be reset.

Let's look at this from a UL of Relativity perspective: how can you shift your wealth consciousness, career experiences, and all aspects of your life? Stop comparing and start observing. We are trained to "compare" everything. We compare ourselves to everything and everyone. It is all a matter of perception, not comparison.

Universal Law of Compensation

Approaching this UL, I was naïve at first, thinking it was all about the money. This Law says you will always be compensated for your energy and contribution – whatever it is, however much or however little. Interestingly, Ralph Waldo Emerson writes in his essay titled, "Law of Compensation," that each person is compensated in a manner he or she has contributed, and this even exchange is what this Law is all about.

This Law states that everything will be compensated—our time, intention, focus, and action will be rewarded. For every energy we put out into the world—be it opening a door for a stranger or leading thousands of people—it will be repaid, reimbursed, and returned. This Law is echoed in the adage "nature abhors a vacuum." When we grow, we create space and the Universe always fills it. Ralph Waldo Emerson describes compensation like this:

"For everything you have missed, you have gained something else, and for everything you gain, you lose something else...a system of compensations. Every defect in one manner is made up in another. Every suffering is rewarded; every sacrifice is made up; every debt is paid."

Some say this Law is associated with laws of balance and karma. This isn't a bleak Law that says with everything you gain, you lose. It is about balance in a Universal sense. Someone out there in the world is rich, but unhappy, and yet another person out there is poor, but happy. It is the yin and yang of balance. It is said that the Law of Compensation is the abundance factor of the Law of Cause and Effect. It delivers the gifts of what we create.

In Marianne Williamson's book, *The Law of Divine Compensation*, this is how she describes it:

"...the universe is both self-organizing and self-correcting. To whatever extent your mind is aligned with love, you will receive divine compensation for any lack in your material existence. From spiritual substance will come material manifestation. This is not just a theory; it is a fact. It is a law by which the universe operates, I call it the Law of Divine Compensation. The universe is programmed to manifest through you, the highest possibilities for your creativity and joy."

Imagine if you applied this Law to your life. Where in your life can you imagine going above and beyond being of service? In your job, even if you are the largest producer in your field, how could you give more to the people around you? You'd be amazed at how easy it is to invoke the UL of Compensation by sharing a kind word with another person.

These are the **all powerful** Hermetic Principles and Universal Laws. The reason we call them the all powerful is because it is as if the Wizard of Oz, himself, gave them to us when he gave scarecrow his brain, tin-man his heart and the lion his courage. These are our gifts of wisdom, the how-tos of creation. Just as the wizard told Dorothy she had the power to go home within her all along, we too, have the power within us to create worlds. These natural access points are the code, the key to the treasure map, the answer to centuries of questions about the Universe and living within it. These guidelines show us how to work in this closed system; if you listen and pay close attention you can find the solution to whatever you seek, and have an incredible life.

CHAPTER 8

Keep Your Eyes Peeled

"Life is one big road with lots of signs. So when you're riding through the ruts, don't complicate your mind. Flee from hate, mischief and jealousy. Don't bury your thoughts, put your vision to reality. Wake Up and Live!"

- BOB MARLEY

Intuition is with us 24/7. There is not a minute of the day that our intuition is not present. When I first started this work, I didn't really trust this—that we had the ability to always tap into our intuition, that it was always present. I thought things were coincidences, and it took me a while to see that they were actually incidents that were co-operating. One of the greatest realizations I had is that the Divine wants to help us. The Divine wants us to connect with our intuition and wake up this powerful sixth sense. This Divine knows that our lives will be easier, and we will feel supported if it is awake. All day, every day, there are signs that are available to us.

For example, as I am immersed in the final edit of this book, I am sitting on my deck enjoying the sun and feeling excited about it. I am excited about being a part of the project and also connected to helping people heal and step into their mastery with their intuition. Out of nowhere, a feather lands at my feet and a butterfly flies right in front of my face. We can call these incidents happenstance *or* we can see that this is a direct communication from the non-physical realm.

When I first started in this field, I relied on Lynnette's book, *Angel Numbers*, to help me understand the messages I was receiving. When I took my first intuition class, it did not surprise me that I had coincidentally moved into a building with the number 555 (which can be interpreted as big changes are coming). This is the interpretation and understanding *Angel Numbers* gave me. As I paid attention to the moment, I was in the repetitious numbers I was seeing, I started to connect that there was a powerful message in that moment.

Signs take all shapes and sizes. The biggest thing to note is if a sign impacts you. A client of mine got a new condo and right outside her loft was a sign that was hidden earlier by the foliage of a tree. The sign said "Billionaire lottery winner." To her, that was a sign that her next art show was going to be a success. And it was: she sold her work to some amazing people, one of whom realized he needed 12 more pieces and consigned her to do custom pieces to go in his multiple houses.

When beginning to trust your intuition, signs are a powerful friend. In the beginning when I was building my intuition, I would wake up and ask for a big sign each and every day to confirm I was on the right path for my purpose. Some days the signs would be small, like finding a quarter on the sidewalk. Other times, the signs would be big, like witnessing magic before my eyes. Years ago, when I was struggling with the decision about taking on intuitive coaching full time, I would repeatedly see a mouse in my home. At the time, I was working part time in medicine and part time in intuitive coaching. I was the only one in the house who would ever see it. The mouse was a symbol of running around and looking for the scraps. When I made the decision to jump into practicing intuitive work full time, the mouse completely disappeared. Like everything else, signs are what you make them mean.

With time, I have expanded and now I am aware of other signs, including animals, shifts in perception, colors and more. This awareness has helped me to build the consciousness of Divine support that is always around us, which in turn helps with our intuition.

The use of signs is incredibly powerful throughout our lives, and especially when we are first starting. It reminds us that we are not alone. The key is to pay attention to what we are thinking and pondering at the same time we receive the sign. You will be surprised at how bang-on the Universe always is!

Witnessing Miracles

The book *A Course in Miracles* defines a miracle as a correction in perception. It is not about shifting anything outside of us, but looking at how we perceive the world. All miracles happen at a mental level (remember mentalism?) and may or may not have resulted in differences in the external world. When we sit with or consider this definition, can you see and be present with all the miracles in your life? Have you noticed a shift in how you perceive yourself? Have you noticed a difference in how you perceive your family? These are true miracles. A miracle is a change in perception, that is it.

When we realize that we are all connected to the "One Mind," we know and see that our essence is love, peace, and connection. This is available to us at every moment. Are we willing to witness the miracles from our mind first? Can we see that our intuition is always with us through miracles, signs, and signals?

Being Present to Magic and Synchronicities

When we are willing to open our eyes and be present in the now, we are able to be witness to the realization that magic is happening all day every day. Magic is the middle name of Spirit, the Divine, our intuition. We sometimes think magic is something we experience once in a while, but magic is truly present all day, every day. Are you willing to be present with what is and witness it?

Synchronicities are exactly that, things that are synced up. Now, the world defines synchronicity a bit differently. The *Merriam Webster* definition is simply a simultaneous occurrence of events which appear significantly related but have no discernible causal connection. Of course, those of us who understand the ULs know that this is impossible. Everything has a connection, and there are no separations. Energy is energy, and nothing happens randomly.

What this means is that we are able to watch as the Universe works for us. Can we be open to see how the coincidences, synchronicities, and magic are playing out in our lives? Are we willing to notice and be present to the everyday magic that happens all around us? Are we willing to jot these seemingly small occurrences, on a Success List, where we can track all our wins, big or small?

The Daily Success List is a habit that we recommend to boost awareness of the small and large accomplishments of our day. The idea is to list a minimum of five things you accomplished or succeeded in that day. They can be simple things: made the bed, exercised, meditated, showed up to write today, used a process, (from the Divine Prescriptions section) and didn't argue with my spouse. When we start keeping track of the magic, we begin to notice and see that it is all around us.

Patterns

There are patterns in everything. Sacred patterns exist everywhere around us, and they are the fundamental templates of the Universe. Galileo said, "Mathematics is the alphabet with which God has written the Universe." Artists use sacred geometry and create patterns and shapes that help us see that everything is connected and organized. Patterns are the fundamental building blocks of the Universe. As humans, we are simply a pattern. Our DNA is a double helix pattern, and we carry behavioral patterns from our parents, grandparents, and so on. These patterns can be shifted through observation. Are we willing to see the patterns that are constantly occurring in our lives? Sometimes those patterns show up as an intense contrast, which is the Divine telling us it is time to make a change. Many of our patterns originated in generations before us, and yet we still live with them! If they are creating havoc in our lives, are we willing to shift these patterns?

Just noticing our patterns is a success. Our patterns remind us that we are part of the Universal energy of oneness. We are reminded that it is okay to have these patterns and they are inherent in the bigness of who we are. We are not separate. We are a part of something much more. Patterns show us that.

Numbers

Do you see a sequence of numbers repeatedly? What do those numbers mean to you? Numbers are a forgotten language, and they provide insight and access into Divine Guidance. They are a shorthand way we can instantly know the direction the Divine is showing us.

Through receiving messages for my book, *Angel Numbers*, I realized that accessing Divine Guidance through numbers goes all the way back to the ancient wisdom of teachers like Pythagoras, Plato, and Hermes (recognize him? Hermetic Principles!). Pythagoras said everything in the Universe is mathematically precise. Every number has a specific vibration, frequency, and meaning. He wrote that everything in the Universe is constructed from basic geometrical shapes birthed from numbers, triangles (3), and squares (4). The Kabbalah, Jewish tradition, speaks to the energy and vibration of numbers. Numerology is a sacred science that has kept up with modern times. Numbers show us our Divine Guidance on this earth plane, the third dimension, and guide us to the lessons, guidance, and growth our soul needs in this lifetime. I want to point out that this is not usual numerology; this is what we call "angel numbers." When you find yourself noticing repetitive number sequences, you definitely want to pay attention, because the Universe is speaking to you.

Divine Guidance Through Numbers

0. The Alpha and Omega—The Divine, God, the center of ALL.

1. Watch your thoughts the Universe is taking a snapshot of your thought in this moment to bring it into form.

2. Don't give up before the miracle occurs—keep going.

3. Divine teachers are surrounding you to give support; listen closely.

4. Angels and Divine beings are surrounding and supporting you now.

5. Change is coming, or it is time to make a change.

6. Material things or conditions are taking too much of your focus. Notice your attention.

7. Good job—way to go—you are on the right path—keep going.

8. Infinite abundance in wealth, health and Spirit.

9. Get to WORK! Your purpose is calling you!

Animals and Nature

Nature is one of the best ways the Universe communicates with us. Animals and plants are messengers. We can ignore these with ease especially when living in a big city, and yet these messages are loud and clear and always around us. Ted Andrews' book, *Animal Speak* is a great resource to dive deeper into these signs and discover their meanings.

Dreams

Dreams are symbolic ways of connecting and giving us a message. Many times we do not remember the dream in detail, but we can remember the feeling. Those feelings and basic parts of the dream are symbols and signs that the Universe is speaking to you. When we have prophetic dreams or dreams where we wake up and can't discern if it was a dream because it feels incredibly REAL as if the person is standing right there, those dreams are actually true visitations.

Songs

Songs are a great way to access Divine Guidance, because of the meanings, feelings and associations they conjure. Most of us have connections with certain songs and memories. Music brings me back to the 1980s and my years in high school and times of great inner torment. I often receive a sign when certain songs from that time comes on. It generally is there to tell me that my saboteur is fully in charge. I also often receive songs when I'm reading for clients. They are like shortcuts that hit the center of the bullseye. My clients often love it when a song comes through because they'll use it as their "theme" song to move through what they are working on. Pay attention!

Physical Pain

All physical ailments are a sign. A sign that something isn't balanced in our bodies, and that is okay! The physical body is the greatest divination tool you will ever have. Are you willing to listen?

All of the cells in our body move. There is constant communication between the mind, the Spirit and the body. Our body is not stiff like a robot, and the Spirit can use our body to give us messages. Most people have experienced the butterflies in the stomach when walking onto a stage to speak or the tightness in the neck when we have too many things on our mind. These are great examples of how we get signs or messages through the physical. When we get the butterflies, it is the Divine saying you got this and your mind is worried, excited and anticipating. Neck tension is the way of the Divine saying you have the capability of getting through this, but the mind believes that it is too much to handle. This discrepancy between our personality's opinion and the Divine's opinion is the key. Many of us have experienced shoulder pain. Our shoulders can get achy when we feel as if we are carrying the burden of the world on our own. Lower back tension is often related to fears around money and our own self-worth. These are just a few examples of how the body imprints pain to give us messages that we may not be hearing otherwise. For more details on messages through your body, we recommend Louise Hay's book, *You Can Heal Your Life.*

Sirens

Sirens are a great attention getter; it's as if the Universe is shouting, "HEY LISTEN RIGHT NOW!!" Anytime while doing client sessions if I see or hear sirens, I know I need to pay attention to what's being said in that moment as well as what's going on for my client. In my office where I see clients, sirens will go by when I need to pay greater attention to what is happening to my client. This is big. It always works this way.

As you read this section on signs, you may start to think, but really? Could it really be that I saw an eagle and it meant that? And the answer is YES, YES, YES! You are the center of your Universe.

Everything that is happening to you at this moment is to give you information, guidance, a heads up, or a hello from the Divine. You are an important part of the Universe. Your presence matters, and you are loved. You matter, and yes, we all matter. And we are all the centers of our own Universes. As more of us listen to the signs and ourselves, we fill the Universe with greater love and connectedness.

A key to seeing the Universe at work is to pay attention to the signs. Don't dismiss them. As you write them down, you are seeing your connection and commitment to all that is in this world. This helps us shift out of the ego's fear and into connection and love.

CHAPTER 9

Interacting With Energy

"Every feeling is a field of energy. A pleasant feeling is an energy which can nourish. Irritation is a feeling which can destroy. Under the light of awareness, the energy of irritation can be transformed into an energy which nourishes."

- THICH NHAT HANH

We discussed the scientific and spiritual forms of energy earlier. Now, we will delve into how we can start to see spiritual energy in other people. To do this, we must start by understanding and noticing auras.

Auras, simply put, are the energy we can see radiating off of people. Noticing this energy is an important step in waking up our clairsentience. When working in intuitive sessions (on our own or with other people), being in tune to energy helps us feel the Divine, feel the goosebumps and the tingles, and consequently, notice the messages coming through to us. Feeling energy can also help us to be aware of our body cues. Sometimes, we are disconnected from our body and are programmed to ignore some of the subtle cues our body is relaying to us. We get little cues before the big ones. Feeling energy is also important as many times we can feel an energy, but unsure of where it came from. For example, when we walk out of a party, we may feel a pain in our back that was not there before. By being aware of energy, we can notice when someone else's energy is impacting us and use tools to redirect it. Feeling energy has many benefits, and most people already do it, they just may not be aware they are!

Most people have unknowingly felt energy, and if not, we have a really simple and fun exercise to help you where you can get comfortable with feeling and witnessing the energy between your hands. All of the exercises in this book are about having fun and staying out of your head. No analyzing, thinking, or criticizing allowed. Try this little experiment to feel your own energy.

Feeling an Energy Ball

- Close your eyes and focus on your breath. Take a few deep, slow breaths in and out.
- Place your hands about six inches apart and imagine that you have a soccer ball between your hands. Rotate your hands in opposite directions. One hand can move clockwise and the other can move counter-clockwise. As you do this, go slowly and then speed up and then go slowly. You can't get this wrong.
- Start to notice if you feel anything between your hands. You can pull your hands out to make the width even bigger, or put them closer to each other to make the ball smaller. You may feel a sponge like bounce between your hands.
- Continue to do this for a few minutes. Have fun with this invisible yet palpable ball. Start to notice if there are any sensations in your palms, fingers, or body.
- You may start to feel tingling, hot and cold burning, or goosebumps. It may be slight or quite pronounced.
- It may feel sticky or thick or buzzing.
- It doesn't matter if you feel something or not. This is about play! You are getting your body accustomed to feeling energy, and each of us feels it differently.
- If you got the buzzing or tingling or perceived anything, great! If you didn't, you may have dismissed the subtleties of the energy. Go back and try again by simply closing your eyes, breathing deeply and feeling the sponginess between your hands.
- Continue to practice this regularly.

Once we've practiced feeling energy, we can start to practice seeing auras. Energy can look different to each of us. It is unique to every living thing and is very real. On a hot summer day, have you ever seen the heat vapors coming off of the road? That is energy. Just being aware that energy can be seen is important. Examples like this remind us that energy looks different to each of us, but is real. Like rainbows, arguably, from each of our unique perspectives we see different rainbows, but the rainbow itself still exists.

Aura

An aura is an electromagnetic energy field that surrounds people, animals, and living things. And as we open to our abilities we find that we can feel, sense and see energy. Seeing auras requires a softening of our vision, utilizing the cones of the outer parts of our eyes, the same ones we use for our peripheral vision. If you feel challenged by seeing auras, don't worry, the more you practice and work with your clairvoyance the easier it will become. And because we can also feel aura energy you may sense auras from your clairsentience perspective; you may get a sense of texture, colors, etc. The exciting thing about discovering your ability to sense these energy fields is the opportunity to experiment and discover how we relate to the energy, which is completely unique to everyone.

Seeing an Aura

Our eyes—when used all day, every day—get used to focusing on specific objects. When we are trying to see an aura, we need to relax our eyes to redirect our focus. Look off into the distance at a spot for 30-60 seconds. Then relax your focus. Let your vision soften. As you do this, notice the objects outside of your direct line of sight, in the periphery of your vision. Breathe and relax with this soft-focused vision.

To practice seeing an aura, go to a neutral colored wall and ask the person you are viewing to stand in front of the wall. Stand at least 1.5-2 feet in front of them. Now, close your eyes and breathe. Sink into your body, and ask your Divine Guidance to show you the aura and its color. Continue to take deep breaths, assuring yourself and your connection to your Divine Guidance, remembering you are asking to see this aura to build your abilities to be of service.

As you gently open your eyes, look at the wall (not the person) and begin to sense their energy field. Softly gaze at the wall and gaze "through" the person in front of you. As you do this, ask the color to be shown to you.

Sometimes you may not see it with your eyes open. If that happens, try closing your eyes.

Aura Colors

Each color of an aura has significance, and we need to remember that this meaning is not frozen in time. It can shift and be flexible. Auras can change constantly and will change depending on our alignment, emotion, and what we are experiencing in life. Here is a general guideline for the color's associations:

Red. Life force, survival, anger, frustration, determination, feeling overwhelmed

Orange. Sensitivity, creativity, health, vitality, physical pleasure, lack of reason, lack of self discipline

Yellow. Mental alertness, analytical thinking, optimism, childlike, thinking more than feeling, ego driven

Green. Healing, peace, new growth, need for security, jealousy, envy

Blue. Verbal communication, free thinking, emphasis on business, male energy, sadness, possibilities

Purple. Wisdom, authoritative, royalty, divinity, wisdom, sense of control, intuition, feeling of superiority

Brown. Grounding, down to earth, practical, emphasizing body, denying Spirit, feeling worthless

Black. Issues related to death, hatred, unresolved patterns or beliefs, need for self-compassion, unforgiveness, denial

Pink. Self-love, tenderness, female energy, being "nice" at the expense of being real, upcoming opportunities

Cloudy White. Religious energy, lacking consciousness, confusion, being "good" instead of whole

Clear White. High spiritual vibration, Divine inspiration, seeing the spiritual big picture, compassion, auric field of your guardian angel

Gold. High Spiritual vibration, integrity, freedom, clear seeing, integrating Spirit and body, creating as Spirit

Shapes of an Aura

How we respond to our life events affects the shape of our aura. The possible shapes include a multitude. Like the color of an aura, the shape isn't fixed. They change as we change. Here are several we've witnessed and experienced.

The Fuzzy Shape

This is the shape we see if someone lacks clear personal boundaries. There is a tendency for people to take on other people's stuff—other's stress, other's emotions, other's responsibilities, other's anything. Neutrally saying "no" to someone can be hard. We may believe for people to like us, we must always say "yes." regardless of our own needs or concerns. This causes someone to have a fuzzy aura.

The Aura Wall

This is a defensive shape. It happens when someone puts up boundaries. It is a way to "feel safe" and thereby block out other people. This is common in people who assert their will through resistance and judgment.

Spiky Aura

This shape is especially prevalent when we feel threatened and ready for conflict. Often from past wounds whether from abuse, mental, emotional, or sexual or other traumas. People who live in this energy for long periods can be reactive, a way of hurting others as a defense mechanism. They may be threatened by professionals, people qualified in their area who are trying to help.

Aura Size

The distance our aura goes from our body can tell us a lot about ourselves. Auras can be large, small, absent, healthy, spiky or balanced. Generally, we sustain a "usual" pattern or another, but it can change, depending on what is going on in our lives. For example, if we are feeling afraid, our energy may be pulled in. Alternatively, if we are feeling super confident, our energy field may be expanded out.

Large Aura

A large aura may show a desire to control. It can also indicate spreading yourself too thin and taking on too much responsibility for others. When our aura gets too large for us to manage, it can be challenging to focus on things outside of ourselves.

Small Aura

The small aura generally indicates fear on some level. We might be trying to hide, hoping to stay invisible. It can indicate how we are holding our energy back until it feels safe to release. When our energy is pulled in tight, it can be hard to connect with ourselves because the flow of energy isn't consistent.

No Aura

This aura is observed if you are unhappy with your life or are struggling with deep core wounds. With this wounding, we tend to check out and not be in our body. It is a way of temporarily avoiding pain or problems. If we keep the behavior which is causing us to have no aura, then eventually we will not feel present in our lives. We also see the absence of an aura with those who are in the process or approaching the sacred act of transitioning.

Before we transition, our aura begins to draw into the body center as if pulling all the energy into the physicality so it can then launch the soul into the next realm. This is also a time when the aura will not be visible. If you are just developing your abilities to see auras, please don't assume that because you do not see an aura that the person you are reading is going to transition. Take a deep breath and begin again. Sometimes our attachment to seeing gets in our own way of seeing what is there.

Energy Patterns

Energy patterns can appear fast or slow. We all display an energy pattern and similar to auras, they can be seen or felt intuitively. Our energy pattern changes just like our aura does. Depending on what we are doing, feeling and experiencing, our energy pattern will appear differently. Most of us have intuitively felt it. If you live with someone, you can actually see with your physical eyes when they are sad or depressed versus excited or joyful. These emotions feel completely different. You may have felt this with a boss or co-worker, where they were stressed or upset and you could actually see it. If your boss is feeling stressed, you can actually sense it. These are classic examples of energy patterns.

The way in which our energy patterns appear is unique for each of us and often represents things. Energy patterns that appear fast can symbolize fast moving energy that feels frenetic. Other times, you may see slow energy patterns which can symbolize sluggish energy, or it can even be a message to slow down. As we see energy, we start to understand that within each pattern there is something for us to learn, understand, and relay to our clients.

Being Conscious of Other People's Energy

Everyone is an energy field, and when we are in contact with them, whether we realize it or not, our energy fields interact and this is where we can pick up information. What we pick up, how much we pick up, and what we do with it are a subject of big discussion boards, group chats, and so on.

The way we have approached it in our experience is to see energy as something that can change, move, and fluctuate. Energy can move and be transmuted. It is also important to understand that when we work as intuitives, or are just moving through our lives, we do not have to carry other people's energy around with us.

Picking Up Energy and How It Impacts Your Energy

As intuitives, we are naturally sensitive and pick up the energy of people who are in the room with us. We can also pick up their energy simply by thinking of them. Yes, it is that simple. If we are not conscious and not practicing some of the techniques below, we can feel their energy impact us. Sometimes you may suddenly feel extremely tired or yawn excessively, whereas moments before you felt alert. This is because you are picking up someone else's energy field. When you connect with another person, you are literally comingling two separate bands of energy. The following list allows you to understand the message and purpose of picking up someone else's energy:

- **Intention.** Having an intention to understand and be open to knowing the reason for receiving this energy.

- **Ask Your Divine Support Team.** Why you picked up this energy. You may receive guidance that you feel it is what you have to do to be a great coach. It may be to show you that you're overly attached, or that you, too, need to look at this aspect of yourself.

- **Build Your Energy Body.** Within building your energy body, is the work with Light Body. Anything that comes in contact with your energy will be impactful. Light body is a practice to interact with this energy and can be studied through the work of Orin and Daben.

- **Be Present In Your Physical Body.** Regular exercise, yoga, qi-gong, or other techniques are imperative to be present to your body. Sit in your intuitive sessions (for yourself or others) bare footed so your feet can touch the ground. Be in your breath, your feet, and your gut when working with discerning energy. Your Divine Guidance will always give you direct honest answers.

- **Practice Techniques** regularly—from the Divine Prescriptions section.

Energy Vampires

What? Vampires are real? Cue the scary music. These types of vampires are real and they can impact you. The term energy vampire relates to the feeling of depletion when being around certain people. When we speak of being around others and connecting with their energy, the first thought that people have is that this energy must be "bad" if it makes us feel depleted. We make it mean that the people we experience this with must be "bad" people. First off, energy vampires are not bad, just impactful. Often, people don't even realize they are being a drain. This is because without being conscious of it, people who are living in fear, lack and disbelief in themselves want to hitch their boat to your ocean liner and catch a free ride. When we have been exposed to an energy vampire we may feel: overwhelmed, physically ill with headaches, achy, stressed, irritable, or physically and mentally exhausted. An energy vampire may display some or all of the following characteristics: big ego, passive-aggressive tendencies, resentment, narcissism, gossiping, whining, guilt tripping, manipulative behaviors, jealousy, or just being extremely over talkative especially when you aren't interested. Energy vampires tend to be takers rather than givers. There are also environmental energy vampires like TV, internet, social media, and cell phones to mention just a few.

It's important to remember your energy when being around other people so you are aware of where you are giving your energy. It is important to set limits and boundaries, and practice not reacting to energy vampires. Another technique to use with energy vampires is to listen more than you talk. Energy vampires classically like to talk usually nonstop. The more we listen and be completely present without judgment and with unconditional love, the more they feel heard and acknowledged. And if you do find yourself spending time with someone you feel taps your energy out, remember to clear your energy after spending time with them. There are in-depth exercises about how to dissolve etheric cords and other energy clearing practices in the Divine Prescriptions section.

Understanding Your Body's Energy

The more you understand your body and how it receives and disperses energy the easier it is for you to work with it. Within a short period of time, you will discover your ability to hold energy, others' and your own. It takes practice, practice, practice. The more you practice, the more you will expand your own energy bandwidth, which is your ability to hold energy and broadcast it deliberately. As we do this, we can hold it within our own body and thereby not take on other's energy as often.

CHAPTER 10

Chakras Revealed

*"If you want to find the secrets of the universe,
think in terms of energy, frequency and vibration."*
- NIKOLA TESLA

The word "chakra" comes from the Sanskrit language, meaning disk or wheel. A chakra is a disk-like energy center located in different parts of our body. (It generates a part of the auras that we discussed earlier.) The chakras are responsible for distributing life force energy to various organs and glands throughout our body. Despite having hundreds of chakras in our bodies, traditional literature puts emphasis on seven of them. The 7 main chakras run parallel to our spine from its base to the crown of our heads, and they affect our flow of energy, and subsequently our intuition. We also have other chakras besides the main seven that are located in our endocrine glands and nerve plexus, just to name a few. Though we only tend to talk about the main 7, all of these chakras affect our intuitive energy.

Chakras don't operate separately from each other; they are interrelated, like the ULs. The lower 3 chakras are responsible for our grounding, survival and self-image. We block our intuition when any of our chakras are misaligned or out of balance, allowing our body to manifest with physical issues. As we become more aware of our energy system and begin to open our chakras, then our life-force can move, and we feel empowered and safe to open our intuition. In short, understanding our chakras helps us open ourselves up to our intuition.

The chakras start at the base of our spine, which is why the first chakra is called the root chakra. This chakra is represented by the color red and manifests in the world as our basic needs: survival, safety, and security. When our root chakra is out of balance, we may experience feeling flighty, ungrounded, anxious, and insecure. The physical symptoms associated with this root chakra's imbalance could be diarrhea or constipation. We know this chakra is out of balance when there's an inability to trust nature or over-focus on material things.

Our second chakra is located below our belly button. We call this the sacral chakra, and it's represented by the color orange. We affectionately call this the sex, drugs, and rock and roll chakra because it relates to our desires, creativity, and creation, including procreation. When this chakra is balanced, we feel open, generous, and considerate. When we are imbalanced in this chakra we can feel unsure and emotionally unstable, and it can be challenging to express our feelings.

The third chakra is the solar plexus chakra, and it represents our power center and is depicted with the color yellow. This chakra supports understanding the emotions of life. Some consider this area (our stomachs) to be the second brain for the body because this is where we process all of our emotions. When we are experiencing an imbalance in this area, there can be physical imbalances such as anorexia, bulimia, diabetes, or any other digestion issues. This chakra can also reveal its imbalance as a need to control or dominate situations. The emotional imbalances can manifest as low self-esteem, fear of rejection, or indecisiveness. When we are in alignment with our solar plexus chakra we feel a sense of wholeness, belonging, and acceptance—a feeling of balance between the spiritual and physical worlds.

The heart chakra is our fourth chakra, and it represents emotional empowerment, forgiveness, unconditional love, trust, and compassion. The color associated with this chakra is green. This chakra is the center of our clairsentience, Divine feeling. When we experience an imbalance in this chakra we can experience heart conditions, asthma, shoulder problems, lung issues, breast issues, jealousy, anger, envy, and fear. When we are aligned in this chakra we feel harmony and connection, a sense of oneness and purpose. This is the first chakra that synthesizes intuition, and it is the center for clairsentience.

Our fifth chakra is the throat chakra. This energy center rallies around communication, and it is key in speaking our truth, sharing our needs, and making the choices aligned with our truth. When we hesitate to make choices, we create disturbances in our throat chakra which manifest physically as laryngitis, sore throat, thyroid imbalances, jaw, gum, or tooth problems. When this chakra is balanced, we are able to speak and listen to others while easily expressing our thoughts. When this chakra is out of balance no matter how much talking is being done, we are unable to tap into our true expression and communication. Usually people who talk nonstop have a throat chakra imbalance.

Our sixth chakra is the third eye chakra, located between our eyebrows, and it connects to the pituitary and pineal glands (as well as the sinus, eyes, nose, and face). It is represented by indigo blue, and it is our avenue to wisdom—both learning from our experiences and putting them into perspective. It is the second main chakra of intuition and the powerhouse for our clairvoyance. When balanced, this chakra helps us be wise truth-seekers and supports our awareness of the spiritual world as well as our intuition. When this chakra is out of balance, we reject spirituality and tend to overemphasize intellect, seeing only obvious, superficial meanings of situations.

Our seventh chakra is called the crown chakra, represented by the color violet. This energy center focuses on wisdom and knowledge. This is the chakra that synthesizes our claircognizance, allowing us to tap into the wisdom of the Universe. It is believed that this is the energy center that integrates our life force with the lower chakras. It is another chakra that lends itself to intuition, and it is the center of claircognizance. When this chakra is balanced, we live with knowledge and wisdom from the Divine. Balance means we feel connected to our purpose, identity, and bigger picture of the world. When this chakra is out of alignment, there is a sense of dissatisfaction and depression as if something is missing. Chronic exhaustion is also associated with an imbalance of this energy center.

As we've said, there are hundreds of chakras all over our bodies and 7 major chakras, but there's one "minor" chakra we want to address because it is the fourth center of intuition. These are the ear chakras, and they are located above each ear. Their function is to hear the Divine, to allow in the highest vibration of guidance. The ear chakras are shown by a red violet color, and when they are in balance, we are easily able to hear our Divine Guidance. When this chakra is out of balance, we don't listen to other ideas. We adjust our hearing to only hear the negative distrustful things about ourselves and others. This minor chakra's job isn't minor at all. This is the center where clairaudience comes through. All those times when we overhear a conversation that answers a question we have, or the perfect song comes on that soothes our soul, are signs of our clairaudience coming through balanced and clear ear chakras.

Although the fourth, sixth, seventh, and ear chakras are the main energy centers for intuition, it takes a balance of all the chakras to sustain the energy and life of an intuitive. Like the ULs, all of the chakras work together, gracefully interwoven. Individually, they are only a single brick, not the entire building.

CHAPTER 11

Stay Clear

"You cannot change anything in your life with intention alone, which can become a watered-down, occasional hope that you'll get to tomorrow. Intention without action is useless."

- CAROLINE MYSS

As trained intuitives, we have many tools to build our confidence and confirm the intuition we receive, but there's the rub with using tools of divination: for some, they become a crutch. An intuitive who can't tap into their Divine Guidance without their runes, tarot deck or pendulum is not trusting themselves as a vessel of the Divine. I love using divination tools, such as oracle/tarot cards, runes, pendulums and crystals to support my work with my clients, but I never rely on them as my access point. These tools are meant to support not be our source of Divine Guidance. In my career, I learned early on that for my path, I must be able to rely solely on my Divine Guidance without leaning on anything BUT my connection.

I don't mean this to sound ominous—for me I HAD to KNOW that I was the real deal that there weren't any tricks, no cards up my sleeve, no influence from anything other than my Divine connection through my four clairs. But there are tools that are helpful in working with your intuition.

As you continue on your adventure of intuition, you may find some of the tools we are about to discuss handy. But remember that the call of these tools, just like every other tool, lies in how you choose to use it; it is in your hands. The tools we are sharing with you were and are incredibly helpful in our paths as professional intuitives. And like I've said, too much of anything, isn't good; it's all in the dance of balance.

The group of tools we want to share with you here are tools of support to sustain your energy as a clear and tapped in intuitive.

First, we want to talk about "clearing" energy. Why do we need to clear our energy and the energy of our environment?

Studies from UCLA in 2009 showed increased stress levels and depression for those who lived in a cluttered environment. A 2011 study from Princeton found that cluttered homes led to poor focus and attention span. Clutter also comes on an energetic level as well. If physical clutter impacts our minds, productivity, and stress levels, imagine what cluttered energy does.

You wouldn't go out for the day without brushing your teeth, right? Good grooming is essential even for those parts of us that we may not readily see. Our bodies are incredible tools themselves, a powerful divination tool of timeless wisdom, the vessel through which we receive our Divine Guidance. Makes sense that the clearer our body and auric energy field are, the stronger and more accurate our intuitive channels and connections will be.

But first, how do I know I need to clear my energy?

Any time you feel heavy, emotionally or physically. When life seems to be completely stuck. Times when you feel worn out and exhausted. As sensitives, it's easy for us to take on the energy of our loved ones, or even global energy, such as all the uncertainty that's bouncing around with this pandemic; sadness or depression can be a sign you've taken on too much energetically. You need to clear your energy when you feel overwhelmed by even the smallest of things; with Covid-19, the overwelm is the understatement.

Anytime I feel any of those things the first Divine Prescription I reach for is clearing my energy. Because everything is comprised of energy, including physical spaces and land that holds memory. Every time we step into a physical space we are stepping into the energetic imprint of that location as well as into the energies of all the living beings in it, including the stranger who just passed you, that you didn't even pay attention to.

I had a powerful personal experience with a shaman clearing energy many years ago, when we had some energetic disruptions. I had a shaman come to our brand-new, custom-built home to cleanse and bless it. The house had never been lived in, so we knew it was remnant energy of the workers as well as the land. The shaman performed the clearing by doing a couple of different rituals. The moment they were finished I felt better. I felt more grounded and able to focus. My family of course rolled their eyes, tolerating my view, but interestingly enough after the clearing was completed my husband received multiple business opportunities that seemed to appear overnight, and some money we weren't expecting came out of nowhere. I give credit to the shaman clearing the energy. Coincidence? I think not! Though my family wasn't so quick to agree.

Shaman believe the atmosphere of your exterior space reflects your inner space. Clearing the space removes stagnant energy and creates more of a flow that is in harmony with the healing power of the Universe. There is more room for clarity, concentration and harmony.

Here's just a few ways to clear energy and a great place to start. There are as many ways to clear energy as there are people on the planet. Find the way that feels good for you and yields the best results for you, your body, and your auric field.

Clearing the space removes stagnant energy and creates more of a flow that is in harmony with the healing power of the Universe. There is more room for clarity, concentration and harmony.

Here's a general guideline to help you choose how you want to work with them: fresh things are usually the first choice for most shamanic and healing practitioners. Fresh is naturally cleansing, whether used in baths or as a sweeper to brush out the old and invite in the new. On the other hand, herbs that are spicy are considered to burn out the stagnation.

Using Fire as a Clearing Tool

Fire can be a powerful clearing instrument. You can use fire in your energy-cleansing work through actually burning things, through candle work, and through visualization.

Burning

You can write on piece of paper what you are clearing and/or releasing and burn it. (Always bury the ashes off of your home property). This is a great thing to do during a Full Moon.

Smudging

Shaman refer to the act of burning sacred herbs, resins or barks as smudging. They use this act as a primary tool in energy clearing. The way I was taught to smudge was to close my eyes and tune into my beating heart, listening to my heartbeat to connect then with my feet, planted on the earth, which connects me to my surroundings. Then I call on my Divine Support Team and ancestors, asking them to support me in performing this sacred act of clearing. I create my intention, usually something as simple as clearing my sacred sanctuary. I place the herbs I choose in a fireproof bowl and light it, allowing it to burn just enough to make smoke for my smudging. Many traditions use a bird's feather to spread the smoke, but it's not a requirement, you can simply move your fireproof bowl to the areas you are wishing to smudge and the smoke will naturally clear it. As you are smudging, pay attention to all the corners and any places where you have physical clutter, like bookshelves, and give them a good smudge as well.

Candle Clearing

Hold a candle and infuse all the energy you desire to clear and let go of into it by simply visualizing the energy leaving your body and going into the candle. Then take a toothpick and write on the candle what you are releasing. This can be a sigil, (Sacred Sigil p. 452) symbol or the actual word. Light the candle, watch it burn, gaze into the flame and see all this energy leaving, clearing its way out.

Using Water as a Clearing Tool

Makes sense that water would be an excellent tool to clear energy, just washing it away. It may sound simple, but still it is extremely powerful. Perhaps the reason you feel so good after getting out of the shower is because of the water clearing the way. Other ways we use water as a clearing tool is through washing our hands and taking herbal or sea salt baths, as well as making tinctures and herbal teas.

Teas

There are a multitude of medicinal and herbal magic teas to promote any area of your life. Just like any other herb we recommend awareness about what you are consuming and putting into your body. Even if it is natural and organic, some herbal remedies have a wide impact, and if you aren't sure consult your healthcare professional before ingesting.

Florida Water

Once used as cologne and smelling of 1808 from where it originated, this high-alcohol content flowered water is a huge favorite with many shamanic and healing practitioners. It's believed to remove heavy energies, encourage expression, and attracts positive energies because of the sweet smell.

Using Air as a Clearing Tool

Breath work is a powerful way to clear your energy as well. The very breath we breathe clears our body. It is why taking deep breaths are so important in our daily life. It's as if those deep breaths signal our amygdala that all is quiet on the western front. Another way to use air as a clearing tool is by opening up the windows of your home, any sticky energy will be carried away on the breeze.

Sound

Our voice is an incredible healing tool—even Pythagoras recognized the therapeutic power of the human voice. He used the reading of poetry to treat diseases back in his day. Every sound has a resonance, a frequency of wholeness. In his book, *The Healing Aspects of Toning*, Ted Andrews says using the sound of the vowels in our language will open different areas of our body consciousness.

Sounds always break up stagnant energy in any form. Here's a couple of suggestions of tools you might use to create sound:

- Singing
- Singing bowls
- Tuning Forks
- Bells
- Windchimes
- Drums
- Rattles
- Chants

Crystals

A simple technique to clear energy is to place a stone or crystal in your pocket. Crystals are well known to be beautiful ornaments. They are a solid whose makeup is arranged in a repetitive pattern—this includes our everyday salt, sugar, and even snowflakes. The crystals we are speaking about here are solid minerals, gemstones like Quartz, Amethyst or Citrine that have a definite pattern as well as powerful properties. Each crystal has a unique purpose and specialty. Some crystals can help us deepen our meditation practice while others are well known for releasing negative energy. For example, Black Tourmaline is thought to be one of the most powerful protectors. It repels negative energy and sends it back to its origin. And it's also known to remove energy blocks like anxiety, stress, and fear. You can find more information about crystals and working with them in the Divine Prescriptions section.

Nature

Nature is one of the best ways to clear our energy. Returning to nature is like returning to ourselves. Nature has a way of grounding us and helping us calibrate ourselves with deeper vibrations. The power of nature is like a system reboot for our hard drive, our mind and body. When we walk along the ocean or stare at the majestic mountain ranges, we are often in awe of the beauty that surrounds us. It is difficult to stay in our lower vibration when we are surrounded by this beauty. The reboot that nature gives us is really like no other clearing technique as it often leaves our body more centered and aligned.

Plants and Herbs

There are multiple ways to use plants and herbs to clear stagnant energy. Herbs can be digested as foods or essential oils, or burned (also known as smudging). I like to use all the elements (fire, air, water, earth) when I do my clearings. Plants in our home create a beautiful space and help to boost the energy vibe for our home AND for us. Simply touching one of your green friends during your day will lift your mood and give your energy a boost faster than any 5-hour energy drink. The Peace Lily is touted as a plant that improves the flow of positive energy in a space while neutralizing indoor gases.

Pets

Our pets are one of the biggest contributors to our lives. They take on the energy of their owners to support the pack and us. They are big givers in the world of energy. Have you ever held a puppy or kitten and felt happy? This is why. When you want to clear yourself if you can't find a tree, pet your dog or your iguana.

Napping/Sleeping

This is a powerful way to clear yourself and press the restart button. A quick disconnect from the current moment by napping is a great way to clear out the fog. Consistent and regular sleep is essential for an intuitive to keep their engine from burning out. We usually discount the benefits of good sleep. As intuitives, sleep can sometimes be a tricky dance between bedtime and prophetic dreaming, so it is a good practice to make sure you are getting plenty of sleep.

Salt

Salt is a crystal that has the ability to naturally cleanse and remove stagnant energy. By using sea salt in a hot bath, your blocks will melt away. I place sea salt bowls anywhere around our home where the energy feels congested.

Sun

The sun is a magnetic tool to clear away any fog or stuckness. Simply open the curtains and let it in, or walk outside and let the rays of this epic star dissolve anything that is stopping you.

Movement as a Clearing Tool

Kinetic movement is another great way to move and clear energy. Think about how you can feel the vibration from a big speaker: the movement impacts your body, rippling through it in the same way.

This doesn't need to be a difficult exercise; it can be as simple as shaking it off, literally shaking your body all over. The next time you need to clear that heavy or anxious feeling take a few minutes alone and just shake your body all over. Our friends in Hollywood tell me actors use this to help them release tough energy after playing a difficult scene.

There are other ways to use movement to clear you as well:

- Clapping/stomping
- Skipping
- Dancing
- Walking

Stretching

Because we store energy in our bodies stretching is a powerful way to let the energy and emotional tension go. Something as simple as stretching your arms out to your sides and reaching up, turning to stretch your torso, such simple moves bring you back to your body, back to breath, back to the now with clarity. There are multiple processes and exercises to clear your energy in the Divine Prescriptions section, such as Chakra Clearing, Etheric Cord Dissolution, and many more.

CHAPTER 12

An Ounce of Prevention

The number one rule and requirement for intuitives (and all humans) is self-care.

We need self-care for lots of reasons, but most importantly, we need it to sustain our energy. In order for us to connect with our intuition, we need to give ourselves private, personal time. This may seem logical and obvious, and yet, it can be challenging for some professional intuitives to include this habit as a regular practice. The more rested, aligned, and in our body we are, the more easily we can tap into our intuition.

For each of us, self-care can appear differently. This is an overview of common self-care practices and why we need to use them. At the root of self-care is the art of being truly patient and gentle with ourselves as we practice our gift in this world.

Self-Development

Our own personal self-development is very important. We are never finished learning about our inner realm and our relationship with our intuition. This never ends. Ever. Our own personal growth should be our number one priority.

When we are constantly growing and analyzing our inner world, it is essential to have a regular forgiveness practice. When we look at our thoughts, our behavior patterns, and all our inner happenings, we can be hard on ourselves. Forgiveness is key in our self-development. In order to truly sustain our own self-development, we recommend everyone to work with someone (coach, therapist, teacher, minister) who can witness and mirror our growth, as well as hold the space for our goals. This is especially true for those of us who are coaches, we believe all coaches should have a coach. We never get it done, it's never finished: in this thing called growth, there's always room for more. We cannot always see our own patterns as clearly as we think, and sometimes a coach is paramount to our growth.

Meditation and Journaling

A regular meditation and journaling practice are critical in this work. We want to give ourselves time to connect with our Source. Journaling after meditation brings us further clarity as it allows us to extricate and witness our thoughts and truly get present to ourselves and what emotions or thoughts are there.

Movement

Movement of the body is crucial. For those of us who are intuitives and emotionally sensitive, we get stuff stuck in our body! Some of that stuff is not even ours. It can be discomfort that we feel in others' energy bodies or the emotional pains that we feel from being highly sensitive and living in a world of dichotomy. Regular movement of the body is completely your choice. Intuitively, you will be guided to answer what, when, and how often you move for yourself. Practices like ecstatic dance, yoga, tai chi, Pilates, barre, paddling, and running are just a sample of things that may help you truly get into your body. What movement you choose will shift as you grow, but you want to keep in mind that movement is part of your daily self-care and a way to deepen your connection into your body.

Boundaries

Being clear on your boundaries is crucial. If that means you do not work weekends and you only text back during office hours, do that. Many times, we feel like we have to be on call 24/7. Setting boundaries for yourself does two things: it makes others accountable for their own personal work, and it creates the much needed space for you to refuel.

Support Network

Having a support network of people who understand you is incredibly valuable and dare we say essential to maintaining your growth. This work is so different from "normal living." To have people who are like minded, "get you," and who see the authentic you is very important. It is so easy to slip into patterns of the ego, shadow of disbelief and doubt. Having a support group of a few people who hold your vision is inspiring and necessary as we do this work for ourselves, others, and the planet.

Equal Exchange Compensation

Receiving can be challenging for intuitives. We have created this conduit of greater clarity, connection and love to share with anyone who is interested. It is great to receive these messages, and we also need to be aware of what we are receiving in exchange for our gift for sharing. In our modern-day society, we receive money as an exchange for our talents. Remember the UL of Compensation? If we have a distorted relationship with money, this can be challenging as we may feel we are not worth the money. We may create stories of lack, poverty, and so on. We want to work through these beliefs with a coach and be truly present to the financial exchange we are allowing in our lives when we give our gifts to others.

Play

Play is a part of life, and as funny as it may seem, many of us are scared of it. We may feel afraid to "look like a fool" or not appear grown up. Play is a part of what keeps us young, vital, and alive. Play is a part of the joy of living. Games of strategy allow us to use both the left and right hemispheres of our brain, logic and creativity. Fun is essential to every intuitive's toolbox. Even if it seems like you have to "work" on it, go play—cut loose, laugh. I had a friend once who told me it's impossible to skip without smiling. She's right. So, if you're hard pressed to bring play into your life—skip around your house. See what happens. Regular retreats are an easy access point to fun, play and meeting like-minded people.

Unfortunately, as we sit with the Covid-19 pandemic, gathering in groups in person isn't considered a health-conscious option. This is why it is so important to live ULs, knowing that everything is of the mind, Hermetic Principles of Mentalism, that we are the creators of our experiences. We can create our own personal virtual retreat. Create a habit to ask yourself what you can do today to increase fun can infuse more fun and play into your life. It can be small things like going to the dog park, playing a game of backgammon, or hopping on the swing at the park. Adding play into our lives not only increases our intuition but also invites in health and vitality. Playing and having fun keeps us in the present moment.

Solo Time

Encoded in the meditation and self-development sections are the importance of solo time. We can see solo time as the 30 minutes of meditation and journaling we do daily, or you may take a retreat by yourself or go for a walk on the beach to collect your thoughts. This type of regular inner focus is important to develop that self-reflection. Solo time increases our intuition. Solo time is essential for professional intuitives. Own it now—put it in your calendar—or experience the burnout and chaos that comes with overwhelm. That may sound harsh, we're sorry, but we are being honest here. It is amazing what 20 minutes of alone time will give a sensitive intuitive. The best thing is, it's easy and free!

Body Work

Regular body work is also helpful. This could be a massage, cranio-sacral therapy, reiki sessions, acupuncture, and energy healing, amongst other things. Body work, like exercise, is important to keep our energy cycling through us and not stagnant. If you trust your guidance, you will know what practices to do and when. Making them a regular part of your life can be incredibly therapeutic for sustaining our gifts on this planet.

Sleep

I'm sure you are asking yourself, "didn't they just talk about sleep?" Absolutely, and it bears repeating because we overlook its value. Consistent and regular sleep is necessary for an intuitive to keep their engine from burning out. Often, we discount the benefits of good sleep. As intuitives, sleep can sometimes be tricky, so it is a good practice to make sure you are getting plenty of sleep. Possibly even creating an evening sleep ritual so your body consciously knows it is time to replenish. Leaving electronics, especially cell phones, outside of your sleeping area will allow sensitives to rest more easily. Whatever methods make sure you are getting solid sleep. Your body and your intuition will thank you.

"Fear stops our intuition in its tracks."

CHAPTER 13

The Danger Zone

"Vulnerability is not a weakness;
it is proof of feeling the uncertainty of life—
the risk and emotional exposure we all have at stake."

There are a number of reasons why intuitive abilities can get blocked: being out of touch with the physical body, emotional blocks lodged in the chakras, and **FEAR**. The most common block to an intuitive's abilities is unrealistic expectations. Because of all the media portrayals of intuitives and the vivid visual descriptions those clairvoyants give, we fall into the trap of expecting our visions to compare to Hollywood's, but it just doesn't work that way. The key to releasing these expectations, in our experience, is surrender. Surrender means to give up expectations, give way to the process, and give in to the reality of our personal experience. Be willing to accept that our way of receiving Divine Guidance is valid and of service; by allowing our perceptions to flow freely, trusting our connection, and practicing articulating our perceptions, we develop confidence in our abilities, no matter which form they take.

Fears

Fear stops our intuition in its tracks. It really is that simple: our fears are stopping us. This is why the regular consciousness practices of meditation, mindfulness, and self-awareness are so important. We all have voices in our heads that stop us from putting our hand in fire, or similar dangers. The downfall of these lifesaving voices is that they also hinder us from succeeding in our lives. For example, the voice that says, "Who are you to do this? What makes you special? What do you know?" These fear voices are the biggest blocks.

If we have trained ourselves, aligned our lives to what we feel deep within ourselves, and gone through the steps of waking up our intuition, then why wouldn't we use it? It is a gift of service to the world. It is a "fun tool" to have in our back pocket. We can use it for work and for our daily lives to make things easier. So why don't we use it?

These voices are collectively called our ego, and they have a role in our lives. The ego takes its role very seriously. These voices really think they are helping us and trying to keep us safe, and while at times our ego can help us relate to the outer world, the main role of the ego, spiritually, is to prevent us from connecting to our Divine Guidance. Take a moment and read that again. The role of the ego is to prevent us from connecting to our Divine.

You may think, "Why would I have ever developed such a crazy idea?" *A Course in Miracles* teaches us that as we entered the human body and "left God," there was a human thought that we were the one who "killed God." This was the formation of the ego. It is taught that in the killing of what we call God, we have been isolated and are bad. In turn, it tells us we do not deserve to find God. This is why the ego does everything in its power to prevent us from returning to our Divine. Most spiritual teachers go through this journey only to discover that they are stopping themselves. We discover we are our greatest friend, and we can also be our greatest enemy. Making friends with our ego and understanding its role and importance in our life is required homework for any intuitive. And we have a question for you: "Are you willing to see the how and why of these fears being there?" We have a choice to listen to them or not. We can never get rid of fear, completely, but we can transcend and live through it.

As a society, we are fed fear. Fear is an epidemic in our culture. We are taught to fear our body, to fear its limitations, to fear our neighbors, our boss, our partner, and ourselves. Especially now (during COVID-19 pandemic) we are afraid to hug each other; we are afraid to gather together, to travel or even leave the supposed safety of our homes. The fear wave of COVID has rippled across our planet. Times like these is when our connection to our inner being, our relationship with ourselves, and the Divine give us impeccable guidance through our intuition. We can stop, listen and follow our Divine Guidance, trust with certainty instead of listening to millions of different theories, ideas, or suggestions about what we should do. In times when nobody TRULY knows the answer, Divine Guidance, your intuition, is the best compass to get you out of the storm. Follow it even if it looks like it's taking you into the storm; it's the most direct way.

My teacher, Ingrid, tells a story of how the Norse watched the reindeer and followed them, even when they would head directly into a storm, because somehow the Norse knew it was the best way through. Fear can feel like a fast and powerful force. And yet, the most powerful force in the world is the energy of Divine love. When you use your intuition in your professional business or choose to use it in your daily life, you are giving yourself a great gift. The gift of allowing your life to be easier, living more in trust, compassion, love, and flow. Let's explore fear and what it tells us.

Vulnerability

Being vulnerable is at the heart of our fears, and yet, it is the best pathway to love. Ego's view is this: vulnerability = death. Fear of being vulnerable is a huge fear with which we all struggle. We fear being exposed, being a fool, being ridiculed. Trusting our intuition can feel like we are walking around naked. It could feel this way because we are relying on something that cannot be proven or statistically analyzed. And yet, our intuition comes from half of our brain. The brain we were given at birth for a reason.

Dr. Brené Brown defines vulnerability as "uncertainty, risk, and emotional exposure." And yet vulnerability she says is "the birthplace of love, belonging, joy, courage, empathy, and creativity." Practicing our intuition can feel vulnerable and intimidating. We can be afraid of looking like a fool. We can be afraid of looking like a "snake oil salesman," and yet, all we are wanting to do is to help and serve others. This fear can keep us in our box and prevent us from connecting with our Divine Guidance, intuition. When wondering if that is you, consider this: are you afraid of having a free, happy, joyful life or are you actually afraid of your intuition?

"Our deepest fear is not that we are inadequate. Our deepest fear is that we are powerful beyond measure. It is our light, not our darkness that most frightens us. We ask ourselves, "Who am I to be brilliant, gorgeous, talented, fabulous? Actually, who are you not to be? You are a child of God. Your playing small does not serve the world. There is nothing enlightened about shrinking so that other people won't feel insecure around you. We are all meant to shine as children do. We were born to make manifest the glory of God that is within us. It is not just in some of us, it is in everyone. And as we let our own light shine, we unconsciously give other people permission to do the same. As we are liberated from our own fear, our presence automatically liberates others."- Marianne Williamson

Feeling vulnerable can cause intuitives to activate their protection modes. Most of us have been at the brunt of some trauma which gave us fuel for our purpose but it also made us say "Uh no. I'm never going to let anyone see my weak spots."

Vulnerability is not a weakness; it is proof of feeling the uncertainty of life, the risk, and the emotional exposure we all have at stake. It is something we all feel, but few admit to feeling. Acknowledging you feel vulnerable is powerful, and looking at it and accessing its origin is where the magic happens.

Isolation

All intuitives feel "set apart," different, weird, and odd sometimes. We feel like we don't fit in. Our heightened sensitivity feels like a curse not a gift. It feels awkward to walk up to a group of people and interact, much less tell them what you do for a career. And yet, the number of highly sensitive intuitive people on this planet is huge. We are a gift to the world, and we are here to help, lift, and engage the world through our service. Yes, it can feel lonely at times, but the greatest connection we have is with our Divine intuition. When we allow ourselves to remember this and create a community of like-minded souls, then we will no longer fear feeling odd.

It is natural to practice intuition and the more of us that wake up to this, the easier it can feel for us to move through our life not isolated or alone.

Shame

We can run into shame when practicing our intuition. The majority of our Western culture teaches us to think and rationalize. We are taught to back up our decisions with reasoning, but how can we explain our intuition if by definition it is *"the messages our unconscious mind gives us which cannot be explained with the conscious mind"?* We can easily enter shame as intuition is difficult to explain or validate in a way that is respected in our culture. Yet, it is the muscle in our life that, when used, can create great ease, joy and freedom.

Losing Control

As humans, we are compulsive about control. We have been taught consciously—or we decided ourselves—that control is a good thing. "If I can control things, life will be better. If I can control things, then I won't be disappointed or upset." Control is the bedfellow of a perfectionist mindset, and it is rooted in fear. With it, we learn to not trust, to not flow, and to plan everything. Eventually, control only makes us sick. Control stimulates our sympathetic nervous system and can create rigidity in our physical body.

Intuition is all about trusting. If we listen to our intuition in our daily life, we learn to trust the moment, the expansion, and the growth that is found in the unknown. It is about allowing our intuition to guide our life the way a flashlight leads us through a dark alleyway.

Seeing or Receiving Scary Stuff

This is a real fear that many people have and it stops them from opening their intuition.

First off, all of this originates from our belief systems—make believe, lying, or scary movies. I grew up as a Hindu, and my own religious upbringing did not speak of scary entities. All of the Gods and Goddesses that I was introduced to were from love. Because of my own experience, I do not have fear of receiving scary messages. Of course, we all have different belief systems and upbringings. If we encounter anything scary or things we don't want to see, we can easily call in any energy that feels protective to you, be it Michael, the bouncer from the angelic realm, a relative, or a Divine sacred being. We say "call" because it feels like you're actually calling for them, simply by thinking of them. And as we know by working with ULs anything we send out there is reciprocity; the Universe responds always. Your call is answered, and the energy of the scary stuff dissipates. Sounds like science fiction, but it's true: we've both experienced this in our lives personally. The Divine will protect you, surround you with energy, and have that scary stuff dissipate.

Impostor Complex

Impostor Syndrome is more common than you might think. If you have ever heard the voice in your head saying things like "You just got lucky. You can't do that again" or, "Who are you to do that? Who are you to write a book?" or "Who are you to start your own business?" you may be experiencing impostor syndrome.

The term was coined in 1978 by psychologists when they saw that well-accomplished people could not accept their success. Instead of being able to embrace their success, they had an intense fear of failure. Consequently, they didn't experience joy from their accomplishments.

Through research, it was found that the impostor syndrome is rampant in everyone, especially CEOs and COOs. It is especially common in high-achieving women. Our fear of failure can affect our personal lives as well, our child rearing, our relationships, and more.

What a lot of people try to do is to push through it. We try to ignore it, push past it, and tell ourselves "Fake it until you make it" or "No pain, no gain." This type of approach only perpetuates the impostor voice. When we ignore it, it yells at us louder. To work with the impostor, we first need to be aware of its presence in our life. When we become mindful of it (aware it is there, noticing it without judgment), then we will no longer be trapped by it. As soon as we shine a light on it and see it, it loses its power over us, and the rest of our mind can relax. Here are a couple of remedies for the impostor voice inside our heads:

Meditation. Are you seeing a pattern here? Regular meditation is a must to be able to mindfully be aware of ourselves as intuitives. With meditation, we wake up our true essence, our Divine Mind, and the impostor can lose its grip on us.

Success Lists. As we mentioned earlier, these lists are imperative in building and trusting our intuition. Writing a daily success list of 3 to 5 small things you are doing to take care of yourself can have an impact on your awareness. It can be anything from making your bed to taking a shower to working out. By doing this regularly, you can be in touch with your success. You will likely notice that when you don't do this regularly, your impostor starts to show up, doubting your own experiences.

Third Person. One thing that really helps me is to just talk about imposter syndrome. My husband and son both know that inside of mom is an impostor who doesn't think she is capable of doing what she is doing. Talking about it in the third person by saying things like, "That part of my mind," allows me to distance from the impostor's voice and helps me bring awareness to it.

CHAPTER 14

FAQs

"Building your intuition is an evolutionary skill that captures the relationship between you and the Divine within you."

What if I don't receive anything?

This is actually impossible! Our intuition is always there giving us answers, always! As an intuitive, the most important thing to do is to use your primary clair and ask from that place, what am I feeling, seeing, hearing, or thinking. There is always something to receive. It is impossible to get nothing.

How do I know that I'm not making it up?

The way intuition shows up (feeling, hearing, knowing, seeing) in our body tells us that we are receiving. Over time as we open up our other clairs, what we are receiving will be validated in many different forms—hearing, sensing, seeing, even knowing. We will start to get two hits at the same time, and there is no disputing that! With intuition, the message is direct, and it comes in a form and language our own mind can interpret. The more we practice our intuition, the more real-life evidence we have for its validity, and the more we decrease our doubt and increase our trust in ourselves.

How do I know I'm the real deal?

The more we practice intuition, our connection and our relationship to the Divine deepen, supercharging our clarity. And here's where the "real deal" comes in: the real deal is why and how you use this gift of intuition. This gift is meant to be used to direct and support you and your purpose. The gift of intuition is service. To ask "How can I love and be of service to this person?"

When I was first learning how to trust my intuition, my teacher drilled this into my head: "When you get nervous, focus on service." Because everyone gets nervous. Everyone. The more we practice, the more confident we become. This is a knowing that is beyond words. The more we practice, the more confident we become, and the more we learn to trust our intuition. This practice is always expanded when we do readings for people we don't know, and we are able to collect our hits—confirmation from the person you are reading that you are "spot on." This makes it easier and clearer that we are being of service to the Divine.

If you are so intuitive, why don't you have all the answers—the lotto numbers, for example?

Our intuition is a gift designed to help us in life, but it is not a shortcut to a life of fame and fortune. In all the stories of myth and magic, anyone using the shortcuts for personal gain are always met with certain disaster, and the same is true here with intuition. It doesn't give you a bypass on the freeway of life. It's more like the navigational system that lets you know there's an accident ahead, so prepare to slow down. We are each on our own journey, and within that journey is consistent, never-ending expansion and growth. Our intuition is meant to help us along our life's path. It is a compass unique to each of our lives. While intuition is a powerful tool, we still live in a human body and have a human experience. Intuition doesn't rid our lives from conflict or tension, but using our intuition makes this journey easier to discern, helping us see our path and purpose with greater ease and flow.

What will other people say?

It is within our societal training to be worried and concerned with other people's opinions. We are trained to adjust our image of ourselves based on what others think and say. For me, becoming a physician by the age of 25 should have brought me great joy—at least that's what others told me. They told me it was something I should strive toward. But, despite achieving that goal, these external accolades were short lived, and I was left struggling to find what would truly bring me joy. Through this, I learned external approval never brings internal satisfaction. Since then, I have tried to make decisions less based on what others think and more on what feels good to me, but at times, I still struggle at times with the thought, "What will they think?"

In my own work, I'm always blown away by the power of the intuitive messages and the improvement people have in their lives. This dissolves any thoughts I, or they, have about my ability to accurately connect with my intuition. When I lead workshops, clients always make comments that show they feel understood, acknowledged, and heard. Isn't this the greatest gift we have to give and receive from others? When we work from our Divine Guidance, we are providing a channel of clarity for our clients where they can feel heard and understood.

There is a principle in the Rules of the Cosmos Chapter that we discussed earlier that I'd like to revisit called the Hermetic Principle of Correspondence: As above, so below. As within, so without. Remember it? What this means is that people outside of us will be a reflection of us. If we are fearful and self-critical about our gifts, then the people around us will mirror that back to us with their judgment and criticism. What does that mean? This puts us in the driver's seat! It is up to us. How we feel about our gift determines what others will say about it. Create what you want to receive!

How does my past impact my present?

Many intuitives have had difficult experiences around their intuition growing up. The traumas of being teased for making things up, being a "know it all," or being "too sensitive" can lead to self-doubt, judgment, and low self-esteem, all of which impact our connection to the Divine and our Divine Guidance. Because our culture has trained us to shut off our feelings and shut down our intuition, we tend to push these past experiences into the deep crevasses of our mind and body. It's foolish to think that our past doesn't impact our future; our past contrasting experiences have made us who we are today. In fact, we would even venture to say that those experiences had to happen to get you to where you are today, reading this book about intuition.

If your past starts creeping into your awareness, it is best to address it sooner rather than later. There are many ways to address it: forgiveness, energy work, and developing an understanding of it. In the Divine Prescriptions section, there is a beautiful Inner Child Exercise which supports clearing all the lower vibrations of past experiences while leaving us with all those experience's lessons that brought us to who we are today.

External Factors

We often disregard the impact of our external factors on our psyche and intuition—external meaning our home, office, community, and greater environment. What you surround yourself with is what you become, and this is why being present to outside forces and characteristics is crucial to developing our intuition.

War, COVID pandemic, social uprisings—these could upset anyone, but for an intuitive, the energy is tripled. In times like these, it's not unusual for sensitives to check out by leaving their bodies—start emotionally eating, over sleeping, drinking, or smoking. All of these activities that take us out of the present moment.

Our external environment might be a toxic home where frustration, stress, and anger are ongoing. It might be an unorganized work environment where co-workers are constantly talking about fear, anger, clutter, or scary movies. Everything has a frequency and vibration. Living within the confines of an area that is filled with the energy that is a toxic vibration impacts mindset, perspective, health, and success. Even if you aren't listening to the negative talk or the movie that is blaring on the television, the energy is there. Being present to our environment is imperative, because what we surround ourselves with is what we become.

CHAPTER 15

Take It Easy

"Most of us are in touch with our intuition whether we know it or not, but we're usually in the habit of doubting or contradicting it so automatically that we don't even know it has spoken."

- SHAKTI GAWAIN

As you begin practice using and strengthening your intuition, we want to remind you of a couple of core philosophies that will keep you on track. We've found them helpful in our practice.

Don't Try

This may seem counterintuitive, but it's true. When we try, we put our focus and energy on "doing" or "making" something happen. This type of energy shuts down intuition in a heartbeat. When we can remember it is not us that creates intuition, we realize we are only the vessel through which it flows. Trying is like saying you have to make it happen—force it. Don't try, just show up. Be open to receive whatever comes forward, even if it doesn't make sense at the time to you. It will make sense, eventually.

Be Open To Being Present

When we are concerned about getting it wrong, we are inviting in energy that is contrary to love and intuition. With a single thought, we invite the energy of fear. Most mistakes that happen with intuition are in our translation of energy. If we are concerned that we are not getting it right, our translation of energy will be amiss. A very valuable thing to remember is this: you can't get it wrong! What? How is that possible? When we are standing in the intention of unconditional love and service, everything that comes through is accurate! And while it may take a moment to translate your message or symbols, the message always comes through.

Play

When we can be in a flow state, ease is present. Of course, that energy allows our intuition to abound. It also helps to relax and not take the process so serious, despite where your Divine Guidance is leading you, your client, or your audience. Holding the freedom and ease of play allows your intuition to be loud and clear.

Pretend

As children we didn't block our receptors of intuition, we let it all flow. We laughed, played, and allowed it all to blossom. Much of our work as intuitives is getting back to that child-like awareness, where everything is magical, and nothing is impossible—if we believe.

All these aspects are a part of stepping into the belief that it is possible to receive these messages, and you are also an integral part of the process as is your mind. As we mentioned before, your brain is divided into two lobes, left being analytical, right being creative. With these practices, we are building the zone between the two. If the left is red and right is blue, we are standing in the purple zone. As we play and test the intuitive waters, our mind begins to believe and have confidence.

CHAPTER 16

The Cost of Resistance

"For the spiritual being, intuition is far more than a hunch.
It is viewed as guidance or as God talking,
and this inner insight is never taken lightly or ignored."
- WAYNE DYER

When we ignore our intuition, we tend to shut down all aspects of our inner voice, and often that leads to depression, stress, disease, anxiety, and a lackluster life.

We are trained to ignore our intuition. Our inner voice is screaming at us, but when we disregard it, to follow the path we think society wants us to follow, negative physical symptoms present themselves. When we follow a life path because everyone else is, we can suffer not because the path is inherently wrong, but because it isn't ours. Shutting down our intuition to go along with the norm is like cutting off our arm. It doesn't make sense to not utilize a skill that is naturally and innately within us, and one that also benefits us greatly in leading a life that we love.

There are multiple side effects of not listening to our intuition from gaining weight to eating disorders. For now, just know that you were meant to use this incredible skill, and it doesn't require you to become a PhD or an Olympic athlete to receive its benefits. Intuition doesn't require professional accreditation; it requires training to be open to listening, and anyone can do it.

Over my 2 plus decades of teaching this work, I have witnessed patterns from overusing, and yes, also underusing, intuition. Consider this analogy: "When static electricity builds up, it shocks you." This is what happens to our body when we disregard or underuse our intuition. Our channels are open and receiving, yet when we are oblivious to it, the energy builds up and impacts our physicality. The same is true of overuse, or overloading. Whether it is eating, lifting weights, using your intuition, or running, even machines will fail if overloaded. Overload typically manifests as physical exhaustion. When we are tuning in 24/7, we are receiving many messages. It is okay to turn down the volume of your intuitive messages to take a break and rest.

There are also emotional impacts to be aware of when under and overusing our intuition, such as emotional outbursts and mood swings. This is especially strong for empaths and those who utilize clairsentience. After I opened up to my intuition and began practicing regularly, I found myself having a breakdown at the grocery store. Why did that happen? Well, I went to the grocery store with my daughter, who was very young at the time. When we walked in, I felt great, but within a short amount of time walking around the store, I became incredibly emotional and upset. It came on like a freight train out of nowhere. I didn't understand at the time that walking into a big public place with my intuitive channels wide open would impact me in that way. The good news is it passes quickly when we are conscious of the situation. I finished up my shopping, headed home, and took a long, hot sea salt bath and didn't "tap" into my intuition for the rest of the evening. I learned to create a boundary so that I could rest and slowly acclimate my body to the powerful energy of intuition.

I share this experience to show you it's helpful to understand the personal challenges that come with being an intuitive. It's also important for your community, your loved ones and friends, to understand this, so that when you have overloaded your intuitive channels they have an idea of what's happening for you. I can't tell you how many partners I've supported in understanding their intuitive counterpart. And we don't want to condone nor encourage emotional outbursts, nor judge them: as they are simply a reflection of an overworked energetic system begging for refueling. Eventually, the longer we work with our Divine Guidance, the quicker our responses to an overused channel happens. That being said, this doesn't mean that partners of intuitives are meant to be whipping posts; should this be happening in your world, please get coaching and support for yourself. Inner work is a MUST so that the outbursts, and other side effects dissipate.

Overuse and underuse also affect our mental state. We can lose focus and experience a scattered mind, which often lends itself to getting an attention deficit diagnosis. Practicing daily energy exercises and processes keep our mental state clear. Because these scattered states create more worry and stress which tends to cumulatively build on itself so it's important to practice self-care frequently.

Our discernment given through our Divine Guidance is a valuable tool to transmute and transform the overuse and underuse of our intuitive abilities. With it, we have the ability to understand what is ours and what is another's.

If you are not sure what you are experiencing is due to overloading or underuse, here are some typical physical impacts we've seen over the years.

- Sinus infections
- Allergies
- Anxiety
- Exhaustion
- Overweight
- Emotional outbursts
- Eating disorders
- Dis-ease in the body

Everything relates to energy, vibration, thought and while you may believe that your emotional outbursts are solely because your boss is demanding, actually, there's more to it. What is happening is your Divine Guidance is bursting forth to get your attention and is finding any outlet it can to be expressed.

Experiencing these impacts doesn't mean that you did it wrong. These signs are our body's way of informing us, letting us know that there is more at work here than what meets the eye. Because our body is our largest divination tool, it is essential that we are present in it, aware of it, and taking great care of it. And we would be remiss if we didn't remind you that if you do experience these impacts, just as you would in any other situation where your health is on the line, consult your healthcare professional.

With that, we encourage you to use the gifted skills that you have (and that you are learning to use), and remind you to use this superpower to cultivate love and service. When we use this gift from a perspective of "How can I be of service?" and "How can I love this person?" we will always hit gold!

PART 3

Intuition

Stepping Out

Staring at a painting at the Getty Museum, I was jolted from my trance by my phone buzzing in my pocket. It was Divi calling from Vancouver. I knew immediately something was awry. I could feel it before I pressed the button and said hello. Divi's voice was calm and resolute (you know like all doctors when they're about to give you bad news). My claircognizance was activated. My head buzzing, I began to focus solely on her voice. The Getty and the drone of people moving in and out fell away as she said, "I'm sorry to bother you on your trip, but we have an emergency." Even as she said the word emergency, I felt perplexed. What kind of emergency, I wondered. I couldn't imagine what was so important that Divi, of all people, would use the word emergency. I listened intently.

One of the clients we shared, who was in our year-long course, was in an extremely difficult place and exhibiting multiple signs of suicide. She hadn't threatened it. It was worse; she was tying up loose ends and disassociating from her community and friends.

I immediately stepped outside because I needed some air. I felt like I had been kicked in the stomach by a bull. My clairsentience could feel our client's pain; she felt as if she could leave the earth and no one would miss her like she didn't matter. Her pain was palpable. Divi and I began to discuss our options and how we could best support her in getting the help she needed. We knew our professional accountability. We had to let the authorities know if there was a possibility that she could endanger herself, and still, we wanted her to know she wasn't alone in this situation—there were options.

Divi and I decided on our strategy. She was going to call our client and see if they could meet in person so Divi could make a professional assessment of the situation. We hung up and she was going to call me as soon as she spoke with our client. While I was waiting to hear back from Divi, I told my friends, Heather and Jeanne who were at the Getty with me, what was going on. We immediately stopped what we were doing and walked solemnly down to the Getty gardens. As we walked along the roses that were in full bloom, the massive planters overflowing with colorful flowers, we felt the heaviness of the situation.

Soon Divi called back, and as we continued our conversation, it became clear that we had to follow professional protocol to assure her safety. During every call with Divi, my friends sat with me on the green grasses of the Getty. We took our shoes off and let our feet touch the emerald turf.

Each of us were speechless and fully present to what was happening in Vancouver—thousands of miles away. It felt like we were listening for a pin to drop. I heard a thought in my head, send her love, love, love. The green grass of the Getty became a magic carpet of healing as I sent love to my client. I could feel Jeanne and Heather joining me. I felt a warm sensation come over my entire body, as if I was being swaddled in a warm blanket I knew it was the power that my friends and I were building and sending to my client.

Sitting in silence as we waited, I began to notice how this energy was impacting my friends and I. And then I heard in my head: "Look around and see with your Divine sight. What do you see?" I saw the 3 of us sitting there on the green earth of the Getty with our legs laid out, bare feet, painted toes, holding our breath while we prayed.

We began to look around and point out the sweet things we saw as we waited. A cute little Asian girl barely 2 years old in a big yellow dress who was insistent upon her daddy chasing her around, only to catch her and swoop her up in his arms as she laughed. I can't remember which of us said it first, but we each started saying "Look over there; see that couple laughing? That's love. See the pregnant woman waddling across the greens and her partner helping her to sit on the ground? That's love." In the distance, a couple was dancing a waltz in their shorts and tennis shoes while Mort Garson's song "Plantasia" played over the outdoor speakers throughout the gardens. After the couple danced, they bowed, curtseyed, and continued on their way. We began to notice in every single place we looked, there was love. It was surreal; it felt like we were in a Felini film. We began giggling and laughing, sending this energy to my client and Divi as we continued to watch the love around us.

Then in a flash, the wait that had seemed like a lifetime, was over, and Divi called. The professionals arrived at our client's house, and she was okay. Our client was alive, well, and going with medical professionals to the hospital to get some help. My body felt heavy like it was encapsulated in cement. I stopped noticing all the love scattered across the Getty lawn. I sat there for a moment letting the realization sink in. Tears began to fill my eyes, and in sisterly fashion, Heather and Jeanne joined me as each of us came to an epic awareness of love. We can quickly forget that we have it all around us and within us. We are LOVE. ***We are loved even when we may not be able to see it.***

CHAPTER 1

Conscious Ethics

"People who truly understand what is meant by self-reliance know they must live their lives by ethics rather than rules."

- WAYNE DYER

If we choose to wear the hat of "intuitive coach," "intuitive healer,"or "intuitive guide," we play an important role in our clients' lives. We are responsible for providing messages with the highest level of love and service possible.

In such intimate connections, it is important to be deeply grounded and holding sacred space of service and unconditional love. That requires us to make a promise, a commitment to ourselves and our work with others. That commitment and promise is first and foremost DO NO HARM. During sessions, we must remember to practice our expertise. If you are not a doctor, don't diagnose, stay in your lane. Know when to use your expertise and when to refer your client to a healthcare expert.

We must discern when ego rears its head through fear and control, and not give into that momentum. This is why our work as intuitives is not only in our sessions with others, but also beyond the scope of actual 1:1 sessions—understanding that every session holds messages and guidance for us as well as for our clients. This is why regular self-care, mediation and success habits are important; they allow us to not be reactive to our ego.

At times, when we first begin, we may want to offer intuitive advice to everyone we meet. We may get so excited and tell everyone what we see, but these innocent bystanders are not asking for our guidance, so why do we feel compelled to give it? We feel compelled because it's something powerful that we haven't experienced since our childhood, or perhaps ever before, and the freedom and love that flows through it makes us literally want to shout it from the rooftops. Still we need to learn to harness and appropriately direct this information to those who want it, those who have given their permission or have asked to know. Only use your intuition when you are being asked and have permission to help, guide, and support.

The more we practice our intuition and use it with our clients the more confidence we gain. Sometimes, due to the resurgence of this new intuitive energy, we feel electrified and our duty to not only tell everyone about our skill but to cross the line into bragging about it. Of course, we may not see it as bragging. The ego is slippery and wants to be known by others. For example, you may be at a party, having a cocktail with a few people, and overhear a conversation where someone is expressing confusion over a situation in their life. A few drinks in, you may step forward and tell them, "Well, I can see what is best for you."

Stop. Hold up. Pause. Wait just a minute. Can you hear how this is all ego? You have stepped out of bounds and automatically jumped into giving feedback: "Well, I know what you should do because I am intuitive." This example may seem far-fetched, but it really isn't. Sometimes, a false sense of over inflation can develop because we've received many accurate intuitive hits and can share them with ease, but here's the secret: regardless of how excellent your skills, or the decades of experience, we all have to reckon with our egos.

What we have is a gift, and it is a gift to be of service to the highest and greatest good of others. It is never us "knowing." Instead, it is us receiving Divine Guidance and being of service, sharing. This fine line is essential to be aware and conscious of throughout your life as an intuitive.

Another slippery slope is when clients are asking for guidance or steps to take in their lives. As coaches, we never tell people what to do. Rather, we show them their options and allow them to choose their own path. Often, I will use terms like, "I see this, and I see that. Which feels better for you?" We always ask questions, provide direct Divine Guidance so they can then make their choices, as we hold the space of unconditional love, nonjudgment, and service.

Staying in Your Lane

As a physician, I'm well aware that there is a big difference between the work I have done as a doctor and the work I practice as an intuitive. They are completely different. They do not overlap, and if you ever feel like you're being asked to give a medical diagnosis, medical treatment, or psychological advice, please remember you are practicing as an intuitive, not a medical professional. It is important to *stay in your lane*. We can't drive a car in two lanes without breaking the law nor can we bowl in two lanes and win. Remember, when you get faced with this situation, refer out to medical professionals, psychiatrists, therapists, counselors, or psychologists.

It's always helpful to have a list of local therapists, physicians and social workers to share with your clients, should the need arise. When clients work with us, many of them have, for the first time in their lives, experienced Divine love—the space of unconditional love without judgment. Because of this amazing energy they experience through us, they feel love for us. And we love them. Having said that, intuitive coaching is not necessarily for everything. If someone in front of you is bleeding, for example, or having severe chest pains, you're best to send them to the emergency room.

Another key to intuition, especially when doing a reading, is to speak the way you receive the message. I'm a Canadian whose personality has been founded on "being sweet," but sometimes the messages I receive are very direct and much different from how I would ever speak. In session, I may say things like, "This may sound harsh, but I keep hearing." What I find is the clients always respond, "That wasn't harsh. That was accurate!" My mind likes to take the message and make it my own. Don't do that. This is a type of censorship. You need not censor the Divine. The message is direct and clear for a reason. However it comes through, whether it's direct and to the point or flowery, trust it. There's a reason. And that reason is that is the way your client needs to receive or hear it. It is for your client to decipher. Trust what you receive and present it exactly as you get it, and if you do this, you will find your accuracy goes through the roof. There's always a reason why guidance comes through the way it does: it's always for the benefit of the client. Say it like you hear it, and don't make it your own. We aren't meant to censor the messages we receive.

In the beginning, I was concerned about delivering messages that my clients might not like or want to hear. The important thing to remember is all messages we receive are for the greatest good of our client. The beautiful thing about this is when we focus on being of service to support this person who is desiring connection and healing we can't get it wrong. The magic is that your client's Divine Support Team and ancestors will bring the message through in a way that your client can receive and understand. This is why it is essential that we not censor our symbols or messages. You may think it's strange to see a butterfly flying away with a Monte Blanc pen, but sharing **exactly** what you see, hear, feel and know can give your client the precise message they needed to hear. We live by a creed: **"Above all, do no harm."** Being mindful of your words and speaking with unconditional love are essential, and when you do this without adding your censor to it, you will be of service.

Often in sessions, we are asked questions about a client's health, life purpose, money, and other important matters. Only share what you receive from Divine Guidance. If you don't get anything for a specific question, that is okay. Try to ask the question in a different way, being careful not to use compound questions. It is best to be completely honest; You can say, "I'm not getting anything specific on that, but I am getting this." Honesty is key, in life, in intuition, and in readings. Take the person you are reading through the steps of slowing down, being present, and deep breathing. If you get nervous, focus on service. It's impossible to get nothing...breathe and receive…notice what you notice.

Softening the Ego

The ego's primary job is to stop you from connecting with your intuition, and likewise, it can keep us from connecting authentically with the person we are reading. Being aware that the ego is present deflates it. That really is the first step: awareness. This is why (and yes, again!) mindfulness and meditation are key for anyone who wants to use their intuition regularly.

The ego is not always bad. It is a part and parcel of who we are. We come from an energy that us humans term as "God" or "Spirit," and that energy is oneness. In the human form, we live in constant duality: hot or cold, good or bad, right or wrong, rich or poor, and so on. And yet, we wish for non-duality, oneness, coherence, and harmony. We assume that love is good and fear is bad, but they are both equally important in our return to oneness. We must accept that our ego is part of us and learn to recognize and understand it.

In my personal journey, it was my pain, deep sadness, feeling of unworthiness, and confusion which helped me find a place of Divine love within myself. Not a day goes by that I don't thank my contrasting experiences for getting me to where I am now. The ego is a necessary part of us, and if we are conscious of its presence, we can use processes to slow down our reaction to it. We can live happily, and with a higher sense of intuition, guidance, and flow. We cannot get rid of the ego, but we can befriend it. In befriending it, we automatically soften our resistance to it, having its voice in our head feels quieter.

All parts of our ego actually think they are helping us. For example, imposter syndrome within us thinks that by telling us "who are you to write a book" that it is saving us from potential shame, disgrace, and so on. It is a protection mechanism born from fear meant to help us, or so the ego thinks.

Some techniques we can use to befriend our ego include exercise, dance, and yoga. Regular meditation, yoga, dance, and exercise actually create a much-needed stopgap between ourselves and our ego's voice. These types of activities allow us to breathe, get into our bodies, and get out of the spin of our mind. Just creating a stopgap between ourselves and the mental spins of our ego allows us to witness its voice. Other befriending exercises include things like a subpersonality journey, journaling, and inner child work. These types of active meditations help us to truly see that our ego is not our enemy but instead our friend. You can find more ego-softening exercises in the Divine Prescriptions section of this book.

Feelings of Love and Satisfaction

The feeling of love and satisfaction is within you right now. It is available to you as you read this sentence. Are you aware of that? That feeling of love and satisfaction is what we are all looking for when we get a bigger house, vie for a job promotion, or look for a perfect partner. But we never find it in these physical things. It is always within us, but when we look for it in external, physical things, we may find ourselves caught in a never-ending cycle of buying and not finding fulfillment, love, and satisfaction.

The only love and satisfaction we will ever feel in our entire lives is within ourselves. We can't get it from anyone else, even though at times it seems we can. Some intuitives may go off track by searching for love, satisfaction, and validation from the people they are reading. While our messages come from a place of love, we are not searching to be rewarded with love or validation from another. Giving someone a reading is very satisfying to us, yet we are not seeking satisfaction from them. The love and satisfaction resides within ourselves, and even if we've only touched love once, it wants to be touched repetitively. It wants to be felt daily as that is who we are, and it doesn't take anyone else to feel this. We are a Spirit in a body experiencing this incredible life. Our ability to feel love and satisfaction is key to unmasking the ego and sitting in a space of truth and love.

Validation from Others

In the beginning of building our intuition, it is easy to look for validation from others. Remember that we have two ways of processing energy and intellect: logical/rational and intuitive/sensitive. It's completely normal to feel the need or push to have validation for our intuitive abilities because it's not something considered "rational" in the world we grew up in. And here's where you will hit the wall with your accuracy in your ability.

Consider validation as a tool of the ego, a saboteur slowing your reception, dimming your intuitive hits. When we are seeking approval, we are resonating and aligning with the energy of fear, so it's impossible to hold the polar opposite vibration of unconditional love, and we are not plugged into our Divine Guidance. Instead we are in ego, and the guidance we receive from that perspective will be one of fear. The search for validation is fear based. We are looking for something that no one can give us. This is the ego's ploy to distract us from stepping into our Divine to receive the messages for the highest and greatest good.

If you find yourself looking for a pat on the back, to feel and know that someone else sees you, getting a coach is a healthy strategy to offset that validation bug. A good coach will always mirror back to you your growth. It's helpful to have a healthy mirror in your tool kit.

CHAPTER 2

Seeing the Saboteur

"The cave you fear to enter holds the treasure you seek."
- JOSEPH CAMPBELL

There is a native American adage which tells the story of the saboteur elegantly. A grandfather is teaching his grandson about life. He tells him there is a fight between two wolves. One is evil—filled with anger, envy, sorrow, greed, arrogance, self-pity, guilt, false pride, and ego. The other is good: filled with joy, peace, love, hope kindness, generosity, truth, compassion and faith. The grandson asks, "Which wolf will win?" his grandfather replies, "The one you feed." This is a powerful reminder that we create our world through our choices and where we place our focus, including the saboteur.

We all have a saboteur lurking in the dark corners of our psyche. Ever-present, offering its opinions on how and what we "should" do. This inner critic conjures powerful images that shrivel our commitment and distract us from what really matters. It's mandate? To keep us small. The saboteur keeps us from being vulnerable, powerful and authentic; its protective intention, like an over controlling parent, is to keep us from getting hurt and (here's a big one) from standing out. Keeping us safe it pushes us into the corner shadows to protect us from judgment and failure, in reality it is limiting our freedom, joy, and having our dreams.

The saboteur gets very loud when we move from planning into inspired action. The moment we consider action we are stepping out and away from our safety zone. Like the siren's song, its alluring beliefs, images and desperation send us crashing on the jagged rocks.

So often we want to take inspired actions only to be swept away by "doing", which can be a big off ramp on the highway of accomplishment. Meaning well, we take all the classes and preparations, telling ourselves this is it, only to stop short in accomplishing what we truly desire. This is the saboteur's motive operando.

The saboteur's voice is easy to ignore going through our busy days, only to find ourselves waking up years later finding ourselves in the same place. This voice within us will not go away. Regardless of the exorcisms we may want to perform, we cannot get rid of it. We aren't helpless, we know this is an aspect of ourselves that is here to teach us something. But what exactly does that look like? We can acknowledge and be aware that it is a normal part of our ego that thinks it is helping us. It is all part of the Divine entity that comprises us all.

How do we do this?

1. Notice your saboteur, without judgement or reaction.

2. Be curious to learn about it so you can understand it and you.

3. Pay attention to its voice, perhaps even noting your saboteur's limiting beliefs and sayings. Whether it's I am not worthy, I am alone, I am broken, I can't.

4. Create a vision of your saboteur, draw a picture, build a Pinterest board, or a collage of what your saboteur looks like.

5. Give it a name, like "Hellacious Helena," so you can have compassion for its protective duties—however misplaced and misdirected.

6. Practice mindful awareness in hearing your saboteur so you easily recognize "Hellacious Helena" when she rears her head.

The key to understanding our saboteur is to recognize that it is a natural, normal part of us. By shining a light on it, through our awareness, sharing about it with our coaches, friends and family loosens its grip on us. In A Course In Miracles, there is a term used repeatedly, "atonement" which means undoing. We are undoing our fear of not being enough. We are Divine, pure essence of Spirit, this is truth. Yet we cling to the thoughts that we are not enough. Atonement corrects this illusion, that in truth never was. Practicing the processes in the Divine Prescriptions section will support you in seeing a shift in how you respond to your saboteur's directions.

It is important to see our own patterns, something that isn't easy despite regular meditations and practices because these habits of the unconscious want to remain unconscious; this is when working with a coach is priceless. A coach who holds the space and conditional love for us can witness our patterns and show them to us. One of the most common patterns we find as coaches is the saboteur.

By this point, you can see how your ego plays a role in your life. The ego can wreak havoc on us, and yet, it isn't our enemy. It is just a neural pathway pattern we haven't developed yet. That is it. As soon as we see it as just this, it loses its hold over us.

What neuroscience is teaching us is that we can rewire the brain and ease its hold on us. Meaning we can rewire our reaction to our ego. We cannot take away existing neural-patterns, but we can wire around the existing ones, creating new pathways for information to flow and create new tributaries. The good news is that it doesn't have to take long at all. It is said that it only takes 66 days to create new habits. Sixty-six days and you can have a new life just by making small habit switches. This is not daunting and something you can do. Revisiting success habits daily and looking for the positive in our lives can keep our outlook positive and allow us to make the habit switches we want to welcome into our lives.

CHAPTER 3

Setting The Stage

"Because true belonging only happens when we present our authentic, imperfect selves to the world, our sense of belonging can never be greater than our level of self-acceptance."
- BRENÉ BROWN

There is a big difference between sharing your intuition with a group or audience and sharing it with an individual. When you have outside observers sitting in on a reading, it changes the dynamic of the experience. Science has shown when there is an observer present the energy and dynamic are significantly altered. For most intuitives, having an observer is a scary thought since the experience is intimate. There is trepidation in standing before a group to share information and messages that may or may not resonate with the audience. As with every part of our lives, when growth and expansion are moving us into the unknown with something we have never attempted, it is natural to be a bit nervous. The uneasiness passes the moment we remember our *why*—why we are doing this work, why we are sharing, and why we are here. We are here to be of service and make a big difference. Our mission is to create value by expressing our gifts, right now.

The technique for accessing your intuition in front of a group will be the same as it is for an individual, the steps we reviewed in the Ready Set Go Chapter, and the only difference is there will be an audience watching the reading and rather than internalizing the message you will be saying it out loud. Cue scary music. Because of the group dynamic, the responsibility of holding the sacred space will be greater. We manage to do that through our energetic boundaries, intention, and who we are being when we share a message of unconditional love and service with our intuition. That is what this work is all about, sharing with those who have yet to realize there is love, forgiveness, and possibilities for them in their lives. If we utilize this intention — to be a vessel which shares love and invites others to step into the forgiveness and growth of their lives — the possible fear we may feel about vulnerably facing a group disappears. Love and service dissolve our thoughts about what others may think about us. When you can stand in front of others and let go of judging yourself, opening your heart to love them and be of service to them, miracles happen.

After two decades of sharing this work in front of large and small groups, I can attest to that fear disappearing as soon as I remember why I am there and why I want to share this love, forgiveness, and Divine Guidance with these people. In the beginning, I would worry about how the messages came through and whether or not they would be good enough for my audience, or worry that maybe the messages would be too personal to share in a group setting. I soon learned that won't happen. Let me tell you why: when you are standing in the energy of the Divine, unconditional love, with a pure intention to love and be of service to the person you are reading (as well as those who are watching), the result is perfect. It may sound like magical thinking, but it's not; this is truly my experience. I stood on stage at "I Can Do It," a massive event held by Hay House, face-to-face with 2,000 people, and I can honestly say I didn't feel fear once I stepped onto the stage because I could feel (clairsentience) and see (clairvoyantly) that this audience wanted to receive my readings. They wanted to feel the love. They wanted to laugh, and that's exactly what happened.

It was a magical experience for me and an epic reminder of the point of this work: to be of service. This is why intention is so important, and it bears repeating: Don't get into this work to be famous or recognized, because that is 100 percent ego. In this line of work, your ego will take you out of the game, completely. I have witnessed celebrity status authors and healers fall hard because they let their egotistical side run the show. Always remember this: we are all one. We are the same, and the desires to have fame are more about validation and approval. *Check yourself before you wreck yourself.* Be very clear about your intention of service. This along with humility will lead you toward joy and success.

When reading an audience or group, it is also important to remember that while the reading may be for an individual it is also for the group, because we are one (Universal Law of Oneness). Most people come to a gathering of this sort because they want to have a reading. When there is a large group, like the 2,000 plus at the "I Can Do It," conference it is impossible to read each and every person in the audience. Because of that dynamic, collective readings will serve all of the attendees. For this reason, it is important to let your group know that every reading is for everyone; guide them to see themselves inside another's reading and message. This will ease their angst, so they can actually receive through each and every reading. This group dynamic energy assures that the messages that come forward will be perfect for public consumption. No one will be embarrassed by the sharing of confidential or traumatic information. I always find it helpful to let audiences know this so they can relax. This makes it more fun for everyone. Because holding space and being within a group atmosphere is powerful—and yes, sometimes overwhelming—we have some practices to get you ready before you step out on stage or in front of a group.

Day Before

Rest, ground, and connect to your why.

Self-care is essential for doing group sessions; sleeping and caring for your well-being the night before is important. Showing up to a group looking tired or scatter-brained isn't a great way to get started. Be prepared, know your material the day before, including travel to the location, clothes, and tools. This also includes nourishment—eating in a way that supports your body is important.

The Big Day

Upon waking, step into your intention to be of service and share unconditional love. Ask to receive any guidance that will support you in holding space for the gathering. I find it helpful to visualize myself as I'm getting out of bed and putting my feet on the floor to see myself stepping into my vortex, the energy field of all of my Divine possibilities. It's as if I am putting on ceremonial robes of Divine service. Whether through meditation, visualization, prayer, or affirmation, it is important that you distinguish yourself as the leader and vessel for Divine intuition.

Fuel up on healthy food. Even if you're feeling apprehensive and don't have an appetite, it is essential to fuel your body before extended periods of using your intuition. We burn a great deal of energy tapping into our intuition and fuel is a necessary requirement. The last thing we want to experience on stage is our body having a sugar crash. The quality of group readings are directly related to our well-being. So take note: skipping meals isn't an option, even a few nuts or something light will make a big difference.

Prepare to arrive at the location early. The big idea here is ease! We want to go into our group readings feeling ready, energetic, fueled, and open.

Before Going onto The Stage

Make sure everything you need for your presentation is set up ahead of time. That can include special crystals or tools you may use with participants. Don't forget water. It is surprising how talking so much dries us out. Plus, in those times when intuition may not be throttling through, taking a sip of water resets our channels and gives us a chance to take a much needed breath. As we've said, intuition is fueled by breath, and we sometimes hold our breath in these situations without realizing it. Holding our breath means holding back the pathways of intuition.

Just before going out on stage, I have found it incredibly helpful to do chakra clearing and spinning. There's a great book, *The Ancient Secret of the Fountain of Youth*, and in it, the author Pete Kelder teaches the Tibetan Rites of Rejuvenation. One of these rites is something similar to what the swirling dervish do, spin and swirl. The premise of spinning and swirling is that everything is in movement, even that which seems solid, and when we can swirl in circles keeping our eyes on one spot, it clears and aligns our chakras with incredible swiftness. It also allows us to step out of our thoughts and into the Divine.

Go Time

Walk out and SHINE! Be your authentic self, embracing your style and commentary.

Don't try to be anyone else. Remember, all these souls came here because they were magnetized to you through alignment of your frequency, vibration, and broadcast. These people are a reflection of you; they are you!

CHAPTER 4

Building Your Technique

"Be yourself—not your idea of what you think somebody else's idea of yourself should be."

- HENRY DAVID THOREAU

When we are honored with the opportunity to be of service to another being, we enter into a soul contract with them, and we want to assure we are being of service in greatest way possible. This is why it is important prior to every session to invite in sacred ritual and ceremony by performing certain activities that support you and activate your awareness to the sacred experience that is about to take place. This makes sure you are able to put aside anything that may be disruptive outside of this session, be it in your personal life or a global situation. Taking the time to set up the space and energy for those whom you will be sharing your intuitive talents with makes sure that you are present to your act of service. And should you feel a bit edgy getting started just remember our ditty: when I get nervous, I focus on service and BREATHE!

What do these sacred preparations look like? That's entirely up to you and what speaks most to you. It can be as simple as clearing your energy (see energy clearing section) and lighting a candle. It may be taking some deep clearing breaths and drawing a rune, or an oracle card. We can sage the room, invite in our Divine Support Team and ancestors along with our client's guides, and more.

These types of physical, energetic and mental ceremonies are a great way to bring our energy back to where we are, back to us and our client, rather than having our focus on many of the other things going on beyond the boundaries of the reading.

The methods you might use in ceremony are infinite, and it's only bound by our infinite creativity. You are free, actually *encouraged* to create your own preparation ceremony. The most important aspect is bringing our energy and focus back to the connection at hand. For me, ceremony is a powerful delineation between the sacred space and the rest of the world.

Creating an intention for your intuitive reading is a powerful booster in every session; it allows us to put our focus on something specific. The intention may be as simple as, allow this session to be for the highest and greatest good of this client. Our primary intention ALWAYS is **How can I love and be of service to this person?** Preparing our energy, the energy of our environment, and the foundation of our intention for the reading boosts our focus and reminds us of WHY we are doing this work.

Ceremony and Intent

Having a ceremony when we begin a session is a great idea! For example, we can light a candle, sage the room, invite in our client's guides, and more. This type of physical and mental ceremony is a great way to bring our energy back to us and our client. Rather than having our focus on many of the other things going on in our lives — our husbands, our children, our world.

Ceremony is an important element in directing our energy and focus back to the task at hand. Creating an intent is a powerful aspect of setting the stage for this sacred service to share your talents it allows us to put our focus on something specific. The intention may be as simple as, "Allow me to be the conduit of love for this client to receive that which is for their highest and greatest good." Ceremony creates a sacred space to do our work and brings our focus to being of service to our client.

So, now that we've set the stage for your professional reading, what's next?

Lions, and tigers and bears? OH MY!

Hold on a second! Wait! Don't let the idea of sharing your gift with another individual or even a group (YES, I said a group) get you freaked out. Just because our ship is out amongst the rough seas of fear isn't any reason to jump off.

You've been trained, you know how to do this, and when you are centered in why you are sharing this expression of yourself the tumultuous seas will settle, the waves may not go flat, but they will calm because you are not doing this for recognition or fame. You are doing this because of your love to support others. Your desire and soul mission is to leave the world a better place than it was before you got here. If you think about just that for a moment, the shock of fear subsides.

So, without further ado, let's give those mad skills of yours a go with stepping into sharing your talent professionally, shall we?

CHAPTER 5

Stepping Onto the Stage

"It takes courage to grow up and become who you really are."
- E.E. CUMMINGS

Now it's time to shine. You've prepared and set your intention, and you are ready to read the person in front of you, whether it is in front of an audience or not. Once you're in the spotlight, the experience will usually flow like this.

Create Sacred Space

What is sacred space? Sacred space is a place where you can leave the chaos of the rest of the world behind and go inward with reverence and respect. With groups, your sacred space will be the stage. With individuals, it might be a room in your house or cleared office space. This doesn't have to be the same kind of place as a physical location though. Sacred space is created from within and the more you return to it, your energy builds. If you are doing a professional reading, receiving an exchange for your intuitive abilities, it does enhance your abilities to use the same physical location as your sacred space. You may not know this, but locations hold energy. That is why people make pilgrimages all over the world to go to locations of spiritual significance. These locations hold energy of past experiences. As a professional intuitive, remember to be present to regularly clearing your sacred space—whether that place is in your mind or the physical space where you do the reading. Keep it clean.

Ground Yourself

To deepen your connection it is important to ground yourself, whether that's through working with grounding crystals, touching a plant, or hugging a tree. As we've discussed previously, grounding is a powerful chemical exchange between our physical bodies and the earth. Practicing grounding before a professional reading helps us to feel connected and plugged in; it's a feeling of being held and supported. Outside, you can easily ground by putting your bare feet on the ground, not cement, take the palms of your hands and touch the bark of a tree, and/or lay your entire body down on the green grass, touching the earth (literally). Walk in the grass, lay in the sand, swim in the sea. Indoors, grounding is as simple as touching living plants, use crystals with grounding energy such as hematite, smoky quartz, or shungite. You can find more of these grounding techniques in the Divine Prescriptions section.

As you prepare to connect with your client (in front of an audience or not), allow them to relay their intention for having the reading and remember throughout your session that you are holding space for them and their intentions.

Holding Space

Make sure you are present and aware of holding space for your client and/or audience. The act of holding space for another is a very sacred and powerful gift (and tool). While it seems relatively simple in theory, being completely present with someone can be challenging, especially if we get wrapped up in our ego and that's amplified if there is an audience watching us. In our Intuitive Coach Training's year course, we do an in-depth training on holding space so that everyone becomes comfortable and well-versed in their ability to do this simple and powerful tool. We spend an entire year on this because it is an essential skill. Like any other skill, if we want to improve it, we need to practice it.

When we hold space for another, we are stepping into oneness (Remember the UL of Oneness?) When we hold space for another, we dissolve all inner boundaries. This frees us to expand as well as become deeply aligned with another human and healing happens. This is when we feel the unity of the entire Universe. Vibrations adjust and clarity appears. Holding space for another as we do in these powerful intuitive sessions creates a safe place to share fears so they can disappear from our clients' lives. Holding space also gives us and our clients a place to be completely authentic, our true selves available without feeling the need to change. Holding space is a special experience when done right.

Sometimes it helps to put your client at ease by beginning the conversation by asking them to share their intention for the session. This allows them to become comfortable to ask questions and speak up.

Receive the Question

As we mentioned earlier in the Ready Set Go Chapter, questions you receive from your client (or the person you are reading) need to be specific and about a topic that matters to them. Make sure they aren't asking compound questions, like "Will I graduate and go to college and meet the man of my dreams and get married?" Compound questions can be tricky for beginning intuitives. As you advance in your abilities, you will be able to easily manage compound questions.

Make sure that your client is asking questions that point to what they truly want to know. Often when people receive a reading, they may know what they are asking in their own heads, but their questions can lack clarity. For example, your client might ask, "Is "x" a good company?" Your intuition could respond by saying, "Yes, they take care of their employees by giving them yoga lessons." When in reality, your client wanted to know if "x" is a good company to invest in. These are two different questions entirely.

Using our intuition as a form of service to others is an epic gift, so it's important to be clear on what people are asking us. This requires us to be free of judgment and full of compassion for the fellow human sitting in front of us. We want to deeply understand the questions they are asking. To do this, pay attention and read between the lines. Often, someone will ask questions that tip toe around the question they are afraid to ask. Some of those deep pondering questions can look like, "Will I be happy? Will there be enough (of something)? Is my partner cheating on me? Why do I feel sad and unlovable?"

Receive and Relay the Divine Guidance

The most important thing I learned during my intuitive training was to receive the question and immediately start talking, no hesitation. What I mean by that is as I receive the question, I take a breath, and start talking. I don't censor the information. I don't think about or rationalize what I've received. I simply share exactly what I get. Even if it doesn't make sense to me. Censoring what you say will make your intuition so-so; the true magic happens by simply opening your mouth and sharing. If you start to feel shaky because you aren't getting anything, remember this: As we have said before but it deserves repeating: IT IS IMPOSSIBLE TO GET NOTHING! Everything, every single thing you see, feel, think, hear, is part of the session you are giving. This is why it is important to hold a sacred space. Everything matters: the temperature in the room changing, the squirrel climbing on the tree outside your window, the movie clip you see, or the random song that pops into your head are all a part of the reading. If you're still hitting a wall, remember this little jingle, "when you get nervous, focus on service." When you realize your intention is to love and be of service, your "need" to get it right is overruled by your soul's desire to connect, love, and be a contribution.

Translate the Message

After you receive the message, you translate your intuitive symbols and vocabulary for your client. In the beginning, it is helpful to create your own Symbol Legend. Symbols are shorthand from the Divine that help us understand blocks of information rather than using individual words. They are shortcuts to quick intuitive access points for ourselves and our clients. They have personal meanings connected to them. Remember our previous example about the yellow roses? Some folks may see yellow roses and think of friendship and devotion. For me, they have multiple meanings. The state of my birth, Texas, and the first flowers I ever received from my first love. So, in a reading, if I saw yellow roses, that symbol shorthand would lead me to Texas, and first loves, for someone else it could mean devotion.

If you are just starting to work with your intuition, we recommend building your own symbol legend. It could be something as simple as a list in your journal or a Pinterest Board. Recognizing symbols deepens your connections with the symbology in your life. Often, it is a repetitive symbol that will get our attention and relay a message. Remember only YOU can interpret or decipher your symbols and wording.

Collect Your Hits

Hold on! Like we said before, no violence! We're referring to hitting the mark, the so-called bullseye, with your reading. What does that look like? It looks like the person you are reading shaking or nodding their head and/or having an emotional response. Our job as the professional intuitive is to stay present with the person we are reading so we can support them. In our years of practice, we have seen intuitives who blow through readings too quickly, basically unleashing all this guidance without pausing for the client to take it all in, much less respond and understand the guidance. Being present with the person you are reading will take care of that issue. It's also helpful to pause, allowing your client to experience their emotions around the Divine Guidance they are receiving. We don't want to prohibit or break their emotional connection with the Divine Guidance they are receiving, so make sure you give them the space they need to process. Check in with the client throughout the reading to make sure what you're saying makes sense to them. Space is key in enabling your client to process and digest the Divine Guidance you are sharing with them.

Energy Healing Process

After sharing Divine Guidance with your client, you may also receive guidance to support your client in integrating the information they just received. These healing processes can look like leading them through a brief meditation or energy clearing exercise.

Message of Love

Every message of Divine Guidance includes a message of love. This can look like an array of messages such as: they are too hard on themselves, that they are loved, that they aren't alone. This part of the session is the summit of this journey, and often brings tears to even the toughest people. We all want to feel loved, valued, and purposeful. You will feel incredible when sharing this message. And, in the end, the Divine is all about love.

Completion

As you continue to build your intuitive skills, you will find your intuitive energy will pull back or ease off as the session comes to an end, especially when we set an intention for the duration when we begin the reading. In my experience, I believe our Divine Support Team know how long it is and that's how long they gab. This is why it is important to have strong boundaries as to the session length. Some new professional intuitives forget to hold their boundaries around completion of a reading, which leads to over giving, imbalance and eventually intuitive connections being stifled.

That is why we find it helpful as the session is coming to a close, to tell your client the session is coming to a close and ask if they have any questions about the guidance they received. We usually give a five to ten minutes notice for this by saying something like, "We have five to ten minutes left. Do you have any final questions?" It is surprising to see how many people will talk a mile a minute during their session and wait until the last five minutes to ask the question they had been dying to know. This happens because there is excitement in making this connection and there may be some trepidation in asking what they truly want to know. Since it is such a repetitive and common pattern, we are chalking it up to being human. So, take note, give them at least a five-minute warning and hold tight to your agreement of exchange and time.

As the session comes to a close, it is important to allow your client room for feedback, should they have any. Something to be aware of, though, is that some will use this time to ask another question, this is where holding boundaries is essential. As you progress in holding space, you won't have this issue. Most people will say, "Wow, thank you. That was great."

At session's closure, it is important that you (personally) thank both your and your client's Divine Support Teams and ancestors for working through you to support and be of service to your client.

Receiving Equal Exchange

Make sure you also make the exchange aspect of your interaction clear. An equal exchange is necessary for a professional intuitive reading. Often in the beginning, this can be difficult to receive. If you are having issues or concerns about receiving an exchange, be it financial, energetic, or otherwise, know that an exchange *has to happen*. Remember the UL of Compensation? To provide this service without allowing yourself to receive an exchange will create an imbalance in you and your abilities and will lead you to burn out, feeling exhausted, unappreciated, putting a kink in your intuitive channels.

Clearing the Session Energy

After a reading is completed, the client has left, or the call is over and you are alone, it is essential intuitive hygiene to dissolve any energetic connections or etheric cords with your client. Sometimes people are in awe of your abilities to tap into Divine Guidance, not believing in their own, and want to stay connected to you, literally. Please know they aren't consciously trying to stay plugged into you; it feels so good they want more.

You can simply intend, "I now dissolve any and all etheric cords to this person, and ask that they instead be plugged directly into the Divine, remembering that cords of love can never be severed." The specific exercise, Etheric Cord Dissolution, describing how to do this can be found in the Divine Prescriptions section.

CHAPTER 6

Troubleshooting Your Style

"Authenticity is a collection of choices that we have to make every day. It's about the choice to show up and be real. The choice to be honest. The choice to let our true selves be seen."

- BRENÉ BROWN

Building our intuitive skills requires us to look at what works for us and what doesn't. If we want to develop our skills and move to the next level, it is important to be aware of when and where we get stuck in sharing our talents with others. I've also noticed that at the beginning of practicing intuition many folks are challenged by receiving guidance for themselves. This section will be a resource to support not only receiving intuitive messages for others but also receiving intuitive messages for ourselves.

Here are some questions to ask yourself if you are having a hard time "getting" hits, whether you're reading for yourself, for someone 1:1, or in front of an audience.

Helpful Questions To Ask Yourself

- **Are you ready to receive Divine Guidance? Are you in receiving mode?** Check in on your fear levels. Are you feeling afraid, concerned, worried, or stressed? If so, slow down. Your energy is the most important aspect of your readings for yourself or others. If you are feeling upset or having an emotional upheaval, sort that out: realign your focus and vibration. That doesn't mean to cancel your reading with a client. It means you are where the buck stops; everything is in the space **you** hold, so if you are feeling wobbly, stop, drop, and roll. *Stop* the train of thinking that makes you teeter back and forth. Drop that energy like a hot potato. It is as simple as that. *Drop* it. Know that it will always be there if you decide you want to pick it up again. *Roll* with ease onto the vibration and frequency that lifts you and feels good. This is where the intuitive messages are.

- **Are you breathing?** Breath brings energy. Inspiration comes from the word inspire, which means to breathe upon or into. Breath brings light, energy, and space. This is why breath work is so powerful. Deep breathing is essential to readings as well as deepening our intuitive skills.

- **Are you attached to the outcome of your reading?** As we covered before, detachment is important, dare we say vital. When we are attached to what information comes through, or what others may think, we shut down the flow of intuition. If intuition is a water hose flowing freely, attachment is the bend or kink in the hose that prohibits the water to flow. If you think you may be attached, ask these questions: Are you judging yourself and/or your abilities? Are you comparing yourself to anyone? Are you expecting a certain result?

- **Are you trying too hard?** Remember there is nothing to "do" except be open, receive and ask, "How can I love this person and be of service to them?"

- **Are you second-guessing yourself or the information that is coming through?** Are you hearing "Yeah, but" in your mind? Doubt stops us in our tracks, especially when we are receiving. Curiosity defuses doubt, step into wondering if you could believe in yourself, and in your Divine connection. Believing is receiving. If you believe, you WILL RECEIVE.

- **Are you drawing a blank?** Are you getting nothing? It's impossible not to feel, sense, know, or hear anything during a reading. Even the smallest sensation is a message. The trick is to TRUST it, go with it, follow it, and pull the thread. If you are reading for someone else, simply say something to the effect of, "I'm getting this sense of [x]" then breathe and see what the next clue is and follow it. Sometimes using intuition requires us to play charades or even be the psychic detective to uncover the meaning behind the sensations or views.

- **What if the message that comes through is "bad" or "upsetting" information?** First of all, know this: if there is heavy or difficult information that needs to be shared with your client, or for yourself for that matter, Divine Guidance will ensure that it comes through with love so that you and your client can receive it and move forward. Look again at the Truth Detector Test to make sure you are connecting to the Divine, not your ego or fear. When we are in our ego, our readings can get "dark" because our ego wants to protect us. Once you are sure you are in the Divine unconditional love and service space, move forward sharing what you receive. Trust is vital here; your soul will not desert you, nor the Divine. Speak slowly, tenderly, as you hold the space of connection and healing for your client. We must say what we receive. We can't change or convolute the message with our own words. To do this with compassion requires us to be in alignment and know without a shadow of a doubt that this is coming forward to be cleared. There are no coincidences. It is a big mission to share this work with others, and there are a multitude of people desiring it in their lives. Some of whom have big blocks—blocks that you will be able to support them in releasing so that they can have a magnificent life. When in a place of love, there is no such a thing as a "heavy/dark" reading only perspective changing, which *A Course In Miracles* considers a miracle.

- **Are you grounded?** Grounding reconnects us to the living matrix of the Earth, be it land or water. When we are grounded, connecting to the Divine is much easier.

- **Are you present to your WHY and are you being of service?** Are you connected to the reason why you do this work? Becoming clear on why you want to share these messages with others can help you remember, in times of contrast, why you are here. Your why brings you to your passion, which regardless of the expression distils down to being of service. When you are present to your passion of service, the Divine Guidance will flow with ease

- **Are you coming from nothing?** Are you holding judgments or preconceived ideas about your client: their lifestyle, habits, or career? We need to be able to come from a space of no judgment, assumptions, or preconceived notions. We are a blank slate simply letting the Divine flow through us. If judgment is seeping through a message, that is our ego at play, and we aren't coming from a place of service and love. In this case see number nine above.

CHAPTER 7

Phone A Loved One

"Life is a great adventure … accept it in such a spirit."
- TEDDY ROOSEVELT

We mentioned mediumship earlier when we were discussing the different types of intuitives. Mediumship is when an intuitive communicates with someone who has passed away. Like a long-distance call from beyond, when we connect through mediumship, we are connecting to a deceased human through the Divine. The power of mediumship is the ability to have healing and closure that didn't happen prior to their transition. Keep in mind though, that the human we connect with is still a human. As we said earlier, this isn't the purest form of guidance because the person who passed still bears judgment; they are still a person, holding their human personalities and consciousness. Their opinions, feelings, and emotions are still based in their human consciousness. Since there is still a human aspect involved in the reading, this isn't the purest form of Divine Guidance.

One of the biggest questions we receive regarding mediumship is what happens when we have a deceased loved one who speaks a different language than we do. Don't worry. The Spirit world will always speak in a way that we can understand, whether it is through symbols or phrases. There are no boundaries in communicating when doing mediumship, except for the boundaries we place on ourselves.

I recently did a mediumship session for a couple that only spoke Spanish. With their translator in tow, they sat down and we began. Even though I don't speak Spanish and they didn't speak English, we were able to connect, and their deceased son came through loud and clear. The father sent me a message recently telling me the session saved his life because he keeps seeing the symbols his son gave him during our session everywhere. In mediumship sessions, the intuitive provides proof of life—proof of connecting with the deceased loved one. Once connected, the message the deceased relays is always from a place of love. Sometimes a symbol is also given to let their loved ones know that when they see that symbol it is indeed them saying, "I'm here watching over you, and you aren't alone."

Most people know Theresa Caputo through her television show, *The Long Island Medium.* As a famous and well-known medium, she helps others understand that there is life and healing after death. She was one of those people who had her spiritual talent from a very young age, and she often recounts how being so incredibly sensitive caused significant anxiety in her life. It wasn't until she understood her gift and was able to use it to be of service to others that she finally got relief from her anxiety. She's such a perfect example of not giving into the cultural stigma of sensitivity. So many of us have these incredible sensitivities, and instead of understanding them (from an energy perspective), our culture tells us to take a prescription or dampen the messages our bodies are communicating to us. When asked in an interview with *Parade Magazine* how her skills work, Theresa Caputo replied:

I always say this, I don't mean to quote Lady Gaga, but I was born this way. I don't know any different. For me, communicating with people that have died and expressing what I'm sensing and feeling, describing things that are going on in my brain that other people can't see, hear, or feel, to me is normal. I can't explain it, it just happens. When I put this in God's hands, and I say, "If this is my [soul journey], I will honor it and I will treat it with the utmost respect." Here I am 15 years later. So that's just basically it in a nutshell. I just don't know any different.

She refused to let others tell her that her gift wasn't for a greater good.

Another famous medium, John Holland, realized his proclivity for the "woo" after a car accident changed his life forever. As a child, he had a different perspective than his family, but didn't understand it until his major "wake up call." He said while living in Los Angeles he wasn't living his best life. This automobile "accident" put him on track to studying and developing his skills. Today, he attracts large audiences with his accuracy and messages of life after death.

Because everyone has intuitive abilities, using mediumship is a fast track to heal our issues with our deceased loved ones. It requires us to be open-minded about allowing this healing and forgiveness to happen. This along with an open heart, and the intention to connect authentically with them is all that's required. Here are some ways to start the conversation with a deceased loved one:

- **Automatic Writing.** Set the stage. Sit down and write everything you want to share with your loved one, all the anger, the sorrow, the hurt, the missing. Jot it all down. Notice if you feel them beside you. Can you feel their presence? Invite them to sit beside you. Imagine they are sitting with you. Imagine you are having a heart to heart conversation. Allow them to respond through your pen. You may feel them take over your pen, or you may hear responses that clearly didn't come from you. You have a pen pal in the Spirit world. It helps to relive positive memories you shared with them to build the connection.

- **Meditation.** Connect with your deceased loved ones by accessing the mediumship channel during meditation. Meditation keeps your thought waves at a consistent level, allowing a sustainable frequency and vibration. While meditating, invite your deceased loved one to sit with you. Be open to everything you sense, feel, hear and know. As they appear, feel free to ask questions or just sit with them.

- **Breathe.** Breath is the origin of our vital life force. Failed awareness of it restricts our intuitive abilities, including mediumship. While practicing always be aware of your breath. If you get stuck and nothing is coming through, it's because of your breath; remember, breathe and the guidance will come through.

CHAPTER 8

Being The Conduit

"Their souls never leave you. You may feel like your relationship is over, but you actually have a new kind of relationship with your loved one, thanks to an ongoing bond that will never end. It isn't a physical relationship anymore, but a spiritual and soul bond relationship that lasts forever."

- THERESA CAPUTO

Prior to any mediumship session, it is important to prepare yourself and create a sacred space as you would with any other intuitive reading.

Besides the steps we've already discussed for intuitive readings, here are some other steps to connect with a deceased loved one:

Steps to a Mediumship Reading

1. Set up a sacred space.

2. Be clear on the intention you set for the reading. (Being of service is a great start.)

3. Invite your client's Divine Support Team as well as any and all ancestors who want to connect with them. Specifically request the deceased loved one your client wishes to connect with to join when the session begins.

4. Support the client in feeling as relaxed as possible.

5. Ask them if they have any questions before starting. People often get amnesia when they step into the energy of mediumship, and they will forget they had a specific question they wanted to ask Aunt Clara.

6. Trust and begin to speak. Anything you see, sense, feel, or know, share it. Doing this amplifies your channel and allows the information to

continue to flow. It enables you to have an actual conversation with the deceased. I find it makes it easier to imagine I am truly having a conversation with this person's loved one, by seeing them sitting with us during the session.

7. Speak (either aloud or in your mind) to the deceased, introducing yourself as you would in any social situation, relaying questions, being open to receiving any information through your clairs.

8. Provide information that the client can validate as their deceased loved one (a brooch, the clothes they wore, their name, how they died, their career).

9. Facilitate a conversation between client and the deceased. (This is where the healing begins. The healing comes through the energy of the session.)

10. Share messages of love from the deceased to the client.

11. Time allowing, ask if there are any more questions.

12. Ask the deceased to give their living loved one a symbol or sign. When this sign appears, it means the deceased is with them. It can support their loved one through tough times, or moments of contrast.

13. Close out the session. Let your client know the session is ending.

14. Thank the deceased loved one as well as your and your client's Divine Support Teams for being here and supporting your client's experience.

15. Clear out all energy connections and cords from the client and the deceased. Make sure to plug all of those connectors back into the Divine.

What All Mediumship Readings Have In Common

- **Proof of Life after Death.** The readings validate accurate information of the deceased, which proves you are communicating with their deceased loved one. Sharing characteristics, personalities, and specific information that you (the medium) would not know helps establish a connection between you, the client, and the deceased. This usually activates an emotional response from the client.

- **Healing.** These are words of forgiveness and validation shared by the deceased with their loved one.

- **Message of Love.** Deceased loved ones always share messages of love in a mediumship reading. Even if the client has not forgiven the deceased, or they are unable to hear, receive, or be with a message of love, it always comes through.

Mediumship for Pets

This is swiftly becoming a big practice to support people through the grief of losing their pets. Our pets speak through energy, understanding our energy they show us what we aren't noticing in ourselves, our environment, or our family dynamics. They understand their mission here and after transitioning, they will stick around as they did when they were alive. Because of missing the signs they are showing us, many take on shame and guilt of not being a good guardian for these souls, carrying a lot of blame and shame when the pet passes away.

Dogs usually stick around their owners, whereas cats meander while still being connected. They respond to our intuition and communication whether they are alive or deceased, thrilled to be of service. The beauty behind pet mediumship is that it is handled in the same way as a regular mediumship. To do a pet reading, use the steps for mediumship.

CHAPTER 9

Hanging Your Shingle

"When I run after what I think I want,
my days are a furnace of stress and anxiety;
If I sit in my own place of patience,
what I need flows to me and without any pain.
From this, I understand that what I want also wants me,
is looking for me and is attracting me.
There is great secret here for anyone that can grasp it."
- RUMI

Once you know how to read others, you can start to create a constant energy exchange through your talents as a business. But that isn't the only way to create a business with intuition. You can also integrate the methodology into a business you already have. Many people don't understand how to integrate this work into their business world. This is a big reason why we offer our Intuitive Coach Training (ICT) program. This program supports people in using ancient methodologies to create a new paradigm for their careers as well as other areas of their lives.

What does adding intuition to my career look like for me? First, it requires clarity. Just like working with any goal/desire/finish line, first and foremost, we need to be clear on the "**what**" we are wanting. In the case of business, **what do you want to offer**? You may be thinking that "offer" is an interesting choice of words. I can hear you saying, "Offer?" You work at your job, you fulfill your job description, and you collect your paycheck—where is the "offering" in that?

The offering we are talking about here is what you want to offer by way of being of service to others. Remember the UL of Reciprocity? When we are in service to others, we get out of our own way, we focus on how we can support and make a difference which allows us an insight into deeper compassion and understanding. Everything always goes back to being of service, especially in this work. The way we grow is by being of service to one another in our own unique and specialized ways.

Your offer is your gift and legacy to this world and your family lineage. Despite the size of your offering, it is the desire and intention you create for it that truly makes the impact. An offering can be something as small as smiling at someone you see on the elevator, or as large as creating a new social structure that changes the way we connect in the world. The sky is the limit and every offering of energy matters, no matter how big or small. This offering allows us to step away from "selling" ourselves or our business, and instead, directs us to the new paradigm of "sharing" ourselves, our intention, our service, and our business.

What Are You Offering?

Below are some questions to help clarify what you're offering.

> What do you want to offer the world? What are your passions? Passion is the first place to look. (*I am passionate about playing my guitar. I want to share my music.*)
>
> Why do you want to offer this? (*Because it would be fun to see people being moved by my music.*)
>
> How is this offering related to your purpose and passion? (*I have something to say about our world.*)
>
> Is it possible this offering could be a career? Do you love it that much? (*Yes! I would love to use music as a way to connect people.*)
>
> What benefit would you receive if your offering was well received or successful? (*money, career, adventure, travel*)
>
> Who would you have to be to have this offering BE a success?

(*a professional, expert master guitarist, practice daily, understand and manage my money*)

What is the impact on you—spiritually, emotionally, mentally and physically—should your offering succeed? (*If your passion is to be a rock star, you would want to look at the impact of that lifestyle, such as travel, large groups, planning, management, organizing…*)

What is the impact on your personal relationships with your family and friends if your offering is a success? (*Just as above what is the impact on your family and friends if you're touring the world for 45 weeks out of the year?*)

How will this offering benefit or be of service to others? (*The music would touch people's hearts and maybe they'd forget their troubles for just a moment and sing.*)

Looking back at your answers, how do they feel? Are your answers from your heart, your truth? Clarity amplifies momentum, creating a trajectory in the direction of your desired outcome.

Often, when answering these questions, some answers come easy: "I want to receive a million dollars for my book on eating healthy." But when we get to the question of "Who would you have to be to have this?" we get stuck. Our answers speak their truth, "I'd have to be someone who writes every day, who eats healthy, who walks the talk, who shows up for myself." This is where inspired action makes the difference. Inevitably, the next question is, "Are you willing to be that person?" Clarity creates space for action.

Ask Yourself

What do I want?

Why do I want it?

Who do I have to be to have it?

How will it benefit others?

After you're clear about; what you want, why you want it, who you have to be to have it, and how it contributes to others, you will feel ease and your doubt about stepping forward will subside because you now see in your own writing there is a Divine plan for you.

When we don't know the next step, or how to build something new or unknown, we can strengthen our fortitude by accessing the Hermetic Principle/UL of Correspondence (there always is a congruence between life and the unknown) giving us insight into the unfamiliar. Just the simple awareness of tapping into your consciousness of this UL makes room for something new, curiosity builds and creativity blossoms. Curiosity is the vinegar to doubt's oil. They don't mix completely.

In curiosity there are possibilities and potential—for creative solutions and miracles. The Laws of the Cosmos show us yet again there are opportunities even if we can't see them in this moment. When we know there is an opportunity, even if we can't see it at that moment, there is an opening, and what happens next is as Einstein said, a mind shift which allows a solution to the question. When we can shift our mind, our perspective, it is a different mind responding than the mind that posed the question: "What's next..."

This moment of curiosity fuels creativity and your intuition. Take a moment, right now, to close your eyes. Take a deep breath, and ask: what is my next step in the creation (or sharing) of my offering? Remember to notice any images or symbols you may see, feel, hear, or know. They are all messages directing you toward your Divine potential. Can you trust and follow them? This may sound like it isn't *"goal oriented"* enough; some would say it isn't structured enough because there's no room for measurement. Remember, we aren't struggling. We are using a new paradigm to build our business, our wealth, our success, our happiness. This means we need to try something new, something different, that may feel awkward.

Remember the definition of insanity? Doing the same thing over and over and expecting a different result. We want to be crystal clear: we do not suggest you figure out what you want and sit on the couch hoping for it to happen. No, absolutely not. Remember the Universal Laws of Action, Resonance, and Correspondence? When we are tapped into our Divine, we receive inspiration with ease, and following it is a snap, as long as we don't over think it and put our energy of fear all over it.

If you are questioning your next step, consult the Divine Prescriptions section for processes to help you get back to your sovereign center and trust your Divine Guidance. And that's just the beginning, folks. Imagine that you have access to Divine wisdom in every instance by using your intuition and the Universal Laws, the world is your canvas.

Intuition and Money

What talk of business would be complete without bringing money into the conversation? Money is energy, a symbol of accepted exchange and a tool of enlightenment. This is where many intuitives get stuck. They want to be of service and feel "bad" receiving money for it. In truth, a true mystic, a Divine intuitive living this work, would gladly share their gift without charging a penny because they believe in the healing and growth that comes through it (UL of Reciprocity). They know an exchange will happen whether it is conscious or subconscious. We must remember that money is a tool of exchange, it is not evil, but making it your source could feel that way.

When we refuse to receive an exchange of energy, whether it is money, a smile, or a hug, we are shutting our entire receiving mechanism down. We are shutting off the work of the Universal Law of Compensation. When we shut ourselves off from receiving an exchange, it deeply impacts not only our ability to attract (UL of Attraction) but also leaves us vulnerable to exhaustion, resentment, and a victim mentality.

Money is energy, and whether you have an abundance of it or a lack of it, it is because of your resonance with it. (Remember the ULs of Resonance and Relativity?) I like how Ken Honda speaks about the energy of money in his book, *Happy Money*:

"Money is just a symbol when you think about it. We rarely see it or touch it in its printed form today. The money you think you have in the bank is not really there. The moment you deposit it the bank lends it to someone else. All that remains are the numbers you see when you check your bank account on your smartphone..."

When you use Mr. Honda's insights and acknowledge that money is an illusion, you are dancing with the First Hermetic Principle Mentalism, *everything is of the mind.* You are allowing your mind to shift perspectives, witnessing past wounds around money being healed through forgiveness. Using the Hermetic Principles and ULs along with your intuition will give you freedom from doubt, guilt, fear, shame. It will free you up to create, build, collect, and share your money energy, making the world a better place.

Practicing as an intuitive coach does not have to be a side-gig that you do on Sundays while you work your day job for "real" money. Or it can be, it is entirely up to you and what you want. We are allowed to have our dream careers. Practicing intuition no longer needs to be hidden. We are allowed to use it as a coach, doctor, physiotherapist, CEO, or any career that makes us feel alive. As we wake our talents up, we can live more complete, full, enriched happy lives.

CHAPTER 10

Coming Onto Shore

"There is only one map to the journey of life and it lives within your heart."
- WILLIE NELSON

We are coming into the harbor after our massive journey together in the ocean of intuition. We've sailed behind the curtain of intuition, revealing its ins and out, and before you step a shore, we want to make sure you have your land legs—that you've acclimated and can walk on solid ground.

During our trip, we've taken a long look at what intuition is, and what it isn't; we've talked about how it looks, how to develop it, and its origin story. Intuitives look like you, they look like me, they look like the guy down the street too. As you've found, this book isn't an ancient scripture that comes with a magical pill that will make your life better in the blink of an eye. It isn't the Spark Notes to a better life. Nope, there are no quick fixes, but there are quick realignments. In the blink of an eye, we can align back to our natural way of restoring our power, energy and connection. This book's purpose is to remind you of your Divine natural state and to poke that hidden wisdom in the core of your being into rising into your awareness, beyond the deep recesses of your unconscious mind to stay safe in this world.

And now, you can hopefully acknowledge and feel there is no coincidence that you were drawn to this book and to this work. While we are experts, having lived it for over four decades (combined), we know there is more to uncover and learn in the world of intuition and energy. And it is important to say, and for you to hear, that this is not the only way to work with energy and intuition. We are not saying we have all the answers or even that this is the only truth. This is information that allows you to choose for yourself, to experiment, observe, and witness your own personal experience.

You have seen in our personal stories and the stories of our clients and friends how intuition revealed itself, and you've learned that everyone's journey is unique, as are their experiences with energy and intuition. Which keeps this journey interesting, to say the least. In working with your intuition and sharing it, there never seems to be a dull moment, and something good always comes out of it.

Through this journey, our intention is to strip away the blinders to reveal to you — perhaps for the first time — a new way of perceiving and actively interacting with your life, through creation, through listening, and through following your Divine Guidance faithfully. When we are in union — freely communicating with life around us — there is harmony. That doesn't mean "bad" stuff won't happen, but when it does it will be easier to handle because we have more clarity, power, and awareness of ourselves and the world. This means embracing the ALL of your life: ALL of your choices, conscious or otherwise, and the impact of their rippled outcomes. It means understanding you are an integrative thread in the woven fabric of our Universe, and how you, the individualized form of the Divine, are an important integral piece of this world. For without you, this world would not be complete. Recognizing this, we can actively participate in and with the energy of life. I believe to do this with mastery requires living the Hermetic Principles and Universal Laws — the all encompassing, ultimate guides to consciousness.

Why do we want to expand our consciousness? What's the fuss all about? When we are able to build our consciousness, we become aware of our true, natural being, the individualized expression of the Universe. There's a multitude of benefits. Namely, a type of higher thinking happens when we expand, and solutions are more readily available, inspiration peaks, relationships grow, peace is possible, and inspired action happens. Who am I kidding? Magic and creation happens. This is because our expanded consciousness replaces our old point of view, the "I'm not good enough" mindset, with a new point of view. I know this sounds a bit like Russian nesting dolls, but stick with me. Consciousness helps us regulate our energy, and its interaction with our brain creates cognition — the awareness, observation, and knowing we experience every day.

Our ability to observe our emotions, which are triggered by our unconscious beliefs, show us that there are beliefs we may not be aware of. (Hint,

hint: it's those same beliefs that have been stalling your success all of your life.) We shift these beliefs by working with our point of view, taking on a different perspective, and creating an alternative belief, which changes everything, including your experience.

As we've said, if you practice the processes in our Divine Prescriptions section, you'll see a different world, because you'll be different. Just as Wayne Dyer taught, "When you change the way you look at things, the things you look at change."

As with any other talent, skill, or ability, your intuition will grow the longer you work with it, and just like riding a bike, should you stop using it, it's always there to be picked right back up again. The skill never goes away. Our attention to it may wane, but its power does not. The Universe is always speaking to us. And like Einstein said about riding a bike, you must keep pedaling forward so you don't fall over. Your momentum and practice are what will keep your intuitive abilities sharp and clear.

The beauty of intuition is that we are born with it—all of us. It is a naturally given sense that requires attention as any other muscle or sense does. It does not discriminate, and it is given to all. The only variance in our gifts is our level of skill, which is based wholly on working with it deliberately. Practice builds our trust and confidence in recognizing the Universe speaking to us. When we follow that nudge, sense, guidance, we strengthen our connection to ourselves and the Divine, life becomes much easier, resistance subsides, strength and courage grows. We understand our interconnectedness to the Universe through building our intuitive channels, and we are more likely to face our fears instead of being ruled by them. When we stand in the courage of our Divine connection through intuition, feeling fear no longer delays us because we know true consciousness comes from stepping in and through our fear, our shadow, and the unknown.

Despite what you may have been told or what you believe, you are an essential piece and participant in our world. Waking up your intuition makes you a bigger contribution to our world. When we focus on being an instrument of our Divine intuition, our lives grow beyond any dreams we could've wished, because we are of service to others. This service and love is the heart of the matter in this work. We do this work to support others to see their own power and abilities within themselves, so they can move beyond any limitations they once believed about themselves or the world. When we can embrace our perceived mistakes, understanding we are more than our fears of failure and our struggle, we have the courage and audacity to reach beyond what we know. This is what opening and working with our intuition will bring—possibility and opportunities we never imagined.

Comparison is an intuitive's Achilles heel. The moment we compare our talents to another person's, judgment activates our ego, which makes our clarity and accuracy plummet. The reason some intuitives are more accurate than others is because our intuitive energy is synthesized through our energy field. All this means is that our Divine Guidance is filtered through our beliefs and points of view. When we have unresolved fear and emotions they become crystalized in our energy field, like little chunks of debris floating around us. These chunks of debris become an obstacle course, altering the delivery of our intuitive energy. These unresolved emotions and disempowering beliefs impact our connection and clarity, which throw off our intuitive hits.

This natural ability, intuition, is as unique as our fingerprints—no two are exactly the same. There may be similarities, but each of us is 100 percent unique and individualized. In over 30 years of this work, we have seen all different aspects, shapes, and sizes of intuition. Each is as unique and different as the people who practice it. The one resounding similarity is the basis for it all, and that is to be of service to another, to expand love, and be a contribution to this world. So, please, don't judge your skill. Just like the Avengers and every other superhero team ever put together, everyone has their own unique contribution, and it is essential that every one of us plays our part. Trust and follow the guidance you receive, despite how it looks compared to other practitioners. You will find not only peace and authenticity but also FREEDOM!

You may be thinking, this is all fine and good, but I'm going to leave it be with all these grandiose promises and ideas. You may be thinking, "This energy called intuition is poppycock." That is absolutely okay with us. We just want to remind you that the Universe is always speaking to us, even if we don't acknowledge it. Our Divine Guidance is always present, 24/7, and when we ignore it, doubt it, or pretend it is just coincidence, we are shutting down our flow and connection to life. Like a water pipe that becomes clogged, soon only a trickle is able to flow. Your chakras and energy field become like that pipe, obstructed, congested, which stifles your mana (life force) creating disharmony, and it eventually hinders your body through disease, pain, and hardship.

Ignoring our intuition slowly kills our life force. I always picture it like a dimming light within our body. We are meant to integrate intuition into our being, as a part of who we are as humans so that we can continue to live with deeper connection and explore the unknown. With it, we can experience and expand our understanding of the Universe and our part in it. We are not here solely to learn something, or to work off some karmic debt, or to have experiences, we are also here in this timeline to witness ourselves and each other in the cycle called life.

Every century has its influences, technology, industrial progress, art, and culture. In our century, one of the noted influences is neuroscience, mindfulness, and everything of the mind. We are here to expand our minds, intertwining it with our physical bodies, and evolving into expanded sentient beings. No longer can we ignore the Divine nature that courses through us with each breath we take. Ignoring our bodies as one of the most accurate divination tools is not an option.

You are reading this because you asked for a wakeup call, a reminder of who you truly are in your natural state. As always, the choice is yours. The question here is this: can you say yes to your abilities? Can you say yes to your authentic nature? Yes to ease? Yes to clarity? Yes to a newfound happiness?

A Harvard Psychology study said that 80 percent of people are unhappy with their jobs. Are you a part of that 80 percent? Are you waiting for something to drop into your lap to make you happy? Why do we hesitate to follow our guidance, toward happiness? Is it because we are afraid of failing and being disappointed? Or, is it because we don't want others to see us fragile and vulnerable, missing the shot?

I have been at those crossroads in my life, too many times to mention, and at every fork in the road, I always listened and trusted my Divine Guidance, even when it was logically difficult to understand. The Universe is unwavering, always coaching me through the waves crashing on my shore, songs popping up "randomly," friends reaching out, and even billboards sending me messages. Trusting this guidance, however odd it may have seemed at the time, always eased my mental worries, anxiety, and fears, and it allowed me to move beyond my comfort zone, into the great wide open of being relentless, audacious, and completely free. This is how intuition changed my life. With my clairs, I can easily approach any challenge, obstacle or opportunity instead of bracing myself to "figure it out." Having access to Divine universal wisdom truly makes living this adventure called life exciting. There's never a dull moment when we're in the flow and paying attention. Opportunities, adventure, and the best the world has to offer is available to us, all of us, if we listen.

Building our intuition is something that takes commitment and practice (are you getting tired of us saying that?). When we miss the mark and don't hit the bullseye with 100 percent accuracy, we must remember not to judge our skills, and instead, dive in and be the psychic detective to see why we may have missed some of the messages possibly due to our clogged pipeline. Having the resilience to learn and understand this line of communication means being able to laugh at yourself and not take things so seriously. Like we've said, there's nothing serious going on here! This talent is expanded when we can step into it with a playful heart, respecting and knowing that the Universe always answers.

Especially in this time, as I write this, we are experiencing the COVID-19 global pandemic ripple of chaos. It is in times of confusion and uncertainty that being connected to your Divine Guidance, your intuitive energy, will keep you resilient. In the media, everything is a buzz, no one knows what is true, what is conspiracy, what is factual, and what is fallacy. Actually, it doesn't seem like anyone knows, and if they do, they aren't telling the general population. THIS is when intuition rules! In fact, I believe this is WHY we have our natural abilities, for times like these. Being connected and being plugged into Divine consciousness, you don't need CNN or any other news reports. You can utilize your ability to understand, receive, and synthesize this energy called intuition to get the highest level of guidance for you and your circumstance, whatever it may be. You can trust your intuition. And let me tell you, Divine Guidance never lies!

Speaking of Divine Guidance never lying, we would be remiss if we didn't one last time remind you of the falsehoods of the ego. Ego is fear, plain and simple. When we aren't connected to our Divine Guidance, it is easy to protect ourselves through our ego. Ego is frightened of the unknown; it wants to keep us safe. Unfortunately, there is no growth in staying in the same place. When considering this, I am reminded of the story about a deer in a meadow. With hunters nearby, the deer hides in the tall grasses waiting for the danger to pass. The only problem is at some point the deer must get up. If it stays there frozen, it will die. Movement is essential to continue life, but ego wants you to stay still, to not venture beyond your comfort zone.

One of the biggest downfalls for an intuitive is the ego mindset. It's not unusual, when first tapping into your intuitive guidance to begin to feel a surge of power, freedom, and ease. The trick is to not let that go to your head. When we understand that everyone has this ability and access to it, the egoic hold seems to lessen. Nothing will shut down your accuracy faster than ego. When you find your hits are falling short, this is the first place to look—your ego. Have you had thoughts recently that you're better than someone else? Or less than someone else? Keeping it simple, when we step into separation through judgment and comparison, we have unplugged from the impersonal and unbiased Divine Guidance we call intuition. These thoughts are signalling that we are in our ego.

This is why our focus when sharing intuition with others is always based first and foremost on "How can I be of service and love this person?"

When our focus is on service and unconditional love, ego will stay in the background. And like every other part of our shadow, ego is a piece of us to acknowledge and love, not to resist, hide, and compartmentalize. This practice in and of itself requires a more expanded view than perhaps you've had before. It may feel uncomfortable at first, but once you walk through it and find the amazing benefits, the discomfort fades.

By igniting your intuition, you will have a completely new experience of life. Gone will be the days of wanting to look back. You will start to feel and experience life as the creator of your Universe rather than a victim to chance. It is the most empowering, incredible dance of existence that you can possibly imagine from our perspective.

Intuition deeply impacted both of our lives, and it took some time for us to arrive here. It wasn't overnight. It was one step at a time, through the darkness, tripping on Legos scattered on the ground. Discerning our intuitive symbols, delving into the language of our ancestors, the Divine, and our Divine Support Team has been a journey. If there is only one piece of guidance we can leave you with, it is this: building your intuition is an evolutionary skill that captures the relationship between you and the Divine within you. You can't do it wrong. Just breathe and begin to notice it. That's all. When you show up, the Universe will always meet you.

We hope you had fun on this voyage connecting with your intuition, and perhaps you even learned a thing or two. Maybe you've traveled this journey before and you remembered something you forgot. Regardless, we are grateful and honored that you chose us to take you on this tour.

Remember your world may look different from when our ship first left the shore. So be kind and gentle with yourself and others as you integrate and adapt to your new superpower.

And as party favor, for making it all the way through the journey, we're going to leave you with some processes, explorations and suggestions, in the following Divine Prescriptions section. It includes processes we personally use and recommend to our clients and friends. These exercises lead to other trailheads so you can carry on your exploration of knowing yourself as a mystic, an intuitive, a powerhouse, and a gift to this world.

So, if you'll humor us with one more parting question, as our paths diverge, and you go onward in your quest, living your best life, looking to the sky for signs, feeling the energy of the Universe rising up to greet you, we have to ask, in the way only Mary Oliver can,

> *"What is it you plan to do with your one wild and precious life?"*

Until our paths cross again, be well and know you are loved.

PART 4

Intuition

Divine Prescriptions

In this section, you will find a listing of many processes, meditations, and sacred ceremonies to support you in building your intuition, vibrational alignment, and broadcast. We believe all of these processes and ceremonies are sacred, steeped in intention and Divine direction. The way you "hold" these will be a direct correlation of what you will receive from them. In other words, if you treat and honor these processes, you will reap big results. What you put into it is what you will get out of it.

If you want to deepen the meditations we recommend, recording them in your own voice and then tune in—it will definitely give you more bang for your buck! Because these processes are multipurpose, we created an index with some cross referencing to get you started.

Divine Prescriptions Contents

MEDITATIONS

PROCESSES

INTUITIVE TRAINING Clairvoyance

INTUITIVE TRAINING Claircognizance

TAKING CARE OF BUSINESS

SACRED CEREMONIES

Divine Prescriptions Index

There are a multitude of aspects to the processes, exercises, meditations and ceremonies included in Part Four, Intuition—Divine Prescriptions. We thought it would be helpful to give you a breakdown of them by category to help you find the perfect tool for the moment you are in.

General

These general processes are helpful to use on a regular basis for clear intuitive hygiene.

- Belly Breathing
- Chakra Clearing Exercises
- Crystal Magic
- Grounding
- Etheric Cord Dissolution
- Energy Vacuuming
- Mirror, Mirror
- Mindful Eating
- Morning Vibration Exercise
- Momentum Awareness

All Clear

Each of these processes groups supporting, building and strengthening ALL the intuitive channels.

- Amplify Intuition
- Belly Breathing
- Card Play
- See the Future
- Chakra Clearing Exercises
- Crystal Magic
- Energetic Attacks
- Energy Vacuuming
- Etheric Cord Dissolution

- Ho'oponopono
- Mind vs. Spirit
- Morning Vibration Exercise
- Momentum Awareness
- On the Road Again
- Shaking/Dancing

Clairvoyance

These processes build and strengthen your ability to tap into your Divine vision.

- Belief System
- Chakra Clearing Exercises
- Clairvoyance Energy Activation
- Crystal Magic
- Etheric Cord Dissolution
- Grounding
- Imagine If You Will
- Laugh Lines
- Poker Face
- Seeing Oneness
- Signs
- Third Eye Activation & Amplification
- Third Eye Clearing
- Yogi Training

Clairaudience

These processes are designed to activate and strengthen your Divine ability to hear your intuition.

- Belief System
- Boosting
- Clearing Ear Chakras
- Crystal Magic

- Etheric Cord Dissolution
- Chakra Clearing Exercises
- Grounding
- Intuitive Ear Muffs
- Jammin'
- Silence Is Golden
- The Sound of Answers
- Toning

Clairsentience

Each of these processes activate and build your ability to connect with your Divine Guidance through your senses, feeling, touching or smelling.

- Belief System
- Crystal Magic
- Etheric Cord Dissolution
- Chakra Clearing
- Grounding
- Clearing Heart Chakra
- Mindful Awareness
- Mindful Eating
- Picture is Worth a 1000 Words
- Psychometry
- Shaking/Dancing

Claircognizance

These focus on building and strengthening your connection to receiving your Divine Guidance through your intuitive channel of your mind and thoughts.

- Activating Claircognizance
- Chakra Clearing Exercises
- Crystal Magic
- Etheric Cord Dissolution
- Grounding

- Grounding Cord Exercise
- Mind vs. Spirit
- Receiving Divine Downloads

Stopping Momentum in its Tracks

These are designed to stop the action of a downward spiral of momentum before you jump into an old patterned behavior.

- Being In The Now
- Belly Breathing
- Contrast vs. Clarity
- Energetic Attacks
- Fire Releasing
- Grounding
- Mindful Awareness
- Morning Vibration Exercise
- Momentum Awareness
- Shaking/Dancing

Dig Deep

These processes dive into the deepening of your intuitive connections.

- Belief System
- Driving The Boat Exercise
- Ho'oponopono
- Meeting Your Subpersonalities
- Milking The Moment
- Mindful Eating
- Releasing Vows or Contracts
- Seeing Oneness
- Subpersonality
- Worry Scheduler

Taking Care of Business

These processes and exercises are designed specifically for business building and creating clarity around your offering.

- Amplifying Your Offerings
- Attracting More Ideal Clients
- Belief Systems
- Business Building Exercise
- Business Building Meditation
- Chakra Clearing
- Crystal Magic
- Divine Wisdom
- Driving The Boat Exercise
- Energetic Attacks
- General Magnetizing Exercise
- Releasing Vows or Contracts
- Shattering Glass Ceilings
- Successful Event
- Throat Chakra Clearing
- Worry Scheduler

Cha-Ching

All of these processes and exercises are designed to strengthen your wealth consciousness as well as your beliefs around money.

- Belief Systems
- Chakra Clearing
- Driving The Boat Exercise
- Energetic Attacks
- Feng Shui Wealth Activation
- General Magnetizing Exercise
- Meeting Your Subpersonalities
- Mind vs. Spirit
- Money
- Money Speaks
- Releasing Vows or Contracts
- Shattering Glass Ceilings

- Worry Scheduler

Let's Get Specific
We have created a couple of processes with specific intentions and focus:

Addictions
- Addiction
- Energetic Attacks
- Ho'oponopono
- Mindful Eating
- Release Old Patterns & Blocks
- Releasing Vows or Contracts
- Subpersonality

Anxiety/Stress
- Being In The Now
- Ceremony For Uncertain Times
- Closure & Completion
- Energetic Attacks
- Energy Vacuuming
- Environmental Grounding
- Ho'oponopono
- Meditation

Feeling Alone or Isolated
- Attracting Divine Partnership
- Clearing Heart Chakra
- Inner Child
- Seeing Oneness
- Mind Vs. Spirit

Feeling Safe
- Closure & Completion

- Divine Wisdom
- Grounding Cord
- Shaking/Dancing

Self-esteem

- Belief Systems
- Meet Your Subpersonalities
- Mirror, Mirror
- Releasing Old Patterns & Blocks
- Subpersonality

Meditations

Amplify Intuition

When To Use It

Use this meditation when you want to wake up your connection with the Divine. Use this meditation when you are feeling you need to add some extra steam to your intuitive engine. It is a great meditation to amplify your connection to your Divine Guidance.

Meditation

Sit or lie in a comfortable position, hands loosely on your lap, legs and feet side by side. Notice the position of your body resting here.

Be aware of the temperature of the air on your skin — any sounds or movements going on around you. Be aware that this is your time to experience and explore the inner recesses of your mind.

And take a deep breath in through your nose. Imagine that breath at the bridge of your nose just between your eyes and then breathe out. Just breathe out and relax.

Repeat this process again two more times — breathing in — becoming aware of the breath and letting go. On the third time, I want you to imagine that breath rising further — to the pineal gland — the third eye center just inside the forehead. And as your breath reaches the pineal gland, you find yourself relaxing more and more as you drift deeper and deeper into comfort and calm. And on drifting deeper, you become aware of your body — resting here — beginning to feel heavy and relaxed, heavy and relaxed and so comfortable.

Begin to relax all of your facial muscles. The muscles in your forehead and around the eyes. The nose relaxes as does the mouth, and inside your mouth, even your tongue becomes relaxed.

Your cheeks relax and feel flat and smooth — flat and smooth — and relaxation is now draining all the way down the neck. The shoulders and arms, and down your upper body and into your stomach and thighs, and your legs relax — as do your feet — until the whole of your body is completely and totally relaxed.

Your mind begins to relax more as you feel yourself drifting deeper and deeper - into a lovely warm and comfortable feeling. A very relaxed and sleepy sort of feeling, but you don't actually go to sleep. You're aware of everything that is said to you. And you become aware that your entire body and mind are comfortably relaxed. From the top of your head, all the way down to the very tips of the toes and back again to the top of your head, deeply relaxed.

I want you to focus once more on your pineal gland, your third eye chakra, and imagine a door beginning to open over your third eye. You can feel yourself relaxing deeper still. Enter the doorway now and find yourself in a very large and spacious room. This is the room where you spend most of your waking life, sorting out problems, making decisions, processing your thoughts ready for speaking or action. You are aware that there is a higher level of awareness — and looking around — you discover a new door that you hadn't noticed before.

See yourself walking over to the door and pushing it open to then find yourself outside standing in front of an infinitely tall skyscraper.

Looking up you can see your name is engraved over the entrance in large, bold letters.

See your name now. This is the skyscraper of your mind and you know that when you enter the door you will want to go up to the highest level possible.

You walk through the door, recognizing that on the ground level you are now at the back of your mind where those conscious thoughts came from, waiting to be sorted out.

It seems different in here — different — but familiar in an odd sort of way.

As though you can recognize where some of those thoughts were coming from — and you could — if you stayed here to explore them further.

But you know that you are here for a reason — to further strengthen and develop your intuition and Divine Guidance — and to do this you need to go higher. At the back of the room is an elevator that is marked, up, and you see that there are seven levels to visit. So you step into the elevator and press the button marked 1, which takes you up to the first floor.

Feel yourself rising higher and higher inside the elevator, until it stops at the first floor, and when you step out, you notice the first door that you see is tinted with a bright shade of red, and upon opening the door, you discover that this level of awareness is concerned with your primary needs. Your desires for gratification in whatever way that may be your sexual nature, your need for substance such as food and drink, and other bodily functions.

You realize that in order to strengthen your intuition you will need to go higher than this, so you leave it behind for now. Stepping back in the elevator, you go higher up to the second floor.

Stepping out of the elevator you notice that the first door you see is a lovely, bright orange and entering the room beyond you realize that this is the room of your creative mind. It is the seat of joy and the place where your inner child resides.

Your creative mind is the place where new ideas are dreamed up. It is the place where stories and pictures are made — as well as being the home of all sorts of skills—from cooking and carpentry to sewing and swimming.

Again, you instinctively know that you want to go higher right now. So you step back into the elevator and go up to the third level. You can feel yourself going up...and up...and up until the elevator stops and the door opens and you step out.

This time you see a yellow door. It is a bright sunny yellow, and upon opening the door and looking around you see that this is the place where your emotions and feelings are based.

Your thoughts will affect your feelings, and in turn, those feelings will add fuel to your thoughts— whether these are positive or negative ones—but especially the negative ones, and right now, you don't need to be here. You want to go higher still.

So you return to the elevator and go higher still - higher and higher - up to the fourth level of awareness, and when the elevator stops and the door opens for you, you step out and notice that you are now facing a green door.

Looking through you see that this is the place of the soul. Your inner guidance and the seat of your higher emotions that are based on unconditional love, such as empathy, compassion, true love, and friendship.

It is a lovely level, still you are guided to go higher so you return to the elevator and go higher still.

You go up and up higher and higher now going up to level five, and stepping out of the elevator door, the first thing you see is a blue door. It's the color of a lovely clear sky and going through the open door you see that this is the level of communication and expression. It also deals with issues of truth and true expression of your soul.

You get the sense that you are almost there, feeling called to go higher.

Return to the elevator and go up—up to the sixth level—and stepping out of the elevator you see an indigo door, a royal blue color, which is the level of intuition and soul knowledge. This level balances the power of mind and mystical knowledge, dealing with issues of developing, strengthening, and trusting intuition in your life—allowing soul knowledge through and developing high sense perception as a life skill.

And if you'd love to stay and explore this level feel free to and you're happy you know that you are being called to go higher still.

You can come back here whenever you like, but you have an important mission right now, to amplify your intuition.

So, you return to the elevator and go up and up—higher and higher—and the higher you go the more deeply relaxed you become, going up to the seventh floor.

The door glides open and you step out—into the room beyond—where you instinctively know that the next door you see will be violet in color, and sure enough, here it is, and you have now reached a state of equilibrium and balance. You open the door and walk through almost floating on air, sensing that you have arrived at last.

In this room, you can observe yourself and trust whatever you see. You can focus clearly on whatever facet of intuition you wish to strengthen and develop your daily connection. You are in a higher level of awareness than you've ever been before in your life, and the most beautiful thing is that whenever you return to this level you will find whatever it is that you wish to know.

Whether it is understanding more about others, developing your Divine Guidance, utilizing all four clairs, communicating with and through whatever means you feel most aligned. You are ready to allow a deepening, you are ready now. Such deepening that you trust your Divine Guidance and all messages you receive through all of your clairs, your intuitive antennae is up and broadcasting the highest vibrational resonance for you and your Divine purpose, that intuitive antennae is expanding now as it receives a broader and more refined channel to your intuition. Whether your desire be to see into the future, channel, or write, you can focus your mind, find answers to all of life's questions, for here is the key to the place where all is revealed. And you easily receive all that is revealed.

And I'm going to give you that key right now. Receive it now. A beautiful golden key, the key to the seventh level.

Whenever you wish to return to this place, just relax, and mentally go through the journey you've travelled today. Take the key and unlock your mind to your higher potential and return to this wonderful place for this is yours to explore and deepen your clairs and Divine Guidance.

Look around you now. Make a mental note of whatever you see and whatever there is bring it back with you now. Everything you see has a message and purpose in expanding your intuition. If you would like you can write it all down. *Pause.*

Okay, we are about to return to your normal level of conscious awareness, before we do remember to bring back your key and any symbols or messages.

Good, now when you're ready, I'm going to count from one to five, and on the count of five, you'll be present and aware in this space and time. Coming easily back into your environment, back into your body. *One, two, three, four, five.*

Belly Breathing

When To Use It

This is an excellent meditation to do at any time of the day. It is especially great when we are in panic mode and want to practice moving into a calmer state. It is especially helpful before you are going to do something that is making you nervous. This helps you to breathe deeply, decrease your blood pressure, decrease your heart rate, increase your sense of mental calm, feel more connected with your physical body and more.

Meditation

Close your eyes and center your breath.

On this belly breathing meditation, we will introduce you to your breath and have you center in the now.

Start to slowly breathe in and out. In and out. In and out. Relaxed, slow, calm, easy breathing.

With each breath, start to follow the pattern and rhythm of the breath.

Invite your right hand to go on your abdomen and your left hand to sit on your chest. Notice as an observer would which hand is moving more.

With each breath, start to focus on your right hand so that your right hand slowly lifts and falls. With each breath, right hand rises and falls with ease. Slow breath in, deep breath out.

Empty the lungs and start to inhale for the count of 1-2-3 and exhale for 1-2-3-4. (Repeat this a few times.)

Slow breath in deep breath out. With the cycles of breath, focus on your right hand lifting and falling and your mind focusing on the breath.

Calm relaxed, slow, easy breathing.
If thoughts are coming, which is normal, imagine yourself sitting outside on a beautiful sunny day.

As you look in the sky, you see blue sky and clouds drifting across the sky.

The clouds come and go, your focus constantly returns to the blue sky.

Each thought is a cloud which with breath starts to be blown away, returning to your slow deep breath.

Try not to push the thoughts away, just notice them, be aware of them and watch with each breath as they get further and further away from your vision – returning to the blue sky.

The belly breathing pattern is starting to get easier, more relaxed.

You are starting to feel calmer, lighter, more relaxed.

Belly breathing stimulates the parasympathetic nervous system. This calms you down and brings you into the now.

For the last few breaths, make the breaths even longer and slower, deeper, and fuller.

Now, as your mind is a bit quieter, your heart fuller and you are feeling more refreshed, start to bring your awareness to your fingers and your toes.

When you are ready, gently open your eyes returning to the brighter, outer world.

Divine Wisdom

This is our spin on a beautiful Orin & DaBen meditation.

When To Use It

Use this meditation when you want some guidance on your life purpose/life path. It will help you to receive messages or clarity on your service on the planet. It will also help you to get clear outside of the constraints and fears of the ego.

Meditation

Imagine that you are standing in your sovereign center, the center of the Universe, the center of your microcosm of life, the center where the Divine wisdom of the Universe is known. In this place every thought you have and everything you do is aligned with the Divine One Mind.

It is almost as if you are standing in a beam of energy and light; energy that holds the Divine pattern and plan. As you are in this light, you are aligned with the Divine energy signature, pattern and plan of the Universe and of your life. Something about your energy is growing stronger, freer; some limitation is being released as you stand in this powerful energy.

As you look outward with your Divine vision, you might sense your Divine Support Team, your ancestors, guides beginning to appear around you. Each of them holds an essence of consciousness—of love, of beauty, of wisdom, and truth, of inspiration, illumination, guidance, and hope.

Each of these Divine beings, ancestors and guides are joining around you, holding this Divine wisdom and love for you, radiating that energy all around you. You are beginning to sense and feel yourself connected to your sovereign center, to your Divine oneness. You are in a comfortable and safe place. Notice how your ancestors and teachers are continuing to join you, more and more surrounding you with this epic power and love.

Notice your breathing, smooth and relaxed; something about your energy growing freer. You are opening up to the energy that is all around you, becoming more receptive to this energy of the Divine; more aware of all the guidance, connections, and assistance that is there for you, right now, in this moment.

Imagine that your ego has been like the petals of a flower and that you have been inside these petals and they have been folded up around your light—the innermost part of your being. As you stand in the center of All That Is with your Divine Support Team around you, something is beginning to open up so that your Divine center is starting to be revealed.

One quality of energy that is being offered to you right now is the quality that awakens and transforms your emotional body and frees you to move to a higher level of consciousness.

If you are open to transform your emotions, to move into a new consciousness, set this as your intention, and open to receive the energy that will assist you in doing this so that some veil can fall away; some of the petals can unfold, and you can transcend your ego through transforming your emotions. Let this happen now.

In the light and energy of Divine wisdom and Divine perfection, if you would like to evolve your intentions, to release anything that would veil or hide your true path from you, to open to the inspiration of the Divine within you, set this as your intention now.

With the power of Divine wisdom and all of the assistance and qualities of consciousness held by your Divine Support Team, ancestors and teachers, open now to let this transformation occur, right now.

You are shifting. It is occurring at a level beyond the mind, so it is okay if you do not feel anything. Simply setting your intention and being open is all that is needed for change to come about.

Sense an inner energy within you growing deeper, the petals of the ego beginning to unfold even more. Something about your path and purpose is becoming clearer, more recognizable, and brings to you the qualities that enable you to follow your dreams.

Standing in the center of All That Is, sense your Divine Support Team, teachers, ancestors and Divine beings who are holding for you this space of illuminating your mind.

It is part of the Divine plan of your life to have an expanded mind, to have thoughts that show you your path and lead you forward, that bring you the ideas to manifest that which is your purpose, thoughts that inspire you, that come from your Divine Guidance, that open the way and lead you forward on your spiritual path.

If you would like an inspired mind, to begin the process of deepening your mental illumination, set this as your intention right now. And sense your syncing up with all of your Divine Support Team, guides and teachers who have expanded and illumined minds. Open right now to letting this energy wash over you.

Sense your inner light growing as if there were a core or a pillar of light within you, or a sense of peace that is deepening, deepening your roots, giving you stability and strong foundation, that is growing stronger and more brilliant within you.

Imagine the petals of the ego beginning to fall down like a flower awakening, opening, blooming. Each petal folding down and over your shoulders, expanding your Divine essence which is beaming all around you in all directions. The petals of the mind, the emotions and the desires begin to unfold to reveal your innermost being—a being of great depth, power, grace strength, courage, love and wisdom.

All of the Divine Support Team, guides, teachers who are with you are assisting you in holding this space of revealing the deepest part of your being so that you may deepen your connection to this aspect of yourself and know it to be who you are.

This energy and light within your Inner Being, your true Self, is beginning to shine forth into every area of your life. And your ego, the petals, are folding down more and more. In some way your ego is becoming more transparent, so that more of your innermost beauty, the essence of your being, is shining forth. Enjoy right now, for a moment, the infinite beauty, light, and consciousness that is who you are deep within.

You are standing in the center of all that is your Divine sovereign center. Feel, imagine, see, notice your Divine purpose is unfolding within you, in every moment, in your desires, in the illumination and inspiration that unfolds through your thoughts.

You are beginning to rise up out of the ego into Divine consciousness. Attachments are falling away. You see the light above you—the greater light that draws you upward. The light of you, the Divine inner being, of the love, that is everywhere.

In the energy and light of All That Is, with the assistance of all the beings around you, something opens up. With your permission, a new quality of energy is offered to you; one that will move you and guide you to a more harmonious, more peaceful, more loving existence. This is the seed of love.

Take this seed into your heart, if you choose; for it carries the light just for you, to open you to the next steps on your spiritual path, to the next insights, growth, and forward movement.

It is a sacred seed of life that you are awakening. It is the energy that awakens the Divine within you and carries with it all the understanding, illumination, realization, and all that you will need to fulfill your being at this next level of light.

Now imagine as you stand in this light--brilliant, eternal, infinite energy that you are—wise, loving and compassionate, let an area of your life come to mind that you would like to lift to this new level.

As your Divine Self standing in this light of All That Is, in the energy of Divine wisdom with every quality of consciousness that you need being held by the guides and teachers around you, embrace this area of your life. Take it into this consciousness until it dissolves as a separate area. Do this now if you choose.

Keep holding this space until there is a feeling of release or ease, or something opens up and know that as this happens you have changed your reality in this area.

As you come back, remember who you are. Let a sense of that powerful, loving, wise being that you are come into your consciousness more and more often, and remember this is you; this is your true identity. All you need do is make the contact with the Divine and through this contact, all that you need and even more will come to you in every moment.

And so coming back now, feeling wonderful, full of light and wide awake. Feeling the ease of your body coming back into this time and space, integrating this powerful connection to Divine wisdom within you, that IS you.

Ho'oponopono

When To Use It

Use this process any time you feel activated, frustrated, angry or anxious. As part of diving into forgiveness we learn there are infinite levels to forgiveness. We begin to understand the more we forgive the more of our own personal power resurges. A deeper level of this work is when we truly understand that we create everything in our lives. Use this meditation when anything outside of you is triggering you and you want to heal that thing in you that is thereby creating it. This is a powerful process when done repeatedly as a mantra.

The original ho'oponopono process was created by a native Hawaiian kahuna (shaman or medicine woman) Morrnah Simeona (1913-1992) which included 14 steps to reconciliation. This ancient method she brought forward and modernized into Ho'oponopono was believed to restore those who had broken "kapu," ancient Hawaiian code of conduct. Fast forward to the 1980s and her student, Dr. Hew Len, a practicing psychologist working in the Hawaii State Hospital for the criminally insane, creates a mantra meditation that encompasses the teachings of both Morrah and the ancients. He begins to use this healing mantra, and there is a miraculous result: patients heal and nurses and care staff begin to interact and enjoy their work. All of this happened even though Dr. Len never personally met any of the patients. He healed them by healing himself.

The secret to this phenomenon is that nothing is happening "outside of us" or "out there." Everything happens to us in our mind. Everything we see and hear and every person we meet is experienced in our minds. We have only ever been taught to think of everything outside of us as separate from us—it absolves us of responsibility.

We start to understand that we are responsible for everything we think and everything that comes into our attention or focus. If we watch something on the news, we are responsible for it as it is within us. It is not separate from us. So if we are responsible for it, then we can shift it through forgiveness. Given the current state of COVID-19 it may be a good time to practice this method on the pandemic!

Meditation

The ho'oponopono prayer consists of four sentences repeated over and over again. Before beginning, conjure a vision of the person who has upset you, or is in need of healing. See them standing before you as you breathe deeply, close your eyes (if that's comfortable), and say:

"**I'm Sorry.**" This sentence is that of atonement, and it is simply that: I'm sorry for the part of my consciousness that is responsible for the creation of that "thing." That thing we may see is outside of ourselves, and when we realize it is not separate from us but a part of us and an extension of us, we can ask for repentance for the part of us that is creating it.

"**Please Forgive Me.**" This is a simple ask for forgiveness. We are asking for forgiveness.

"**Thank You.**" This simple thank you is exactly that. It is a statement of gratitude for what we have and for who we are.

"**I Love You.**" This simple statement is sweet and to the point, a statement of love for the Universe, for our lives, for our experience. It is simple. It is love. Continue to repeat these four statements like a mantra over and over until you feel an energy shift, perhaps you notice the visual of the person you are focusing on shifting or moving. The more we repeat these four statements, the more we acknowledge what is "out there" is being created by us. As we heal the vibration and our consciousness that is creating whatever we are seeing, that is how and when we start to see and experience miracles.

Inner Child

When To Use It

Use this meditation when you feel ready to heal that inner innocence, your Inner Child. We all have stories from our childhood where we have felt that our needs were not met. We may have felt abandoned, neglected, controlled or any number of stories that are drenched in pain. In order to heal these stories, when you are feeling triggered from something that feels like it relates back to emotions or patterns from childhood, it can be very helpful to connect with your inner child and begin the journey of healing them.

Inner child work is done with the help of a coach or therapist. The main function of this work is to heal and resolve childhood emotions and experiences that the younger version of ourselves are holding onto. As a result of inner child work, we can develop more joy, freedom, innocence, and confidence.

There are many meditations that help us understand the pain of our inner child, and it is something that, with consciousness and love, we can revisit and begin to heal and understand on a deep, cellular level.

Let's begin. If you'd like, you can read the following meditation, record yourself reading it, and listen to it later.

Meditation

Take yourself on a journey. Close your eyes and take deep belly breaths in and out. The long, low, slow flow of breath allows you to settle more into yourself. The deep breaths are your anchor and your home base as you move into deeper levels of yourself.

With your eyes closed and your breath moving, allow yourself to go on a journey. Imagine, sense, see, and feel yourself in a beautiful place in nature. Start to see this place with all of your senses. Notice the colors, smell the aromas, hear the sounds around you, feel the ground underneath your feet. Simply listen and be present. Notice the trees, plants, grass. Notice everything in nature that feels safe and comfortable, comfortable and safe.

Off in the distance, you see a small mountain that you begin to climb with ease. The path is smooth, and your feet easily glide along the path until you get to the top. At the top, there is a beautiful vista. The vista is incredible and captivating. Look at this scene and allow yourself to marvel at the beauty that nature is giving you right now.

Take those deep breaths in and out.

Looking beside you, you see a beautiful bench which calls you over. As you approach it, you see a child on the bench. Sitting on the bench you notice this child is you—the younger version of yourself.

Take a few deep breaths in and out. Get comfortable and sit in your space connecting with your inner child. Notice the age of your child, how old are they? What do you notice they are wearing?

Simply observe these features of your inner child with breath and presence. Continue those deep breaths in and out. As you settle in with your inner child, simply notice. There may be many emotions—yours and theirs. Notice these emotions. Be present to what is happening right now. Just observe it all like a witness. Observe the emotions and allow them to pass through you, stepping more into the role of witness with each breath in and out.

Breathe in. Breathe out. Breathe in. Breathe out.

As you have gotten comfortable with your inner child, you notice that they want to speak to you. They have something they want to say to you. Be present. Being willing to listen. Take those low slow flows of breath in and out. Notice what your inner child is saying. Simply listen and be present.

After your inner child has spoken, notice what they might need from you right now. Listen to what your inner child has to say to you—in words or in other ways. Simply notice what they may need. Perhaps your inner child simply wants to be loved, or hugged. Or maybe, your inner child wants you to laugh and play with them.

Be conscious of what your inner child wants and needs from you right now. Now, spend a few minutes telling your inner child that you are here for them. Allow your inner child to feel safe, to feel cared for, to feel seen. Continue to do this with deep breaths in and out. Allow your inner child to know that they are safe, that they are loved, and that they are seen.

Slow deep breaths in and out. Being conscious of your inner child (and knowing that they need you to protect them), they are safe and seen. Take those deep breaths in and out—low, slow flow.

After you have finished speaking and holding your inner child, you notice, perhaps, a different version of your inner child. They now have a present for you. They want to show you who you truly are, who they knew you were all along. Your inner child is you. They know how powerful you are. They know how courageous, confident, and capable you are.

Look into your child's eyes. These are your eyes. Simply look—eye to eye and see who you truly are. Can you see your power, your genius, and your beauty under all of that? Be present with that low, slow flow of breath.

Now that you've received this powerful message from your inner child, take a few minutes to be in silence with them. Spend some time on this bench simply being present and aware of how powerful this moment is. After a few minutes or longer, you will feel that this is complete.

Take a few minutes to thank your inner child. They will always be here and will always be holding space for you. This bench will always be here for you to revisit

As you begin to come back, take a moment to wiggle your fingers and toes. Bring your awareness back to the now and begin to stretch and re-awaken yourself to this moment. You are more recharged, refreshed, and reawakened.

Subpersonality

This is our own spin on a beautiful Orin &DaBen meditation.

When To Use It

This meditation can be done any time we are feeling incredibly triggered or activated. We all have parts of us that are frozen in time and want to heal. This process is excellent at helping us identify and heal the parts of our ego that are holding a story of fear. This meditation sends bring light and healing to the parts of us that are frozen in fear. For example, when our saboteur is activated and says "Who are you to do a professional intuitive reading?" This is an example where the saboteur is in full swing and can be shifted through energy and awareness.

The concept of subpersonalities is a psychological approach to understanding a principle that states that within each of us there are several parts and personalities trying to run the show. For example, at times, we may have our saboteur telling us that we don't matter to the world or that we will never make it, so why bother? This kind of thing is an example of a part of us (not all of us) that is trying to run the show.

A part of personal development and healing is understanding that these parts of us actually want to help us, and they are within us as a part of our journey. Many times, however, we can spend part of our lives "off course," listening to these inner voices that steer us in directions we may not want to go.

Subpersonality journeys are about acquainting ourselves with these parts of us, deeply understanding their role in our lives, and learning how we can be with them, without being ruled by them.

For this meditation, you can either read it or record yourself and listen back to it:

Meditation

Get quiet. Take a few deep breaths in and out. Go into that space of deep belly breathing—belly rises, belly falls.

Inhale. Exhale
Breathe in. Breathe out.

As your breath starts to center you and you feel your body relax, take yourself on a journey.

Use this journey when you are feeling emotions such as doubt or fear. This is a journey that can be used anytime when you notice yourself out of alignment and a voice is keeping you out of your center.

Subpersonality work is a powerful journey for change. As you become more intuitive, open up to more light, you want to bring all parts of your personality along with you. It is important to remember that all parts of your personality are trying to help. They are trying to help in the best way they know how to. What you will be doing is working with them. You will be giving them a new role. You will show them a new vision of who you are. As these parts of you have a new role, these parts can join us and help us toward our new goal.

As your breath deepens and your body gets quieter, take yourself into a beautiful space in nature. See yourself in this space. See you, you are the Wise Master, your Higher Self, your Divine Self. You are you—pure love and light. You are full of love and light and holding that space now.

As this higher being, your Higher Self, you are going to work with a part of your personality. You will be showing them your greater vision, so that you can bring them unconditional love.

Think now of an inner dialogue, a way of being, a feeling that you wish to transform. As you think of this feeling, think of this as a part of you—a subpersonality that is not all of you— but just a small part of you.

Invite this part of you to join you. You see it at a distance coming towards you. As you see it, start to notice things: How old is it? Is it male or female? What does it look like?

Welcome this part as they come toward you. Send love, unconditional love to this part of you. As you, the Higher Self, welcome this part of you and let love pour out of you.

Notice this part of you as it responds to the love that you are sending. Feel it, accept it, and soften into the love. Ask this part of you now if it would like to journey with you to the top of the mountain.

When this part of you agrees, take them by the hand and journey to the top of the mountain.

Now that you are at the top of the mountain, show them the Higher Vision of your life. Show them what you have as a vision for you.

As you sit and look at your subpersonality, create a conversation with it. Ask it, "How are you trying to help me with this belief?" Listen quietly. "What are you trying to accomplish or do with this thought?"

Ask this part of you if it would like to find an easier way, a better way to do this. Tell it that you appreciate it and you value it. Tell it that you appreciate it's help. Explore together how it can continue to help you in a more appropriate way.

You now sense that a Wise Master has joined you. The master is here to work with your subpersonality. As you acknowledge the Master, your subpersonality goes over to work with the Master. Feel your Wise Master's love for you and your subpersonality. Now, your subpersonality begins to have more light and evolve.

Take a few deep, slow, cleansing breaths as you watch the Master fill your subpersonality with light. Notice now how this part of you is holding more Divine energy and getting stronger.

After a few moments, the Master helps you to integrate this part of you into you. The Master helps you to reconnect with this part of you. You are now reconnected to this part of you.

Watch now as this part of you turns into a symbol. Take this symbol into your heart as you bid the Master goodbye.

Take a few deep breaths in and out.

Slowly, start to reawaken yourself. Bring yourself back into the room and back into your body, back into yourself.

This is a very deep, powerful journey that helps you connect with you and your subpersonalities. It is a deeply transformative process. You have definitely brought a change in your life, and you have transformed this part of your personality to a higher and greater level. Feel yourself become filled with light and the parts of you reintegrate into yourself right now.

As you start to take deep breaths in and out, you will start to come back into yourself and into your body. As you come out of this meditation, you will feel more recharged, energized, alive and filled with light.

Processes

Addictions

When To Use It

When something has our continued focus it can and it results in our lives being out of balance, this energy process can help. We have seen incredible success using this process when clients want to stop a habit or behavior they no longer wish to continue. It could be anything from releasing sugar, drinking, smoking, fried foods or a difficult relationship.

Process

1. Create sacred space. Take a moment and get quiet, take some deep breaths in and out. Close your eyes and center yourself in the present now.

2. Call in your Divine Support Team and ancestors, to be here with you to support you in this process.

3. Use your own words, speak from your heart, ask to be shown this "thing" that you are attached to or have a disempowering habit with. Make sure to continue to breathe deeply.

4. Imagine that object you are attached to (sugar, liquor, caffeine, fried chicken) floating out in front of you, as if you were watching a 3D movie, or virtual reality.

5. Notice wrapped all around this object are these etheric cords (that look like surgical tubing) of attachment, you see that they are all plugged into your solar plexus chakra, your power center. See all these cords coming from your stomach and wrapping around this object that is floating in front of you.

6. Now your Divine Support Team and ancestors ask you, "Are you truly willing to release your attachment to this object/habit/experience/in exchange for peace?"

7. When you say YES, notice how your entire Divine Support Team and entire ancestral lineage come forward and with their energetic swords and in 1 swoop they dissolve the cords. They are not severed they are instantly dissolved and removed completely from your solar plexus and energy system.

8. See this object you once believed you had to have floating up, see it floating away from you, getting smaller as it floats completely out of your vision, dissipating into vapor.

9. As you continue to say yes to releasing this attachment your entire Divine Support Team and ancestors surround you sending energy and love to your solar plexus chakra, which is receiving this energy now. Notice how it is beginning to shine bold and bright—see that bright yellow orb spinning free and clear.

10. As you sit quietly feel free to ask your Divine Support Team and ancestors for any guidance and/or support to continue this healthier way of living.

11. Stay quiet, listen and receive your Divine Guidance.

12. Thank your Divine Support Team and ancestors for this energy and incredible support.

Belief Systems

When To Use It

Do this process when you are living a part of your life that is not how you want it to be. You will unravel the thoughts and beliefs that are creating it and then create affirmations to redirect them to create something new.

Our beliefs are often formed passively. By the time we are adults, we may be surprised how many beliefs we carry. Only upon reflection do we realize that many of our belief systems are "inherited" by parents, teachers, friends, society and culture. Why is it important to unravel our belief systems? Because what we believe, we live into, we create. Our beliefs are an energy that literally build our energy field and they create our reality.

Thoughts ➻ Belief Systems ➻ Reality

How do we know what our belief systems are? Look at our reality.

Process

1. Take a few minutes and look at an area of your life to see what your reality is. (ex. Shortage of money in your bank account)

2. Write down the beliefs and thoughts you think consciously and unconsciously may be creating your current reality. (ex. Money is hard to come by. Money is evil. I have to work hard for money)

3. Based on your writing, start to create new statements or affirmations that are believable to you. (ex. There are some kind people who have money. Money is just energy. I am open to receiving the energy of money.)

4. Affirmations are best repeated and are effective when we are feeling aligned with our Divine Truth. Affirmations done from a place of not feeling good can be counterproductive for our growth. So remember only use affirmations that you can believe are possible.

Card Play

When To Use It

This is a fun way to strengthen your Divine Guidance. It uses all the channels, so tap in and have fun! When you want to practice with all of your clairs.

Process

1. Take out a deck of playing cards and shuffle them.

2. Place the deck in front of you take the top card and place it face down in front of you.

3. Put your dominant hand over the card and imagine you can "**SEE, FEEL, SENSE, or KNOW**" what the card is.

4. Once you choose, turn it over and see if you're correct. Sort your hits and misses.

5. Once you've mastered Level 1, go to Level 2 and so on.
   Level 1: is the card Red or Black?

   Level 2: Is the card a Spade, Club, Diamond or Heart?

   Level 3: What is the number on the card?

   Level 4: What card is it? Include suit and number. ex: Ace of Diamonds, etc.

6. Lay out all the cards face down—use your clairvoyance to pick matches.
   Level 1: Pick the same color

   Level 2: Pick the same suit

Level 3: Pick the same number

❋ This exercise can also be used to build all of the clairs. Simply by keeping your focus on which clair you are deliberately directing, the options are infinite!

Chakra Clearing Exercises

When To Use It

Try it every day for two weeks and take note of the changes or shifts you experience in your energy. The great thing about these are you can use them on the go or some deep diving.

Rainbow Waterfall. Imagine there is a rainbow waterfall coming down into the top of your head, crown center. As the rainbow energy enters the top of your head, watch it move through each energy center, clearing and cleaning out old debris. It moves its way from your crown through all the way down to the root chakra and out through your feet into Mother Earth.

Color Therapy. There are multiple light therapies out there these days, backed by science helping with depression and even wrinkles! On days when you want to feel stronger in one area such as power, ie: solar plexus, try wearing something yellow, even if it's socks or underwear. It will make a shift in your energy.

With Breath. Take a deep cleansing breath all the way down to your toes, and release. On the next inhale imagine, visualize, and allow the energy of your breath to move through each chakra center. As it does, see your breath blowing away any remnants of imbalance, like sand being blown away on your exhale.

Pendulum. Use a pendulum to "see" the size and direction of each of your chakras. Scan each chakra with your pendulum, asking "please show me the size and direction of this chakra," and then follow with a chakra clearing visualization. Check each chakra again to see results.

Despite the 4th, 6th, 7th, and ear chakras being the main energy centers for intuition, it is a balance of all the chakras that helps sustain the energy and life of an intuitive.

Contrast vs. Clarity

When To Use It

Use this process when you are curious about what you want out of life. If you are getting a lot of what you do not want or if you're simply desiring clarity, this process is powerful for you to see what you do want.

Most of us are used to looking at things that are not going well. What we forget and don't often realize is that when we have things that are not going well; this is simply contrast. Contrast can be simply defined as that which we do not want.

Whenever there is contrast there is also clarity launched forward. What we focus on expands. The knee jerk reaction is to look at what is going wrong, talk about it and blow it up. Unfortunately, this just brings more of it into our experience. How can we see it differently?

We want to train ourselves to see that contrast as a good thing, a sign that things are moving. Contrast never stops—and because of contrast, we have access to clarity. Whenever we experience contrast, we literally send a 'vibrational rocket' forward towards clarity. For example, when you have less money in your bank account, you send a thought, a rocket, an idea forward asking for more money.

At every moment, it is our choice as to whether we look at the contrast or clarity. It is habit and taught to us to stare at the contrast. And as we know, what we focus on we actually make bigger. Our world trains us to habitually look at the contrast. With a little bit of focus and practice, we can focus towards clarity and experience it. As we feel the clarity, it is confirmation, we can feel what we have actually created with those vibrational rockets that we shot out. When we feel clarity—the Universe creates it immediately.

Our emotions are our guide to whether we are going moving towards clarity or contrast.

Follow the emotions — the what we want and the why we want it — then we will FEEL our way there. This is very different than trying to figure out how to get there. This concept will completely change our life, a profound truth. With practice and patience, we will remember that contrast actually launches rockets of clarity forward and we respond without reaction or haste.

If we look at the past we realize that the contrast as a child launched huge rockets forward. For example, the contrast of family who didn't believe in us as children creates clarity of us as an empowered adult. Most people look at the contrast, and make it their mission statement to either live in resistance to it or become it.

Use this contrast-clarity process below whenever you feel contrast and are stuck.

Process

1. Write down what you do not want (contrast).

2. Why do you not want this? What do you feel?

3. Write down what you do want (clarity). Perhaps it is the opposite of what you are currently experiencing.

4. If you had the clarity what would it feel like?

Contrast

"I don't want this." (Ex. House with small kitchen)

Clarity

"I do want this." (Ex. House with big kitchen)

Crystal Magic

When To Use It

To amplify your intuitive channels as well as soothe your energy when things feel wobbly or just want some extra umpf.

These energy prescriptions with crystals are really fun and incredibly effective. If you aren't sure where you land on the crystal conversation, that's ok. Just play with it, experiment, and see what you notice. Notice what you feel, maybe it'll be nothing, but it could be something. Every crystal has a different energy signature, just like us! And their vibrations and frequencies are measured through their wavelengths in KHz. Imagine as you align a crystal's frequency with yours, the sky's the limit!

Wearing crystals is a great way to receive this powerful energy. You can wear them close to your body (in your bra) or as a piece of jewelry. This can be a fashion statement of course, or it can be very covert, by placing a crystal in your pocket.

You can even meditate with crystals. It can be as simple as holding the crystals while meditating or placing your crystals on the chakra for the particular clair you are wanting to amplify.

Take them to bed with you by placing crystal on your nightstand or even under your pillow so you can bask in its energy while you are in dreamland. There are many direct and indirect ways of using crystals.

Crystals To Amplify Clairvoyance

- Sugilite
- Amethyst
- Moonstone
- Tigers Eye
- Fluorite

- Aquamarine
- Labradorite
- Herkimer
- Diamond

Crystals To Amplify Clairaudience

- Selenite
- Phantom Quartz
- Blue Kyanite
- Blue Apatite
- Turquoise (natural)
- Selenite
- Sapphire Moldavite
- Fulgurite

Crystals To Amplify Claircognizance

- Citrine
- Labradorite
- Green Prehnite
- Shattuckite
- Amethyst

Crystals To Amplify Clairsentience

- Rose Quartz
- Pink Tourmaline
- Dendritic Opal
- Blue Tourmaline
- Blue Qpatite
- Celestite Elestial Crystals

For a complete listing of crystals that create the clair amplification properties: *Love is in the Earth* and the *Crystal and Mineral Encyclopedia* by Melody, a crystal specialist extraordinaire,

Creating a Crystal Grid

A crystal grid is when you arrange a specific group of crystals in a deliberate pattern with the intention to create a specific outcome. Because each crystal has its own vibrational frequencies when you combine multiple crystals and place them in a group formation it literally harnesses the energy and power of each of them. It is such a fun and creative way to build your energy channels of Divine Guidance.

The most important thing in creating a crystal grid is following your intuition. As you're making your crystal grid, be sure to follow your guidance when it comes to choosing your stones, placement, layout, and location. This is one of the most personal things you can create as an energy amplifier.

Preparation

- Write your intention on a piece of paper

Process

1. **Determine Your Layout.** Using the intention of increasing your intuition, start to envision your crystal grid. Some people use sacred geometry and very intricate designs, still I have found what makes the biggest punch is simple elegance. Like that little black dress that can be worn anywhere, powerful.

   Trust whatever shape or design that comes forward. What kind of layout do you sense? Is it a circle? A square? Or a spiral? Or maybe it's a star shape!

   Allow your mind to wander. Breathe deeply and go with what feels right to you and your intention.

2. **Find Your Crystals.** Once you've received guidance on your energetic design, you'll want to choose what crystals you feel guided to use. This

is a fun and creative play part! You can purchase pre-designed grids, online and in crystal stores, but honestly, I feel the power of your intention is more deeply infused when you create it from your own Divine Guidance—using the crystals that are most aligned with you and your Divine intention.

Depending on which clair you are building—use the crystals listed under each clair or intuitively choose the ones you feel most aligned to use. *As a side note*: I always like to include at least one clear quartz in my grid somewhere, to amp up the clarity.

Because creating this grid is completely intuitive, you may receive the guidance to add bits of nature, flowers, leaves, or maybe even a rune or two to your design. Trust your creative and Divine Guidance you cannot do it wrong as the designer of this energetic prayer.

3. **Choose Your Location.** Now that you have your layout and crystals, it's time to think about where you want your crystal grid to live. Whether it be on the ground, on a shelf or an altar.

   Tune in to see where it will best serve you. I also like to tap into Feng Shui to see what area would better amplify my purpose. So, if I am wanting to build my clairvoyance and working with clients, I would build a grid in the quadrant of my bagua that represents being of service, or helpful people.

   Another great place for a grid is under your bed because you will receive this powerful energy while you sleep. The other up side of this is if you're in the intuitive closet so to speak—your grid is outta' sight.

4. **Clear.** Before you start putting your crystal grid together, clear the energy of the area you will be placing your grid as well as any of the items (crystals, runes, feathers, shells) you will be using in your grid.

You can do this with sage, lavender or rose essential oils. While you are clearing your grid components, call on your Divine Support Team and ask that they support you in clearing the area as well as infusing the crystals and area with your Divine intention (amping up your clair). This makes sure the location of your grid as well as your power source (crystals) are ready to roll with your intention and focus.

5. **Start Building.** Use your freshly charged crystals to start laying out your crystal grid. As you create it, be sure to keep your intention in the forefront of your focus and energy. Remember this is you creating the sacred space and awareness of amplifying your Divine Guidance.

   Lay all of your stones out and select the crystals that will be on the exterior.

   Working from the outside in, begin to develop your crystal grid for your intuitive development.

   As you get close to completing it, you want to start with the center stone. (Consider this is at the **heart of the matter**, it represents the apex point of all the crystals together, like the building of a mountain, this center stone is the epicenter.) You can choose it based on its unique energetic properties or simply use your intuition. The message here is to TRUST!

6. **The Final Touches.** Take several deep breaths, as you exhale see your energy infusing the paper with your intention, focus and desire. Then put it in the center of your grid and place the center heart stone on top of it.

   If you'd like, you can use crystal generators and natural points to activate the group energy of the grid. To do this, point crystal in the outer point of your grid and trace the pathway to the center point. See the energy of each crystal begin to connect, circulate, energize and synchronize with the others. Imagine this powerful energy is circulating around your entire crystal grid.

How long should I leave my crystal grid in place?

This is all intuitive. If you feel your grid's power has diminished, you may want to tune in and ask if the grid's purpose is complete, as everything that has bloomed, it must disassemble so that something new may come through. As long as you feel the grid is supporting your focus and intention—it's a safe bet to let it be.

Crystal Elixir

When To Use It

Anytime you want to consume crystaline energy via drink.

There are two primary methods to make crystal elixirs: One is the Direct Method in which the stone is immersed "directly" in the water; and the other is the Indirect Method, in which the gemstone is "separated" from the water by a barrier. After doing this, you'll consume the elixir.

Crystal elixirs are a simple form of energy healing, based on the theory that the water blends with the crystal's vibrational frequency and resonance, tuning the liquid to the crystal's healing properties.

You can use elixirs to support you in challenging times, such as we are experiencing now with COVID-19, because there's so much confusion, chaos, and concern. This is a perfect time to use elixirs and tinctures to support our bodies and minds so we continue to feel and allow energetic shifts.

Note: Some crystals can be toxic. Consume with caution. Only use the Direct Method with crystals you are positive are safe. Here is an extensive reference of crystal toxicity online (https://www.gemsociety.org/article/gemstone-toxicity-table/)

Direct Method

1. After assuring your crystal of choice is not toxic, safe to submerge.

2. Clear and cleanse the crystal.

3. Charge your crystal with your intuition by holding it in both hands, placing on your heart and infusing your intention.

4. When charging is completed, place your crystal in a clear glass bowl or bottle and pour in clean spring or purified water.

5. Place your crystal in a clear glass bowl or bottle and pour in clean spring, or purified.

6. Cover the bowl and allow it to rest for 4-24 hours.

7. Then place it where it can absorb the sun and the moon's energies.

Indirect Method

1. Clear and cleanse your crystals, charge them with your intention (as mentioned above).

2. Place your cleared crystals into a clear glass bowl or bottle. Then place this bowl into a larger bowl.

3. Carefully pour the water into the larger bowl, without getting any into the bowl containing the crystals.

4. Cover both bowls and allow to rest for 4-24 hours.

5. Place your charging bowls in a place where they can absorb the sun's and moon's energies.

6. You now have your Divine crystal elixir ready to use. Store it in a dark glass airtight bottle.

☼ This elixir is good for one week. If you want your tincture to last longer than a week you can add an equal amount of vodka to your elixir tonic, creating a 50/50 mixture.

Driving The Boat Exercise

When To Use It

Use this process in conjunction with the process of Meeting Your Subpersonalities to understand your subconscious patterns. These are the patterns or the voices from your saboteur and subconscious that are running your life.

This work is truly about you getting better acquainted with yourself. When we understand all of our aspects, whether it is ego, saboteur, or just outright shadow we can begin to heal the things that have stopped us from having the life of our dreams.

As your "boat" moves through life –we can direct it consciously, where we want it to go. Or we can remain in our unconscious pattern letting the boat go wherever it wants, into fog, rain, places we don't desire going.

If our saboteur is driving our boat, then we will struggle to see our wins and continuously doubt our abilities and talents.

Getting to know your inner personalities is pivotal to your journey of success. Author, Carolyn Myss, says we all have 4 archetypal patterns, the Inner Child, the Saboteur, the Victim, and the Prostitute. Unpacking these can help you notice other limiting belief patterns. It is not necessary to name the archetype. Usually it is a very strong energy that takes over and runs the show.

Because we have many archetypal patterns the easiest way to begin is to identify the ones that are showing up.

these four, we have many more. For example, a common one can be the "damsel in distress" or the "knight in shining armor."

Process

1. Read the descriptions of the archetypes below.

2. As you read each one, take a breath in and notice if there is anything within you that perks up with a sense of recognition.

3. As you identify which archetype is emerging, ask

4. "What are you showing me about myself?"

5. "How is this aspect of me helping my situation right now?

6. "What wisdom is this blind spot teaching me?

7. Journal any guidance that comes through so you may witness first-hand the protection this archetype is trying to provide.

8. Have a conversation with this part of you. Let this aspect know you are moving forward with the desire to allow this part of you to evolve so it may grow with you.

   Ask this archetype is there anything it needs to move forward.

   Ask, "What is your symbol or language so that you will recognize it when it peaks into your consciousness.

9. Create an agreement between yourself and this archetype, to be in communication and understanding with each other.

Archetypal Descriptions

Inner child archetype is the part of us formed in our earliest years with our family of origin. Its main issues are responsibility and dependency. This archetype may show up through the feelings of abandonment. They may be dependent on relationships while fearing abandonment. We all have our own inner child that is usually hurt and in need of attention with the desire to heal.

Saboteur archetype are based in low self-esteem which causes us to make choices that block our own success. The core issue for the saboteur is the fear of inviting change into our life

Prostitute archetype shows up to sell our morals, integrity, body, word, and our soul for physical security. This pushes us to find our own inner strength and faith within ourselves.

Victim archetype lacks inner courage and inner strength. When we are in a situation and feel threatened either emotionally, mentally or physically, the victim comes forward. This gives us an opportunity to stand up to our fears and build our own sense of self-empowerment.

☼ Also try the meditation, Subpersonality (p. 317) in addition to this process, they are powerful together at helping us become acquainted with all the parts and pieces that make us who we are.

Energetic Attacks

When To Use It

An energetic attack is when your auric field gets bombarded by undesirable energies projected onto you by someone else. Energetic attacks are not always intentional. Sometimes, the person who is shooting energy at you is not aware that their thoughts and/or feelings are actually going to impact you. You may not realize that you've energetically attacked others, have you ever flipped off someone who cut you off in traffic? Yelled at someone standing too close to you in the grocery store? (6' or more mister). That middle finger being waved around is a sign of battle, agitation and anger. Any time we entertain jealous or angered thoughts towards another it is a type of energetic attack.

Symptoms/signs of an energetic attack can include: nightmares, irrational mood, feeling a dark cloud around you, a heaviness in your heart, not feeling like yourself, intense fatigue, a feeling of being watched and/or experiencing mishaps, hardships or setbacks. The ways to deal with these energetic exchanges is first not going into fear or blame. If we think we are cursed and/or we are blaming another person, we are perpetuating the energy of the skirmish on ourselves!

Simple Steps To Clear An Energetic Ambush

- **Recognize The Shadow.** Our shadow self is the side of our self we keep in the dark. It isn't bad, it is the part of us we don't want to see or acknowledge about ourselves. An energetic shot can enter into our energy field through that unconscious part of us. All of our fears, shames, limiting beliefs, judgements, hatreds are parts of our shadow unconsciousness.

- **Acknowledge With Love.** This shadow aspect is part of our whole being, and it is important to acknowledge it. When an energetic drive-by slams you, it is because that shadow side has a blind spot that is ready to be seen and healed.

- **Be Open To Witnessing The Blind Spot.** When we don't resist seeing blind spots we are able to expand our personal energy and power. It is important to explore the aspect of this unseen area that reared its head to allow healing of this deeper part of you.

- **Claim Your Power.** When we can consciously acknowledge the blind spot it can no longer be hidden. Once something has been seen, it can no longer be unseen. This once hidden aspect will never be that again because of your conscious awareness brings in your Divine connection. In this connection you find yourself perfect, complete and whole.

Process

1. Create sacred space.

2. Call in your Divine Support Team and ancestors to support you during this process with the intention to acknowledge any blind spots.

3. See a massive spotlight being pointed and centered entirely on you. Notice as you stand in this spotlight your entire Divine Support Team and ancestors are surrounding you. As you stand in this spotlight they begin to scan your auric field, your personal energy field for any energetic blind spots.

4. Standing here the complete focus of your Divine Support Team and ancestors notice how each disruption, obstacle or distraction, begin to rise up and out of your energy field like dust particles in a bright light they disappear. Your Divine Support Team and ancestors are removing the energy lodged in your system.

5. Breathe deeply as your Divine Support Team and ancestors continue.

6. Notice as these disturbances release any messages or information that may come through.

7. Allow this process to continue until you feel, see, hear, or know it is complete.

8. As the energy is winding down, thank your Divine Support Team and ancestors for this incredible healing and restoration.

Energy Vacuuming

When To Use It

Energy vacuuming is a powerful technique to use on yourself when there's an accumulation of heavy energy and/or difficult situations. This energy vacuuming can be used regularly to release the heavy energy, allowing love to replace it. It can be used to release negative energies and/or attachments. It can also be used to clear and repair damaged energy systems. You can use it before and/or after a session to prepare the room and clear your own energy field. The technique is written as if you were directing it to a client, but it can also be done personally.

Process

1. Close your eyes, breathe and center your attention in love. Create sacred space. Bring in your Divine Support Team, ancestors and your client's as well.

2. Imagine a column of light that is parallel to your client's spinal cord. See the light and allow in the Divine energy and your Divine Support Team and ancestors to come into the session.

3. Open the column of light allowing your Divine Support Team and ancestors to assist in the vacuuming and deep cleansing needed in your client's energy field. Imagine seeing the vacuum being inserted into your client's crown chakra, vacuuming up all the debris the client is willing to release.

4. The vacuum's suction can move from the crown of the head to various parts of the body to further assist in the releasing of dense energy that is ready to be released and allowing any energy blockages or disturbances to be dissolved.

5. See all of the debris released into the vacuum and being transmuted by both Divine Support Teams. If you feel or sense a tug of resistance intuitively ask your client if they are willing to exchange this pain for peace. This will ease your client's attachment to the old dense energy. You can also adjust the vacuum speed and clearing depth. Use your Divine Guidance and adjust as appropriate to support your client's ease and comfort.

6. You will have a sense, feeling or knowing when the process is complete. Then imagine.

7. Your Divine Support Teams are flipping the switch and reversing the direction of the vacuum. Instead of it pulling it is now distributing this beautiful green iridescent light, that is the texture of a gel, minty fresh clearing gel. See this gel going in through your client's crown chakra and it is moving to all the places and areas that released old energies. This soothing green gel energy, infuses love, and the highest energy to re-enter the body. This further synchronizes the energy of the body's natural well-being and helps to rebalance on a deeper level.

8. Continue to take deep breaths, as this process is happening. Allowing this powerful integration of healing energy. When you feel the energy pull back or you hear a click, you know the session is complete.

9. Thank your and your client's Divine Support Teams and ancestors for their assistance in this exercise.

10. In conclusion, advise your client to drink water and get fresh air to assist in releasing further on a cellular level.

Grounding

When To Use It

Grounding is an essential exercise to help you feel rooted and connected. It involves doing things that ground or electrically reconnect us to the earth. Earth science and grounding physics explain how electrical charges from the earth have had a positive effect on our bodies over time. Certain exercises transfer the earth's electrons from the ground into our bodies. Researchers have found there is an electrical conductivity within the earth that functions as an immune system defense, much like antioxidants. While there isn't a great deal of studies done on this, it sure sounds cool, doesn't it? There have been some studies that suggest grounding influences our healing. Grounding is a series of therapeutic techniques that reconnect us to the earth. When our energy is a little haywire or off, it is important to ground into the earth, reconnecting to our oneness and purpose.

Process

1. **Create Sacred Space.** What is sacred space? Sacred space is a place where you can leave the chaos of the rest of the world behind and go inward with reverence and respect. This doesn't have to be the same kind of "place" as a physical location. Sacred space is created from within and the more you return to it, your energy builds. If you are doing a personal reading, it does enhance your abilities in the beginning to use the same physical location as your sacred space. You may not know this, but locations hold energy. That is why people make pilgrimages all over the world to locations of spiritual significance. These locations hold energy of past experiences. As a professional intuitive, remember to be present to regularly clearing clutter and bottled emotions out of your sacred space.

2. **Ground Yourself.** Make sure you are completely clear and present.
   - **Sit (or stand) in a quiet place.** You can do this outside in nature, anywhere you would like.

- **Visualize.** Imagine roots streaming from the bottoms of your feet, continuing to grow downward, connecting the soles of your feet deep into the core of the earth. Breathe in through your mouth and out through your nose. Visualize all the toxins, anxiety, and stress flowing through these roots and dissolving into Mother Earth. Visualize green healing energy coming back up these roots through the soles of your feet, running up your legs to your heart, moving up into your chest, down each arm, then up through your throat, head, and through your crown chakra, filling you with healing, grounding energy.

- **Be Present With Yourself.** Feel the sensations in your body. Breathe deeply to become present with yourself and your surroundings. Checking in with your breath is an effective way to make sure you remain grounded. Connecting to your body through breath enables you to ground yourself and be present to any Divine Guidance, signs or symbols that may come through.

Environmental Grounding

When To Use It

Use this process if you feel anxious, stressed or experiencing social anxiety.

Often people who are anxious tend to pick up a lot of energy from their surroundings. Anxiety in social situations can come from subconsciously picking up on the energy around you without being aware of it. And the anxiety isn't just limited to social situations because energy is all around us; it's easy to pick up. Often when this happens, people can have difficulty grounding themselves and become reactive to what is happening around them, rather than deliberately directing their own momentum.

This Cognitive Behavioral Technique is excellent to help us ground in any situation. This technique grounds as and allows us to feel connection, love and support with tremendous ease and especially when faced with new situations or environments.

Process

1. When walking into a new room—find something in the room that feels good; a picture on the wall, a flower arrangement or a tree outside.

2. Spend a few minutes gazing at this item, being present.

3. Ask your mind and emotions to find a few things about this item that feels good and that you appreciate. It may be colors, what it represents or even the sound.

4. Feel yourself ground as you gaze at this item and breathe.

5. Return your awareness to the environment, people and atmosphere.

6. If you feel at all, worried or anxious — return to the item and continue to ground, center and acquaint yourself with the good feeling place you created at the beginning.

A Grounding Quickie

Another way to feel grounded quickly in your surroundings. Play this little game with yourself.

Name…

…5 things you can see.

…4 things you can hear.

…3 things you can feel.

…2 things you can smell.

…1 thing you can taste.

Etheric Cord Dissolution

When To Use It

It is important after offering an intuitive session to dissolve all cords of attachment between you and your client (or the person you are reading). We can develop attachments with the people in our life, so it's helpful to use this process regularly.

Etheric cords are energy cords that are connected to your energy body as well as your physical body. They extend out of you and connect to other people, places, animals, and even objects in your life. They can affect your energy and physical body which is why you want to clear them frequently.

Process

1. Take a moment, get quiet, and take several breaths in and out. Close your eyes and center yourself in the present moment.

2. Call in your Divine Support Team and ancestors to support you in dissolving any and all etheric cords.

3. You can say, "I call upon you to ask for your support and assistance in dissolving and removing any cords I may have. I ask that any energy of fear be released." As you set the intention to unplug from your client's energy, imagine your hand going to your solar plexus area and imagine you are taking the cords and unplugging them from yourself and then are plugging them into the sky, into the Divine, Universal wisdom. Your client is now plugged into their Divine connection.

4. Feel free to change the words, simplify or expand this process as you feel fits you best. The primary focus is for the intention to be clear with love.

5. As you sit in this energy, visualize the Divine connection between you and your client, thanking your Divine Support Team and ancestors.

Grounding Cord Exercise

When To Use It

To ground your energy before or after an intuitive session or any time you feel sacred, flighty, confused or frustrated.

Energy Process

See a beautiful golden sun over your crown chakra shining this golden iridescent energy into your crown chakra.

See this golden energy moving through each and every chakra, third eye, ear, throat, heart, solar plexus, sacral, and root.

When this powerful energy gets to your root chakra, allow it to move through the base of your spine. As it does, notice you have this gorgeous grounding cord that plugs you deep into the core of Mother Earth.

Imagine, notice this cord. How wide is it?

Make it a little wider than your hips and see that it's plugged deep into the core of Mother Earth, to the magma into the Divine sovereign center of our world.

See yourself deeply rooted into the core of the earth.

Notice how this beautiful golden energy has moved down, through your grounding cord. It is now activating and inviting this Mother Earth energy to stir and move up your grounding cord toward your root chakra.

Breathe deeply as you open to receive this green Mother Earth energy as it moves up your chakra system all the way to and through your crown chakra.

As it moves out of your crown, notice it is circling that golden sun above your crown chakra, amplifying it.

As these two energies work independently together, feel your body amplified with this deep connection to the core.

Meeting Your Subpersonalities

When To Use It

Use this process when you meet up with a part of yourself that you want to heal. It is typically a pattern within yourself that you may not like and is not necessarily serving you. This process is meant to be used in conjunction with the process called "Who's Driving Your Boat?"

It can take time, awareness and practice to explore life to truly become acquainted with these sides of ourselves. The reason we want get comfortable with them is to heal your relationship with them so that we can truly live life consciously. These energies are from the Divine for the Divine.

Process

1. **Observe.** Taking the observer's mind is key—as for most of our lives are intertwined with these energies. The more we can observe with love, the greater perspective we have. We observe without judgement and with unconditional acceptance of these parts of ourselves. As we learn to observe then we can create a relationship with these parts of our personalities.

2. **Journal.** Start a journal from that "personalities" viewpoint. Writing down—how they truly feel. In this part—you may be able to isolate an age at which this personality was formed. How did they feel? What was going on for them?

3. **Reflect.** Can you see that the formation of these energies was from the energy of love? Ultimately, they are all trying to help us—but we can only see that and be with that as we can create a new relationship with them.

4. **Allow.** This is where the healing begins. As you connect with your subpersonality, consider taking it further with the Subpersonality Meditation on p. 317.

Mirror, Mirror

When To Use It

Use this process when you want to increase your self-esteem or just want to feel good.

Mirror work is an excellent process to increase self-esteem. It helps you to hear the thoughts you say to yourself. Most people have little awareness of the mind's chatter. We are busy distracting ourselves from the thoughts and when we hear them, we don't like what we hear!

Most of us have self-loathing and self-defeating thoughts. We don't believe that we are capable of anything and we may put ourselves down. This just holds us in a pattern of resistance and does not serve us at all. Self-judgement, self-criticism is an energy that is dominant in many illnesses including cancer, auto-immune conditions, allergies & more.

Most people look in the mirror but never actually look into their eyes. The eyes are said to be the seed of the soul. When people look in a mirror, it is often a quick check of the hair, the outfit, the makeup and so on. In fact, within these quick checks, there is often some criticism, judgement and self-admonishing mixed in. Little attention is placed on how we truly feel about ourselves or any soul reflection.

What You'll Need

- A hand-held mirror (not your phone with camera mode)

Process

1. Hold your hand-held mirror in front of your face. Look at yourself for about three minutes.

2. Just notice what happens. Begin to speak out loud all of the thoughts you are thinking about yourself. (ex: your nose is too big, that is a lot

of grey hair etc). Be honest with yourself and give voice to the thoughts that are circulating in your mind that you may not speak.

3. After three minutes, close your eyes and take a few minutes of deep, slow belly breaths. Get calm, centered, grounded and conscious in your body.

4. Open your eyes and look again in the mirror directly into your own eyes. Speak out loud speaking from your Divine. What does the Divine want to say out loud to you? Speak these words. You may notice this voice is quieter, less words and possibly even tears nay show up. Allow and be open to anything that arises.

5. After a few minutes of hearing your Spirit voice speak to you, close your eyes and be still.

6. Repeat this exercise as often as you like to access your intuitive voice with ease and increase your self-esteem.

Milking the Moment

When To Use It

Use this process when you want to increase your mental focus and ability to be present in the now.

Children, between the ages of 2 and 5 show us this process with ease. Have you ever watched a 2-year-old with a new pair of rain boots in a rainstorm? All they do is stand in the water with their boots excited about the puddles and the boots. As the human mind starts to develop past, present, future and planning—we lose the focus of being present in the now. As adults, we find that we are often thinking about the next moment. Even on vacation, everything is planned. Many have lost the art of "milking the moment."

Process

1. Hold a hot cup of tea, coffee, or hot chocolate.

2. Place it between the palms of your hands.

3. Feel the warmth from the cup permeate your hands.

4. Imagine your cells receiving the energy of the cup. The cup and the drink have a vibration that is entering your hands now.

5. Smell the drink. Feel the warmth of this moment.

6. Close your eyes and savor this moment. Remember this now. It is like a polaroid shot in your mind of this moment.

With regular practice, this training of the mind to be in the moment can be taken into our other activities—driving, working, being with our children etc. Practice, practice, practice!

Morning Vibration Exercise

When To Use It

Use this process when you want to wake up and start your day off on a higher note. This is a great daily practice to take on when you want to build consistent momentum.

This is an easy and excellent process to train the body-mind to feel better. The technique is simple and based on the fact that we break our momentum when we sleep, meditate, exercise, stroll in nature etc. First thing in the morning is the best time to start your vibrational set point. After you wake up—be mindful to stay in today—as the mind wants to grab yesterday or the closest contrast.

Process

1. After rising, take paper and pen, sit in meditation for 15 minutes.

2. As you come out of meditation, pick up the pen.

3. Write down any emotions you are feeling (peace, ease, well-being, calm, connected).

4. Next, write down the thought that is creating that emotion.

5. Place your pen down and read what you have written.

6. Close your eyes and sense your feeling place.

7. Write this down—it may be the same as the first—regardless write it down.

Momentum Awareness

When To Use It

Use this process when you are learning to build new ways of feeling. After you notice you have the habit of waking up anxious, this is an excellent process to teach you to build new ways of feeling in the morning and throughout the day.

1. Practice observation of momentum and direction of your thoughts first thing in the morning.

   Notice how long did the upwards momentum last?

   If it went downhill, what technique did you use to break the momentum? (ex. dancing, singing, meditation, laughing, exercise etc)

   What was it like to start bringing, that momentum back up?

   What did you notice—was it hard or easy?

   Did it get easier the more you practiced?

   If you felt stuck, what hooked you?

On The Road Again

When To Use It

When you are in your vehicle and want to play with your intuition.

Think you can't play with your intuition when you're driving? We're not suggesting you close your eyes and tune in while sitting at a red light, that could cause some traffic jams. Because our intuition is always with us, we are able to receive the Universe's messages—even when we are driving. It's especially helpful when there's traffic. I used this game ALL the time when I first started working with my intuition and it was a **game changer** for me!!

There are some rules, first, eyes on the road, present to what's going on around you—at all times. This exercise can be done in your car—with claircognizance because you are receiving blocks of thoughts such as instant responses like yes no, etc. Again, with all of these exercises, playful detachment will bring you many surprises and delights.

Process

1. When driving down the road, ask yourself, which way is the car in front of me going to go at the next intersection?

2. Take a breath and get your answer. Then watch and see what happens. It's so exciting to watch your confirmations happen right in front of you, almost automatically.

3. Notice the ease of practicing this connection, it truly makes the commute time fly.

Quiz Your Clair

What does this person's license plate number say about them?

Is there a better route for me to take to my destination?

Releasing Vows or Contracts

When To Use It

To release contracts, old beliefs or patterns that keep you stuck in your life.

Process

1. Create sacred space being in the now, present to your breath and body.

2. Call on your Divine Support Team and ancestors with clarity of your intention to release any restrictions, promises, vows or contracts that are limiting you.

3. As you breathe deeply feeling completely relaxed, ask your Divine Support Team and ancestors to show you where in your body you are holding this restrictive energy from a past life. Breathing deeply allow yourself to imagine, see or know where it sits in your body.

4. As you see this limiting energy notice how your Divine Support Team and ancestors has circled around you, sending you energy and Divine support with clarity without any attachments to any trauma or contrast. They assure you will only be shown that which you are ready to see, feel and know.

5. Imagine the area where this vow or restrictive past energy is receiving all of the light from your Divine Support Team and ancestors, breathe this in—deeply.

6. As you allow this Divine energy to do its work, ask your Divine Support Team and ancestors to remove any and all vows, contracts or limiting energy that is prohibiting you from living your greatest version this lifetime.

7. Make sure you relax and allow the energy to expand as you continue to release these old outdated past promises. Releasing it all to this light that is expanding all throughout your body.

8. You can ask your Divine Support Team and ancestors to share with you the information from these blocks or vows, if you so desire, but it is not necessary.

9. You will know when the energy is completed. You may hear a click or even a pressurized sensation.

10. Thank your Divine Support Team and ancestors for this gift of freedom and expansion.

Throat Chakra Clearing

When To Use It

When you are having challenges building any of your intuitive channels make sure you are paying attention to your chakras, especially your throat chakra. While the throat chakra is all about communicating it also supports us sharing what we "get" with our intuitive hits. If your throat chakra is out of balance it may be hindering the growth and clarity of any of your clairs.

Signs That Your Throat Chakra Needs To Be Cleared

- It seems hard to communicate clearly.
- Find it difficult to express your thoughts, feelings, and emotions.
- You're experiencing creative blocks
- Other people talk over you (interrupting you consistently).
- Struggling to hear your Divine Guidance.
- Struggling to trust your intuition.
- Feels like the "weight of the world" is on your shoulders.
- You often feel misunderstood when you do speak up.

Quick Strategies to Clear Your Throat Chakra

- **Sing It Loud and Proud.** Seriously singing, whether in the shower or not is a powerful way to open up your pipes, put on a great tune and sing along!

- **Say Empowering Affirmations Out Loud.** Make sure you believe your affirmations, keep it simple!

- **Use A Crystal on Your Throat Chakra.** (Any listed in crystal magic will work). Lie in savasana, breathing deeply into your throat and seeing the energy of the crystal amplifying your throat chakra. Feel notice and acknowledge your willingness to share your clairaudient abilities.

Process

1. Create sacred space, as you sit in a relaxed and comfortable position with your eyes closed.

2. Notice your thoughts and align your thoughts with the intention of opening and balancing your throat chakra.

3. Call on your Divine Support Team and ancestors to energize and support you.

4. Be present to your breathing, notice as each breath enters through your nose and then passes down the back part of your throat and into the lungs and the sound it makes, like "**so**";

5. Then exhale this breath slowly out of your mouth, making a conscious awareness to listen to the "**hum**" sound that is associated with the air leaving our body.

6. As you become comfortable noticing the sounds and watching the breath move through your throat and into your lungs, call to yourself the beautiful color of blue light. Notice how this energy follows along with your breath, as you continue the rhythm of your inhale and exhale, repeating "**so, hum**...."

7. Continue this process until you are present to "hearing" the subtle sounds of your inspiration—energy breath moving in and out.

☼ The yogic **mantra** "**so hum**" is not only a reflection of the sound of the breath but also carries a contemplative **meaning:** "I am that" (**so** = "I am" and **hum** = "that"). Here, "that" refers to all of creation, the one breathing us all.

Worry Scheduler

When To Use It

Use this process if you are a worrier and can't break away from your worries or perpetual anxieties.

This is an excellent process when we insist on returning to the same worry over and over. This CBT (cognitive behavioral therapy) technique can often help us to understand habit our amygdala is in which takes us down the worry path. There are those who do this habitually having no idea there is part of themselves who does not worry!

Process

1. Recognize the worrying is not serving you.

2. Also acknowledge that part of your brain needs to worry to feel functional.

3. Schedule a time in the evening or late afternoon when you can let that part of your mind worry.

4. Schedule a maximum of one hour (ex. 6-7 pm). Do not schedule this too close to bedtime.

5. During the day, carry a notebook or use a note app on your cell phone.

6. When your mind goes to that worrisome thought—notice it and write it down in your notebook or your note app.

7. Your note is the list of things that your mind wants to worry about.

8. Remind your mind that you are going to worry about it—you haven't forgotten and you will do that during the allotted time (ex. 6-7pm).

9. During that allotted time, pull out your notebook and read the list and start worrying.

10. The more you practice this—you will find during that hour, you don't really feel like worrying. Your daily worry level will drop with regular practice of this process.

Forgiveness

When To Use It

Use this meditation when you are feeling anger, shame, guilt, judgment or overall frustration.

Forgiveness is a gift we give ourselves. Often, we are holding onto something that we don't need to hold onto and we don't know how to release it or what to do about it. The following meditations can be extremely helpful and comforting in almost any circumstance.

On the following pages, there are three forgiveness meditations: 30 Day Forgiveness, Novice and Advanced.

With these forgiveness meditations you will feel a sense of ease with the situation or the person that is troubling you.

We suggest you first, begin these forgiveness meditations with yourself.

30 Day Forgiveness

As you move through this meditation, please remember that there is only one spot where you can place your emotional foot—into fear or into love. Every time you have a thought that produces an emotion, you are manifesting a reaction that is fear-based or love-filled. As you do this meditation, you are asking your mind to stay in a space of love, regardless of what you have felt in the past. Some days this will be easier than others. Despite this roller coaster, please do not give up or stop. It is imperative that you keep going without missing a day for 30 days. When you make it to the 30th day, you will find this experience has shifted you.

The meditation is designed to be done first thing in the morning and last thing in the day, prior to bedtime. When you first start this exercise, we encourage you to pick one person to place your focus to work with to release any unforgiveness.

Novice Approach

When To Use It

This approach is used for those of us who find using the word forgive and sorry difficult. This gentler way is a perfect way to start. Even if you are a mastery at forgiveness we encourage you to start here and then proceed to the intermediate level.

Process

1. In the morning, choose the person you wish to feel forgiveness with or about.

2. Bring a visual of that person into your mind.

3. If it is difficult to visualize the person, without creating a lot of emotional reaction, simply bring a visual of the person's energy.

4. Send or sprinkle this person with love, light, joy and peace. Realistically, regardless of what they have done to you, ultimately you recognize it in some part of your being. Knowing everyone benefits from greater doses of health, love, joy, light, peace and abundance.

5. As you visualize this person, sending them this energy, take a deep, calm, breath, stay in the moment.

6. Allow yourself any reaction physically or mentally should one arise.

7. Imagine snow sprinkling on the person's head. Each snowflake brings them health, love, joy, light, peace and abundance.

8. Notice as you send this energy out to them, as per the Universal Laws, you are sending the same energy back to yourself.

9. Stay with this meditation for a few minutes. If you are able to, try to stretch this to 10-20 minutes.

10. In the evening, prior to bedtime, return to this practice. Again, work for a few minutes or if possible stay in this meditation for longer.

11. During the evening meditation, start with the main person you are creating forgiveness towards and then add anyone that you feel may have wronged you throughout the day. It could have occurred in the form of little things, like when someone cut you off in traffic or when you felt someone was rude to you. As you do this regularly, you will get more adept at releasing and stepping into forgiveness mode in the immediate moment.

This will become easier with time and then you will not have to wait until the end of the day to clear the energy.

Advanced Approach

When To Use It

When you move up to the advanced level, it is easier for you to visualize the person and feel comfortable with this energy.

It may have taken you 30 days on the novice meditation to get here, or perhaps you are ready to start here right away. It may be easier now for you to visualize the person or see their picture without feeling activated or triggered by your experience of them. You have a much better, finer and a firmer grasp on the energy and you are much more comfortable dancing in the space.

Process

1. Similar to above, bring a visual of the person into your mind in a morning meditation.

2. As you look at this person, take a few breaths in and say—"I forgive you, I hold no unforgiveness back."

3. Take a few deep breaths and say—"I honor the Divine spirit within you. I am free and you are free."

4. As you do this meditation, start to feel the similarity between yourself and this person from a Divine perspective as two spirits. You will notice that there is no separation (Universal Law of Oneness). When you work in the domain of the Divine, you will find it easier to release judgement, criticism and anger. Stay in this space and allow yourself to feel the love that you have for this other soul.

5. Repeat this until you feel the lightness and ease that it creates.

Similarly, in the evening, repeat the meditation along with anyone that you may have felt wronged by or hurt in any way.

These meditations work so profoundly because the energies of the Universe that are around you want to feel love, light and a space of ease for yourself and everyone around you. Holding onto unforgiveness does not help anyone. Releasing this heavy energy will bring forth a sense of ease, love and peace.

Being In The Now

When To Use It

The great thing about this process is that is a multipurpose process. You can use it to support you when you want to strengthen your upward vibration and momentum. It can also be used to help break the energy when you are in a downward spiral. And you can use it to expand your mindful awareness of your own broadcast. Also another important thing to note about this process is that it can be done anytime, anywhere at the spur of the moment.

The key to this process is to remember the only moment we have is now. Often, what we are experiencing and living is old energy—from old vibrations from last week or 6 months ago. By looking at what is now, observing and responding exclusively to it, we keep creating the same experience and don't shift or create what we truly desire. We direct our awareness, focus & energy to realign ourselves energetically through our vibrational broadcast to create a different reality tomorrow. Non-judgment is essential with this process. S0 please be gentle with yourself

Process

1. Slow down, get present and notice what you are experiencing in your now. What is going on around you in this moment? If you are having a hard time being present to what is happening, maybe you are thinking vs. observing, or gotten caught up in momentum taking you down a road you don't want to travel any longer.

2. Take a deep breath, slow the action down, by notice your body, your thoughts and your environment.

3. Take another look at what is happening for you in this moment.

4. What is the vibration? Or the energy essence? Does it feel like anger, frustration, stress, etc.? Or is it an essence of joy, excitement, happiness?

Whichever end of the polarity stick you are on matters not. What is important is that you can notice the energy and vibration you are experiencing right this moment,

5. Going inward, ask yourself, how is this current experience aligned with my desire, my fears? Because this experience is old energy (UL of Cause and Effect) how is this something you used to resonate with? Perhaps you have a propensity for drama or a flair for sabotaging yourself, no judgment. This is where we are able to come face to face with our manifestations.

6. If you can't figure it out—don't freak out!

7. Stop for a moment, look at something different. Take some deep breaths, relaxing your body as much as possible.

8. Go back to noticing the NOW, see if you can feel it in your body, as you take another deep breath in, being open for this new awareness about yourself.

9. Journal and take note of the Divine Guidance you receive, the awareness that comes forward and the ease of being present to the now and the more often you practice this—the more you will see proof how the Universe is responding to you in every moment.

Intuitive Training

Clairvoyance

Clairvoyance Energy Activation

When To Use It

A very simple yet powerful activator of your clairvoyance channel. Use this anytime you want a boost or feel your clairvoyance needs refueling.

Process

1. Sit in a quiet place of reflection, where you will not be interrupted. Close your eyes and imagine a ray of BOLD purple light with blue sparkles around it.

2. See this ray of light and energy building and coming into your 3rd eye chakra.

3. Breathe in deeply, as you do notice how the purple and blue light amplifies and grows as you breathe it deeper into your brow chakra. Imagine your 3rd eye chakra is opening up, larger, as its soaking in this Divine energy.

4. Relax and see yourself absorbing this Divine energy and light—as you do notice how your chakra begins to spin slightly. Make sure to take several deep cleansing breaths—your chakra is clearing, decalcifying, if you feel a tinge of dizziness, take a sip of water make sure you are grounded and breathe deeply.

5. Continue to absorb this Divine light and energy until you feel a slight tingling or witness your 3rd eye energy center begin to move, ever so slightly, as if its breathing, awakening.

6. As you continue this energy process, notice how your chakra is beginning to spin stronger and faster. Make a note if you feel a sense of discomfort (a twitch, pressure, possibly even a slight ache), it may be due to fears

that are dislodging. If this discomfort distracts you, it may help to acknowledge you are willing to see your Divine truth.

7. When the process is completed you will feel a pull back or even hear a click. Open your eyes and slowly look around, notice if you see anything differently.

8. Acknowledge and give gratitude to your Divine Support Team and ancestors.

Imagine If You Will

When To Use It

This is an easy exercise that will boost your clairvoyance in a jiffy. The practice here is to utilize your mind's eye to expand your visualization through picking an image and practicing seeing it. After choosing your image stick with it until you can see it in your mind completely in great detail, try to see as much detail about the object you can, including texture, color, size, shapes.

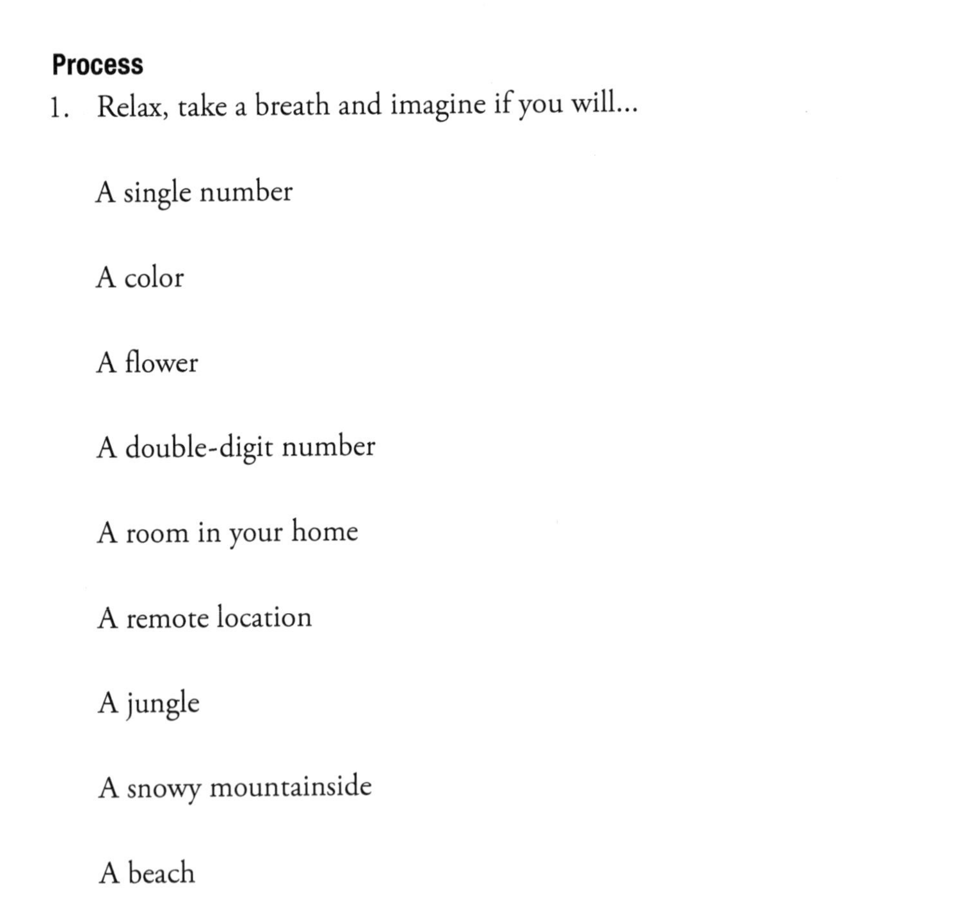

Process

1. Relax, take a breath and imagine if you will...

    A single number

    A color

    A flower

    A double-digit number

    A room in your home

    A remote location

    A jungle

    A snowy mountainside

    A beach

Level II of this Exercise

- For an advanced version of this game see if you can add other objects to your object, including people, animals.

- Now you have mastered seeing single individual objects, see if you can add additional objects to your vision. For example, if you are imagining a color, add texture, a shape—layering more objects into your scenery. See if you can move the objects; see it as a movie. Perhaps it is a scene from your favorite movie, or dice flying through the sky, the context isn't as important right now as the strengthening of your 3rd eye, it is all in the visioning.

Level III of this Exercise

Without looking at the pages prior to answering, use these questions to dive deeper into seeing your answers through your clairvoyance:

What title do you see on page 207?

What, if any, images do you see on page 122?

What images do you see when you tune into the subject on page 175?

What do you see when you use your clairvoyance to access images of the person quoted on page 271?

What characteristics do you see or witness when you tune into the person quoted on page 156?

Laugh Lines

When To Use It

This process is a great way to practice building your clairvoyance. The beauty of this exercise is you can use it almost anywhere and take as much or as little time as you would like.

Process

1. Go into a quiet space of relaxation.

2. Close your eyes and call forward a vision of one of your favorite loved ones.

3. See them smiling. Notice how their cheeks shine, see the sparkle in their eyes when they see you.

4. See if you can deepen your vision by looking even closer. Can you see their laugh lines? Notice how deep they go. If they have dimples notice them, the beautiful expression of laughter on their face. Make note of what you experience

Poker Face

When To Use It

This is a fun exercise to do with a friend who wants to amplify their clairvoyance. You can use any type of card you'd like: oracle, playing or even notecards you scribbled on. This exercise also amplifies your broadcasting abilities.

In Person

1. Each person chooses a card and doesn't show it to the group (or the other person if there is only 2 of you). Choose who is going to go first.

2. The first person look at your card, close your eyes and see your card in your mind's eye. When you have the image crystal clear. Let the others in your "game" know you are sending the image to them. You can do this by imagining a gigantic size of the card literally floating to them, or being handed to them. Make sure you see them receiving it, seeing it. Then let them know when you are finished sending the mental image.

3. Each person goes around saying what they saw.

✺ It's important that this game be played like children do, with no attachment, just fun, this isn't about comparing or judging your abilities.

Remotely

1. Set up a time with a friend to play this game remotely. The time aspect is important as you will be sending the visual and you want to make sure they are present to witness it.

2. Choose a card, sit with it and visualize yourself sending the image of it to your friend and them receiving it.

3. Then text or communicate with them what they received. Then it's your turn to receive!

When You're Out and About

You can do this exercise anywhere you can sit for a moment with your eyes closed. So no driving while trying this one out!

1. The next time you're sitting at your local coffee hangout, or even the DMV, take a moment and look around, take in the entire environment. Time yourself for 1-2 minutes. Then close your eyes and see if you can see your surroundings in your mind's eye, notice how much you can visualize, see how much detail you can conjure.

To accelerate this practice, see if you can send the visual of your environment to a friend without telling them. Then see what synchronicities happen.

Seeing Oneness

When To Use It

When feeling isolated or separate to restore the awareness and feelings of your connection.

The *Bhagavad Gita* states, "If you can see God (the Oneness) in everyone, you can never do harm to anyone." Whatever you experience through your senses, remind yourself it is all a part of the same Oneness. See if you can begin to see the world as a reflection of yourself.

In the Hindu belief Vedanta, Indian literature, it says, "The ignorant man (engrossed in duality) desires material things; the intelligent man (seeker on the path) desires enlightenment, but the wise man (knower of Oneness) just loves and receives everything."

Process I

1. Stand in front of a mirror, pause for a moment, and look directly into your eyes.

2. Say silently or aloud "AHUM BRAHMASMI" (a-hum-brah-mass-me), which means *I am the Universe* or *I am the totality*. You can say it in English, if you prefer. This is your soul reflecting back onto itself and reminding you of its oneness.

3. Practice this at least once a day or whenever you catch your reflection in a mirror.

Process II

1. Stand in front of a mirror as you pause, take a deep breath

2. Say "Namaste" (nam-ah-stay), the Indian blessing which means, *I recognize the Divinity in you which is also the Divinity in me.*

3. Bringing the palms together in front of your heart center as you repeat, "Namaste," feel the power of knowing we are the same oneness.

4. Practice this at least once a day or whenever you catch your reflection in a mirror.

Process III

1. Sit in a comfortable position.

2. Take a deep breath in

3. On the exhale chant the word "OM," through your entire outbreath.

4. Repeat

In every moment of existence, the whole of creation is constantly emerging from the silence of Oneness. The first sound or vibration emerging from the silence is "OM." This vibration then expands into all the sounds and vibrations of the Universe.

When we chant "OM," it draws our awareness back to the dawn of creation and into Oneness.

Signs

When To Use It

Use this exercise to build your clairvoyance while also strengthening your confidence in your connection to your Divine Guidance. Practicing seeing signs.

Ask your Divine Support Team for clear images, signs and symbols. One of the things I always specify when placing these orders with the Universe is I ask that the images, signs and symbols be LARGE and CLEAR, like a billboard, I ask that they come through so big that I CANNOT miss them.

You can do this in your own way, whether in your meditations, prayers, journaling or in your mind.

Process

1. Create sacred space.

2. Clear your mind.

3. Call on your Divine Support Team and ancestors.

4. Make your request to receive clear images, signs and symbols.

5. Acknowledge what you receive—remember it may be subtle so be present.

Always share your gratitude for their assistance and support! I mean it would be rude to not thank anyone who helps you out, right?

Third Eye Clearing

When To Use It

This energy process helps to remove obstacles interfering with our 3rd eye vision with Divine clarity. Typically we shut our clairvoyance down because of fears we listed in the Clairvoyance Chapter. These fears and our continued unwillingness to see creates a calcification—a barrier that impedes our 3rd eye from seeing. All the times you watched scary movies and turned away when the shock came...that slams your 3rd eye shut. To open that up try this exercise. You can do this energy process on yourself, and we find it's fascinating when our participants use it with a friend or client because of the interesting information that comes through.

If you are practicing on someone else, you'll want to tell them that you will be lightly touching their forehead between their brows, 3rd eye region, briefly.

Process

1. Create sacred space.

2. Call on your Divine Support Team and ancestors to assist you, if working with another, call in their Divine Support Team and ancestors as well.

3. Have your client sit and relaxed with their eyes closed. Ask them to take some deep breaths.

4. See, imagine, pretend energy and light is coming through your dominant hand (the hand you use to write with or, if you were born left-handed and made to use your right—use the hand you naturally lead with) into your fingers. Place your hand to your client's 3rd eye area, and energetically rip off the calcification and fears the way you would remove a bandaid—FAST AND QUICK! Yank it off! Sometimes it helps to even make the sound a bandaid makes when it's being torn off.

5. Then place your dominant hand in a cuplike manner and hover it over your client's 3rd eye brow area. Send energy through your hand to your client's brow chakra. See both Divine Support Teams and ancestors sending energy and light through you. As you are giving your client energy, remind them to breathe, as if they are soaking in this Divine energy through their 3rd eye.

6. Ask for any guidance as to why this 3rd eye is closed, what was it frightened by, why is it protecting your client, was it from this lifetime? Allow any Divine Guidance that will support your client's continued open clairvoyance to come forward. Sometimes this could be in the form of self-care (like sleep).

7. Finally ask your client if they are willing to exchange these past fears for love? Are they willing to exchange pain for peace? When they respond yes, ask them if they are now willing to see through their Divine clairvoyance? When they say yes, continue to give them energy through their 3rd eye chakra until you hear a click or get a sensation of the energy subsiding, signaling that it is complete.

8. Thank your client for being open and give them any final Divine Guidance that came through. Hug them, send them on their way AND THEN....dissolve any etheric cords that may remain. (See Etheric Cord Dissolution p. 350)

Yogi Training

When To Use It

This exercise comes from the lineage of yogis, while quite simple don't discount its power. This practice uses the subtle focus of our eyes to build clairvoyance. The more you practice the easier it is to see the subtleties of energy.

What You'll Need

- Candle or incense
- Lighter

Candle Process

1. Light the candle, allowing it to burn,

2. Soften your gaze to the very tip of the flame.

3. See if you can look through the flame, not at it.

4. Practice noticing if you can see the heat energy coming off the flame.

Incense Process

1. Light incense

2. Allow it to burn for a couple of minutes.

3. Soften your gaze.

4. Practice watching the smoke rise up from the incense.

5. Follow the smoke with your softened gaze until it dissolves.

Intuitive Training

Clairaudience

Boosting

When To Use It

In this exercise, there will be a list of questions that you have no idea of knowing so you can practice your subtle art of hearing the Divine. As you begin the exercise do NOT look ahead at the questions…use this as your laboratory, your playground to expand your experiences.

What You'll Need

- Pen
- Paper

Process

1. Create sacred space.

2. Go into a relaxation space—deep breaths—being present to your body and being in the now.

3. Calling on your Divine Support Team and ancestors to support you to hold the energy and space that you expect to hear your clairaudience.

4. As you read each question, take a deep breath and ask to hear the response, being present and in the now, then listen…before checking to see if you're correct. Make a note not to expect or anticipate a voice per se. That can be scary and off-putting.

5. You may receive your clairaudience through other sounds rather than an actual voice. For example, it might be the sound of a revving engine. That could reflect start your engines, or birds singing. It could also be hearing something that isn't actually there as well.

6. As you read each question, relax your body and *write down* anything you hear, even if you "think" it isn't related to the question you posed. What

you hear may be inside your mind, even sounding like your own voice, or it may be outside, like birds singing, phone buzzing, or engine revving.

Quiz Your Clair

What new experience will I have in the near future that will positively impact my life?

Describe a new person I will meet soon.

Who is my next spiritual teacher?

What area of my life needs my attention?

Describe any changes or actions that I can take that will enhance my Divine abilities and talents.

When you've written everything down and the energy subsides, step back and take a look at your notes. Use your intuitive sleuth to detect and decipher your message and answer.

Level II of this Exercise

- Without looking at the pages prior to answering, use these questions to dive deeper into seeing your answers through your clairaudience:

What is the first word that appears on page 327?

What is the last word on page 249?

What is the topic in the center of page 90?

What page of this book do you need to turn to feel a boost right now?

Using your clairaudience, what do you hear when you tune in to page 397?

Clearing Ear Chakras

When To Use It

Use this any time you want to strengthen your clairaudience or when you feel you need an extra clarity in what you're hearing. The main chakra for clairaudience is the ear chakras, clearing and balancing them supports your ability to hear your Divine Guidance.

Process

1. Take a moment and get quiet, take some deep breaths in and out. Letting go of the day or outside world. Go into your relaxation space by closing your eyes and centering yourself in the present.

2. Call in your Divine Support Team, ancestors, guides and angels to be here with you to support you in this process as you acknowledge your intention for this experience.

3. Being in the now, imagine your ear chakras, 2 energy centers lying parallel to your physical ears, see this beautiful red-violet energy within them, like 2 reddish purple Frisbees spinning.

4. Do you notice anything about them? Are they symmetrical, spinning in balanced movement?

5. Allow your intuition to direct you. Trust whatever you receive, through hearing, seeing, feeling, knowing, or sensing.

6. See yourself bringing alignment energy to your ear chakras now, as you do notice this beautiful gossamer white-gold ray of energy and light beams flow into your ear chakras.

7. Take a deep breath and allow your body to absorb this healing energy to remove all the painful memories of harsh words logged in your ear chakras.

8. Continue to keep breathing, long and slow deep belly breaths.

9. In this beautiful powerful energy, your Divine Support Team suggests this is a perfect time to release and offer up any fears you have about hearing your Divine Guidance to this powerful healing energy.

10. Notice, witness yourself releasing any anger, verbal abuse you may have heard over the years, any dark feelings or fears you may have held lodged into your ear chakras which keeps you from hearing your own Divine alignment. You may feel a release of pressure, see or experience a shift as this old energy clears.

11. Releasing and giving any unforgiveness you may have held onto from the origins of those toxic things you heard, to this beautiful and powerful energy. Notice as you give these they are instantly transmuted by the powerful healing love and light energy. Forever dissolved, no longer stuck to you.

12. Continue to allow this energy to run until you have a sense that it is complete. You may hear a click, or even a powering down sound. You may even notice your ears hearing the slightest subtle sounds.

13. As you complete this clearing thank your Divine Support Team and ancestors for holding the space and intention for you to be open to your clairaudience.

Intuitive Ear Muffs

When To Use It

When you are feeling overwhelmed by the environmental sounds around you. Even when you're not at a loud concert, clairaudience elevates our sensitivity where sounds can irritate. We are "receiving" these sounds unconsciously which can create an energy depletion and before we know it we're exhausted and agitated, without even knowing why. It's not because you're moody, it's because your clairaudience was bombarded. Use this anywhere, any time.

Process

1. Take a deep breath in, hold it briefly for a count of 3, and then exhale. Repeat this three times.

2. Call on your Divine Support Team and ancestors to surround and support you.

3. Being clear in your intention to quiet the noise, and amplify the sound of the Divine; imagine before you are a pair of magical earmuffs, activate your clairvoyance to see their color, size, shape, texture.

4. When you are ready, imagine placing them over your ears and notice there's a silence that comes forward. You are still able to hear the sounds around you, but there's a difference. It's as if the static has quieted, even vanished.

5. Breathe into your ear chakras, see the energy of the Divine move through them from these magical earmuffs.

Continue through your day, no need to remove these, they are not a boundary of the Divine, just the static that takes us off course. Your clairaudience is raring to go!! Pay attention!

Jammin'

When To Use It

If you're having issues trying to expand opening of your clairaudience, make sure to check your chakras, especially your throat chakra. Even though clairaudience comes through the ear chakras, sometimes having an imbalanced throat chakra keeps us from being able to share or say what we hear. Try this exercise to clear your clairaudience.

Process

1. Play some music from a "jam band" like Widespread Panic, Dave Mathews, Grateful Dead, Stevie Ray Vaughn or some classical music, as you turn it on, set the intention to amplify your clairaudience.

2. While the music is playing, choose 1 instrument or sound to focus on, listen for **ONLY** this instrument's sound throughout the entire song.

3. Once you've mastered that—choose another instrument and possibly a different song!

Silence Is Golden

When To Use It

Use this process to build and strengthen your clairaudience.

Process

1. In this exercise, sit in a place that doesn't have much ambient noise.

2. Then see if you can imagine "hearing" a sound. Perhaps it's a train, or a horn. See if you can bring the actual sound in your hearing awareness.

Level II of this Exercise

- Call forth your Divine hearing and see if you can "hear" an instrument (remember the room is silent—no background atmosphere). Play with this sound until you can hear it totally.

Level III of this Exercise

- Call forth hearing an orchestration of music. Be it your favorite band, or song, see if you can hear the song all the way through.

The Sound of Answers

When To Use It

Use this when you want to strengthen and play with your clairaudience. The idea is to get clear on your question. Remember no compound questions, get to the heart of the matter and ask what you truly want to know.

Process

1. Call on your Divine Support Team and ancestors, while you hold the intention to expand your clairaudience, feeling relaxed and calm, pose your question.

2. Turn on the "radio" or any music app (Spotify, Pandora, Satellite Radio). If using a music app, please do not use one of your "play lists," instead go to your "Liked Songs List" which is a compilation of all the music you've liked across all genres.

3. While holding the thought of your question, close your eyes, press the shuffle or channel scanner button (where the station doesn't go to a pre-set, but jumps to the closest station).

4. Sit quietly and listen to the song that is playing. Pay attention to the lyrics, the tempo, everything in this song is answering your question through clairaudience.

Level II of this Exercise

- Before pressing the shuffle button to play, intuit the number of times to press the shuffle button to receive your Divine Guidance. While posing your question, also ask how many times do I need to hit the shuffle button? Let's say you get 4, you would press the shuffle button once, twice, three, and four times and the 5th song will hold the answer to your question.

Toning

When To Use It

Use this when you to amplify or gain more clarity with your clairaudience. It's great exercise to use in your car or in the shower where no one can hear you.

Using our voices to amplify our clairaudience may seem like an unusual choice. Our voice is an incredible healing tool—here we will be as Pythagoras, recognizing the therapeutic power of the human voice. Every sound has a resonance, a frequency. In his book, *The Healing Aspects of Toning*, Ted Andrews says using the sound of the vowels in our language will open different areas of our body consciousness.

I love how he compares toning to a restoration exercise of bringing the natural vibrational patterns of our energy field. We are all too quick to disregard the healing power of our own voice, not only is it a part of our physicality but a tool to help others as well. It is also one of the most magical healing instruments we have. Too often we forget how our voice can lift the load of another, how it can support another's healing and growing. Connecting our voice with our body, breath, intuition, and mind we are naturally building our natural Divine alignment.

We have learned and experienced the power of toning through Ted Andrews' work. Using the sound of the vowels in our language will open different areas of our body consciousness. Breath is one of the most important aspects of toning, opening your chest and diaphragm, creating space.

Vowel	Area of Body Opened by its Sounding
"U"	Pelvis, hips, legs, feet, and lower body in general.
"O"	Lower trunk, abdomen area from solar plexus to groin.
"A"	Chest cavity, heart, and the body as a whole.
"E"	Throat, upper chest, and head regions. Back of the skull.

Process

1. To practice toning, it is as simple as sounding out the vowel and holding it as long as you can. If you want to open up your heart area, take a deep breath in and chant, sing "AAAAAAAAAAAAAAAAAAAAAAAAA…"

2. Notice when you are syncing your toning up with your breath. While this is opening up your heart chakra, chest area, etc. you may also feel a tickling in your ear chakras.

Toning OM

The first sound or vibration emerging from the silence is OM. This vibration then expands into all the sounds and vibrations of the Universe. When we chant or tone "OM," it draws our awareness back to the dawn of creation and into Oneness.

- Notice when you are syncing your toning up with your breath. While this is opening up your heart chakra, chest area, etc. you may also feel a tickling in your ear chakras.

- Toning supports our Divine hearing. Be present to your clairaudience expanding.

Intuitive Training

Clairsentience

Shaking / Dancing

When To Use It

Use this process whenever you want to break the momentum and move energy. It is also a great process to use when you feel stuck or just blah.

The process of dancing and shaking can really move energy allowing us to use movement in a very therapeutic way. Shaking and dancing are powerful ways to shift energy and dissipate it quickly, where you feel good almost immediately. These types of rapid movements get you out of your head and into your body. They have the added benefit of releasing tension and breaking up habitual emotional holding patterns as well.

Shaking

1. Plant your feet solid on the ground.

2. Let your arms hang loosely at your sides, making sure your knees are soft not locked.

3. Allow your body become loose as you begin to "shake."

4. You can even bounce your entire body up and down as you keep your feet planted.

5. Drop your jaw, let your head rest entirely on your neck.

6. Give your body permission to make whatever sound it wants to make. You may find anything from no sound to screaming. Nothing is off limits.

7. Feel free to express yourself and allow the sounds to move with your body.

8. Continue for 5-10 minutes.

Dancing

1. Plant your feet solid on the ground.

2. Allow your arms to hang loosely, knees soft.

3. Put on some music of your choice.

4. Let yourself move freely in whatever manner your body wants to move. Nothing is off limits.

5. Express yourself through movement and in response to the beats of the music.

6. Shake it up!

7. After the song has finished, stand quietly as you notice and listen to your body. How does it feel?

Clearing Heart Chakra

When To Use It

To amplify your clarity with receiving Divine Guidance through clairsentience. When your heart chakra feels heavy or you feel sad.

There are multiple ways to clear your heart chakra:
Do a full body chakra clearing—paying special attention to your heart chakra. Meditate with a Rose Quartz crystal or a crystal with clairsentient amplification properties. Use Reiki or other energy work to clean out the energetic psychic debris. Do forgiveness work to release the heartbreak you have had over your lifetime. This includes the ego voice you've used to sabotage yourself.

Process

1. Take a moment and get quiet, take some deep breaths in and out. Close your eyes and center yourself in the present, being aware of your intention, being in the now.

2. Call in your Divine Support Team, ancestors to be here with you to support you in this process.

3. Imagine your heart chakra, a beautiful energy center lying in the center of your chest/heart area, see this beautiful emerald green energy within it, spinning.

4. Do you notice anything about it? Is it symmetrical, spinning in balanced movement? Allow your imagination to direct you. Trust whatever you receive, through seeing, feeling, knowing, sensing, or hearing.

5. Call Divine energy to your heart chakra now, as you do notice this beautiful gossamer white and gold ray of energy beaming down into your heart chakra.

6. Take a deep breath and allow your body to absorb this healing energy to remove any and all the painful energy logged here in your heart chakra. Keep breathing, deep breaths.

7. In this beautiful white-gold energy your Divine Support Team and ancestors suggest this is a perfect time to release and offer up any fears you have about feeling love, receiving and giving love. Releasing any resistance or concerns of feeling your Divine Guidance to this healing light and energy. Releasing any unknown restrictions to allowing this healing light and energy.

8. See yourself releasing any fears, anger, hurts you received, any dark feelings (known or unknown) you may have stuffed into your heart chakra to keep you from feeling your own Divine alignment.

9. Releasing any unforgiveness you may have held onto from the origins of toxic experiences, any residual pain you may have harbored and stowed deep in your heart, possibly hidden where no one would know how deeply you feel. Giving all of that to this beautiful energy.

10. Notice as you offer these energies, they are instantly transmuted by the powerful healing love and light energy. Forever dissolved, no longer stuck, trapped inside of you. You may see these energies leaving and dissipating like bubbles or smoke floating out and away from you. Floating out into Mother Earth who receives this energy as her fuel.

11. Continue to allow this energy to run until you have a sense that it is complete. You may hear a click, or even a powering down sound. You will feel a sense of ease, a lightness of being.

12. As you complete this clearing thank your Divine Support Team and ancestors for holding the space for you to be bold and courageous in opening your heart, to receive this Divine connection of clairsentience.

Mindful Awareness

When To Use It

Use this process whenever you want to break the momentum and move energy. It is also a great process to use when you feel stuck or just blah.

The process of dancing and shaking can really move energy allowing us to use movement in a very therapeutic way. Shaking and dancing are powerful ways to shift energy and dissipate it quickly, where you feel good almost immediately. These types of rapid movements get you out of your head and into your body. They have the added benefit of releasing tension and breaking up habitual emotional holding patterns as well.

Process

1. Notice the direction and feeling nature of your thoughts when you first wake up in the morning.

   Which direction did you feel your momentum going?

   If it was upwards—
   How long did it last?

   If it was downwards—
   What process did you use to shift or change it? (dancing, singing, meditation, laughing, exercise, etc)

   What was it like to start bringing, that momentum back up?

   What did you notice—was it hard or easy?

   Did it get easier the more you practiced?

   If you felt stuck, what hooked you?

2. Acknowledge yourself for being willing to practice noticing your mindset.

The most important thing is not to judge your momentum, it is just a place marker advising you of the direction you are heading. You can always flip a U-Turn.

Mindful Eating

When To Use It

Use this process to build your clairsentience. This also helps when you want to build your awareness around fueling your body.

When we eat mindfully, we are giving ourselves a chance to meditate a minimum of three times a day!

With this process, we acknowledge our relationship with food and the stories we have around eating. The relationship with food can be a huge part of our sub personalities and a way for us to tap into our relationship with ourselves.

Our stories around food come from many places: our family of origin, our culture, our societal norms and more. Such as, finishing all of your food, eating as a family, eating on the run, eating in front of the TV, food scarcity versus abundance, relationship with restriction, repetitive judgement of ourselves for our desires of foods. Judging ourselves for what we ate or didn't eat, all the "shoulds" (I should eat a veggie plate—why did I get the fries?) Restricting ourselves for punishment, approval or both. Making ourselves at victims of judgment to what we *should* do.

What You'll Need

- Grapes, Raisins or Chocolate or anything that you can eat in morsels.

Process

1. Normally, most of us eat automatically or mechanically. Now, we are going to experiment with eating differently, paying full attention in a non-judgemental, open way, staying in the present moment as much as possible.

2. Take one of these food items, only one. See if you can entertain the

notion that you are seeing and sensing this object for the very first time. What does it look like? What shape is it? What color is it? How does it *reflect* in the light? Next, maybe investigate more closely how it feels. What is its temperature? Its surface texture? Its density? Perhaps you might also bring it up to your nose. Do you smell anything? Are you salivating? How do you feel about putting this food into your body right now? How does your body feel anticipating eating at this moment?

3. Now, we are going to receive this food into our body. Be aware of your arm moving to your mouth. How is the food taken into your mouth? Experience the food in your mouth. Chew it slowly, deliberately while playing your full focus and attention on the food's taste and texture. Be aware of any desire you have to rush through chewing so that you can have another. Be aware of the intention to swallow before you actually swallow. Notice after you have swallowed how far into your body you can feel the food.

4. Know that your body is now exactly one food item heavier.

A Picture is Worth a 1000 Words

When To Use It

To boost your clairsentience.

This is a fun exercise to do with old photos of family members (or people) you didn't or don't know. You want to be able to confirm the information you receive, so make sure there's someone around who can do that for you.

Process

1. Go into your relaxation space, taking deep breaths.

2. Bringing your awareness into the now and into your intention of receiving Divine Guidance through your clairsentience.

3. Call on your Divine Support Team and ancestors asking for support in opening your heart chakra to receive this Divine Guidance through your clairsentence.

4. Take the photo (**without looking at it**) place it between your two hands, closing your eyes, breathing deeply.

5. Relay your question, "Please give me Divine Guidance to share about this photo."

6. Breathe and notice any physical or emotional responses you may be experiencing.

7. Write down or share what you receive with your client/friend, it could be something as simple as feeling the number 2. (And you find out there are 2 ducks in the photo).

8. Allow yourself to express all that came through including the feelings,

sensations and emotions you continue to experience as you are sharing with your client/friend that is part of the intuition coming through.

9. Play psychic sleuth with any messages and experiences.

Level II of this Practice

- Instead of using a photo, ask your friend/practice buddy to write something on a piece of paper, fold it and hand it to you. Go through the same process while asking to receive the "**feeling**" nature of what is written on the paper, maybe even possibly the feeling of a word or the context of the note.

- Write or share what you receive—then look at the note. This exercise is especially helpful in refining your accuracy.

Psychometry

When To Use It

Use this exercise when you want to build your clairsentience. To practice your intuition by receiving information through touching objects.

Our energy transfers to the things we own and the more we connect with it whether it is by wearing, using or cherishing the object, the more energy is infused in the object.

You will be using clairsentience as the main channel to receive this information. As you touch an object information begins to come forward and you may often be able to see, hear and know additional information through our clairvoyance, clairaudience and claircognizance.

What You'll Need

- Metal jewelry, watch, pen (belonging to someone you don't know).
- Someone to validate information about owner of jewelry.

Preparation

Clear the energy of your hands. You can do this by touching a living plant, a crystal, or washing them.

Process

1. Call on your Divine Support Team and ancestors to amplify your intention and reception.

2. Go into your relaxation space, being present to your breath, taking deep breath in, and out as you bring into your awareness your intention to receive Divine Guidance through your clairsentience, feeling and being present to your body, in the now.

3. Rub your hands together so you can be present and feel the energy flowing. You'll feel your palm chakras "perk" up.

4. Place the metal item (jewelry, watch, tie clip, etc) in your hands. Put your palms together surrounding the item.

5. Call on the Divine Support Team and ancestors of your client as well as that of the owner of the item. Close your eyes, breathing into your palm chakras, imagine, notice and FEEL the energy of this item.

6. Allow anything about the owner of the object to come into your awareness.

   What do you feel or get a sense of? Are there any sensations? Smells? Tastes?

Quiz Your Clair

Is the owner of this item living?

What are some characteristics of the owner of this item?

Is there any information coming through from the owner of this item the person I am reading?

- Write down or share what you receive with your client/friend.

- Allow yourself to share and express all that came through including the feelings, sensations and emotions you continue to experience as you are sharing with your client/friend. That is your intuition continuing to come through. Trust it.

- Play psychic sleuth with any messages and experiences.

- Notice when the energy is "pulling back" or subsiding.

- Be present to your appreciation for the support and connection you experienced during this exercise by acknowledging both your and your client's Divine Support Teams and ancestors. Being grateful for the opportunity to be of service.

Intuitive Training

Claircognizance

Activating Claircognizance

When To Use It

To activate your claircognizance or when you want to strengthen your clarity through Divine knowing.

Take a moment and get quiet, take some deep breaths in and out. Close your eyes, center yourself in the present, aware of your intention, being in the now.

Process

1. Call in your Divine Support Team, including your ancestors, to be here with you to support you in this process.

2. Tap into your grounding cord.

3. Imagine your crown chakra, a beautiful energy center at the top of your head, see this beautiful royal purple energy within it, spinning.

4. What do you notice about it? What do you know to be true about it? Is it symmetrical, spinning in balanced movement? Allow your imagination to direct you. Trust whatever you receive, through seeing, feeling, knowing, sensing, or hearing.

5. Call Divine energy to your crown chakra now, as you do notice this beautiful gossamer white-gold ray of energy beaming down into your crown chakra at the top of your head.

6. Take a deep breath and allow your body to absorb this healing energy to remove all the past judgment or distrustful thoughts lodged here in your crown chakra. Keep breathing, deep breaths.

7. In this beautiful white-gold energy and light your Divine Support Team suggests this is a perfect time to release and offer up any fears you may have about opening your channel of knowing Divine love, receiving any resistance of knowing Divine Guidance to this healing energy.

8. See yourself releasing any old thought patterns of fear, anger, and hurt. Releasing any thoughts, conscious or unconscious, that created judgment of yourself or others which may be crammed, hidden deep in the dark crevasses of your mind. Removing any diversions and distractions from your own Divine alignment now.

9. Deep breaths—keep breathing...

10. Releasing and giving any unforgiveness you may have held onto from the origins of those experiences. Any residual pain you have harbored and stowed deep, deep in your mind, head and neck, back there where no one would know, giving all of that to this beautiful light and energy.

11. Notice as you give these to this beautiful white-gold energy they become pixilated. As they become more and more disconnected from you they begin to sink down through your lower chakras. See this assembly line moving this pixilated energy down into the roots of your grounding cord. Allowing all of this pixilated energy to move down and out of your body through your grounding cord. This energy going as fuel, feeding Mother Earth, fuel to the fire of the magma at her core.

12. See these spots of energy going into the fire—burning and turning Universal fuel.

13. Imagine as you do this, you notice how your mind feels clear.

14. Continue to allow this energy to run until you sense or know that it is complete. You may hear a click, or feel a shift in the energy around you, signaling the completion of the energy.

15. As you complete this clearing thank your Divine Support Team and ancestors for holding the space and intention for you to be bold and courageous to open your knowing, to receive this Divine experience of claircognizance.

Mind vs. Spirit

When To Use It

Use this process whenever you have a negative feeling emotion and you are stuck in your mind. This process helps you to open up to the intuitive voice that may be buried in the string of thoughts you have.

Process

1. Write down the mind voice, the emotion you are feeling and the thought that is creating it. Try to write a general thought which is easier to work with.

2. Practice the Belly Breathing meditation. The more you practice the Belly Breathing meditation (p. 304), the more you are open to other thoughts from your intuitive voice that want to show up.

3. Given that the Spirit Voice always creates emotions of love, joy, ease, appreciation and knowledge, take a moment to intuit, think or imagine what the Spirit Voice may be saying on the same topic your mind is. These thoughts may come to you during the belly breathing meditation.

4. Write down what you sense your Spirit Voice is saying.

5. Return to this process through the day as it will help you to realize that the Spirit's Voice is a steady stream of love and appreciation that you have access to. With some practice and focus, you can access more of the Spirit Voice thoughts.

Mind Voice: Emotion and General Thought

ex: Frustration—Husband always late for dinner.

Spirit Voice: Emotion and General Thought

ex: Love—He is out working and creating money, so sometimes he runs late.

Receiving Divine Downloads

When To Use It

This is a fun way to practice trusting your claircognizance and receiving not only through individual thoughts but also as "blocks" of thoughts, that happens instantly. This is much quicker than receiving individual words or thoughts. This practice helps those who want to be a professional intuitive because it speeds up our ability to share information with clients, making room for more healing opportunities.

What You'll Need

- Pen
- Paper
- Open mind

Process

1. Go into your relaxation space, taking deep breaths, close your eyes.

2. Bringing your awareness into the now and into your intention of receiving Divine Guidance through your claircognizance.

3. Call on your Divine Support Team and ancestors asking for support in opening your crown chakra to receive this Divine Guidance.

4. Relay one of the questions below.

5. Breathe and notice any thoughts, pictures that flash in your head, or even a certain knowing. Pay attention to physical or emotional responses you may be experiencing as well.

6. Write down the message, pictures, symbols and/or knowing you receive even if they don't make sense to you.

If you aren't receiving anything right away—take a deep breath—sometimes these downloads come through as thoughts you've had before—so don't discount them. If that's the case, there is guidance and information around them. Seek those…

Play the role of the intuitive detective and decipher your messages.

Quiz Your Clair

What is my life purpose?

Is my current career the highest expression of my Divine purpose?

How can I be financially successful living my purpose?

How can I expand and improve my clarity? What area of my life needs more of my focus right now?

Level II of this Exercise

- Without looking at the pages prior to answering, use these questions to dive deeper into your claircognizance, Divine knowing.

Is there a number in the body of the 2nd paragraph on page 181?

What do you know to be true about the topic on page 242?

Who do you know that could use a call or a note from you to lift their spirits today?

Name a person we mention on page ix?

Level III of this Exercise

- Master your claircognizance. Pick someone you would like to receive Divine Guidance about, whether it is a family member, friend or colleague. Before beginning this level make sure you are clear who's energy you are tuning into. It sometimes helps to state their name: "I'd like to know this information about Bruce." Even if you know three people named Bruce, focus and align with the energy field of the Bruce you are talking about.

  What would you like me to know about this person?

  Is this person experiencing troubles or challenges right now?

  What is the purpose or reasons for what's happening in their life right now?

  How can I best support and help this person?

Taking Care of Business

Building Your Business Meditation

When To Use It

You can use this process any time you want to create a new offering. It is an easy way to tap into your Divine Guidance for your next project.

Meditation

Go into your relaxation space, allowing your body to be completely supported by the chair you are sitting in, feel your feet, touching the floor. Notice your breath, breathing deeply, notice your body letting go of the outside world, allowing any sounds outside to simply fade away, as you continue to feel more and more relaxed.

Allow the energy of the day to fall away from your body, like small pixels drifting away from your body. Returning back to their place of origin through social media, emails, calling all your energy back to you now. And now releasing any energy that is not yours, allow it to go back to its place of origin. Calling back any energy you may have deposited around the world through social media, interactions, emails. Bringing back all your energy to you now. Good, and continue to relax your mind as you focus your thoughts on the questions and directions of creating your offering.

You are excited to make this connection to your offering so as you relax call energy to you now. Imagine, your body, mind and soul receiving this Divine light, that comes through and permeates every cell and atom in your body and entire energy field.

Process

1. Call on your Divine Support Team and ancestors, to support you in your path and purpose this lifetime. Especially any ancestors or masters of this lifetime you know specialized or mastered the gift you desire.

2. With your paper and pen in front of you. Relax deeper, possibly even

softening your eyes, as you pick up your pen and automatically respond to these questions:

What is this offering you are desiring to create?

What will it fulfill within you?

What service will this offering give your world?

3. Let the pen take over, you are simply the vessel through which the Divine is flowing. Don't over think.

4. Allow your pen to jot down every and all thoughts, feelings, senses you experience. Allow your desires to come into your awareness, and onto the page.

   Have you considered where this offering will take place?

   Can you imagine that place now? Where is it?

5. Take yourself there in your mind.

6. See yourself putting your own personal touches to your work space where you will create and share your offering. Perhaps it is a home office, or maybe an artistic shared workspace.

7. Notice your work space and how you made it comfortable and very appealing.

   Does it delight you?

   How do you feel now that you are empowered with being of service in a way that inspires you?

Can you imagine feeling fulfilled and completely satisfied with your offering?

8. Imagine you are receiving calls and emails from people who are interested in working with you because you are the one they have been looking for in this specialized area.
9. See yourself feeling confident and sharing your offering with them.
10. Witness the ease of how you share your gifts and how much you charge.
11. Notice how easily you tune into your Divine Guidance, to see if they are an ideal client for you.
12. See how easy it is for them to say YES to this Divine adventure of working with you.
13. Now fast forward, a year later from today
14. See yourself established in your offering for over a year now.
15. You have been managing all the requirements as you share your amazing talents being of service to your clients.
16. And you receive another message, this time you have been highly recommended by someone.
17. Your circle of influence is growing and you feel so delighted that the ease of following your passion and providing this service brought you this success.
18. Let this vision soak in, this successful vision of you and your incredible offering to the world that will have a positive impact.

19. Continue to build this vision, see how much color and texture you can add to it. Remember how it feels.

20. You have made up your mind, determined to succeed and you will.

21. Thank your Divine Support Team and ancestors for holding the sacred space for you during this process.

Having taken this trip you now see how your future is going to be and you feel ready and excited to take that first, important step.

You will succeed—because your focus and momentum to succeed grows stronger and stronger, day by day.

Business Building Exercise

When To Use It

There are multiple exercises in this Chapter that will support you in building or creating your business. Keeping Universal Law in mind with a special nod to Hermetic Principle (UL) of Correspondence, as above so below, it is outside as it is inside. To build your business you have to start with the most important aspect of it... **YOU**! *Like my client Bob realized, you gotta start with yourself.*

To create sharing your offering with the world you want to acknowledge Universal Laws and your intention to access Divine Guidance for your specific directions. Whether it's online or brick and mortar, whether it's 1:1 or in big groups, doesn't matter, the most important thing is to trust your Divine Guidance—it will NEVER lead you astray.

What you'll need:

- Pen
- Paper

Preparation

- Before doing the following Divine Prescription, let's make sure you're clear on a couple of basics. Write down your answers to these questions so that you can see them for yourself.

  What is your offering?

  Why are you offering it? (What's your WHY?)

  What is your message? (short and sweet)

  What's your passion?

  What are the benefits of your offering? (WIFO—What's in it for others?) The world listens from the perspective of what's in it for me, am I interested, do I feel drawn, or called to this?

What are the characteristics, values and habits of your ideal client/customer?

Do you feel more comfortable working 1:1, or with groups?

What are some new areas you want to explore that are beyond your comfort zone? (Maybe intuition? Going on a safari? Teaching? Speaking in public?)

How many clients/customers do you desire to impact on a weekly basis?

How many clients/customers do you want to be of service to each month?

- Now that you have more clarity of that we're going to take you through a meditation process that will build on what you've begun. You can record this to use for yourself or use with a friend or client.

Process

1. Go into your relaxation space, allowing your body to be completely supported by the chair you are sitting in, feel your feet, touching the floor. Notice your breath, breathing deeply in, noticing your body letting go of the outside world, allowing any sounds outside to simply fade away, as you continue to feel more and more relaxed.

2. Allowing the energy of the day to fall away from your body, like small pixels drifting away from your body. Calling back any energy you may have deposited around the world through social media, emails, etc, calling all your energy back to you now, and as you do also releasing any energy you may have picked up that is not yours, allowing any energy that is not for your highest greatest good to be released and sent back to its place of origin.

3. Good, and continue to relax your mind as you focus your thoughts on the questions and directions of building your new offering.

4. You are excited to make this connection to your offering so as you relax call Divine energy to you now, imagine yourself, your body, mind and soul receiving this Divine energy, that comes through and permeates every cell and atom in your body and auric energy field.

5. Now call forth your Divine Support Team, all your ancestors and guides on the other side to support you in your path this lifetime. Especially any ancestors or masters whom specialized or mastered the gift, talent, skill you are desiring to offer.

6. Now we will pose several questions as you are plugged into your Divine Guidance to build your connection to knowing and trusting your next step:

   What is this beautiful offering you are desiring to create?

7. Pay attention, allow your guidance to come through with ease. Listen, be present to the sensations in your body as you consider this question. What do you desire to create? Allow the knowing to come forth and be integrated into your being.

8. Breathing deeply…

   What will it fulfill within you?

   What service will this offering give your world?

9. Write down the messages, ideas, desires you receive you will now more easily allow them to materialize. You will be successful in your Divine service to our world.

10. Allow that idea of your service in the world being a contribution to sit with you for a moment. Be with this, consider the value of your gift of purpose.

    What is your message? (short and sweet)

    Have you considered where this offering will take place?

    Can you imagine that place now?

    Where is it?

11. Take yourself there in your mind, through all of your senses, all your intuitive channels are wide open. Receiving all this Divine Guidance. See yourself putting your own personal touches to your work space—the place where you will create and share your offering. Perhaps it is an office, or maybe an artistic shared workspace. See yourself making it comfortable, inspiring and very appealing.

    See your work space—does it delight you?

    How do you feel sitting and being in this beautiful work space—being of service in a way that inspires you—in a way that has you feel fulfilled and completely satisfied?

    How many clients/customers do you want to be of service to each month?

    How many clients/customers do you desire to impact on a weekly basis?

    What are your ideal clients like? What are their values and habits?

12. See yourself in your sacred work space feeling successful as you receive calls and emails from people, these ideal clients, who are interested in connecting with you because they have been looking for, the perfect intuitive guide, teacher, leader, speaker, person for them.

13. See yourself feeling confident and sharing your offering with them. Witness the ease of how you share your gifts and how much you charge.

14. Notice how you are actively listening to what this person is looking for as you tune into your Divine Guidance you see if this is indeed your ideal client, someone you feel aligned to work and collaborate with. See how easy it is for them to say YES to this Divine adventure of working with you.

15. You are already on the way to realizing this desire.

16. Now fast forward, a year from today—see yourself established in your own business for over a year now. You have been managing all the admin requirements—sharing your amazing gifts and talents being of service to your clients.

17. And again, the phone rings, this time you have been highly recommended by someone. Your circle of influence is growing and you feel so delighted that the ease of following your passion and providing this service has brought you this success, this abundance, this joy, this freedom, this feeling of contribution to your community and world.

18. Imagine this as you take some deep breaths in, let this vision soak in, this successful vision of you and your incredible offering to the world that will have a positive impact.

19. Continue to build this vision—see how much color and texture you

can add to it. Be present to all of the emotions associated with this coming to "true". Feel it in all of your being, breathe it in—allowing ever cell in your physicality to know it is your truth.

20. You have created this energy and alignment to succeed—and you ultimately will, succeed.

21. Having taken this trip to see how your future is will be—you now feel ready and excited to take that first, important step.

22. Follow your guidance.

23. You will succeed—because your focus and momentum to succeed grows stronger and stronger, day by day.

Shattering Glass Ceilings

When To Use It

Do this practice when you feel like you need a boost in the abundance department. I helps in any situation where you feel you are being "held down" by a boundary or barrier.

Process

1. Go into your relaxation space, breathing deeply. Create sacred space.

2. Call your Divine Support Team and ancestors to hold the space for you to move beyond your perceived limits.

3. See a beautiful golden sun—the heart of all the light—hovering over your crown chakra, open up your crown chakra and soak up this rejuvenating energy and light. See it being soaked up by every part of your body.

4. Notice how this energy moves out and through your physical body into your aura. As it does it immediately dissipates any fogginess, creating your aura to become clear.

5. As you integrate this beautiful golden light you are present to the energy and support of your Divine Support Team and ancestral lineage. Continuing to breathe deeply, ask to be shown this glass ceiling or the symbol of limitations you have been living in.

6. You may feel a little squished, or uncomfortable when you notice this energy. Imagine this glass ceiling is pressing down on you—blocking you from having the space you want.

7. Bring your attention to this glass boundary, direct your 3rd eye, solar

plexus and heart chakras to send rays of energy into it. Notice the ceiling is expanding with this new energy. Watch as this old glass ceiling begins to pixelate, separate and dissolve.

8. As it dissolves you continue to send the energy from your chakras.

9. Now imagine these pixels begin to swirl. The glass ceiling begins to morph into a helpful tool. Watch as it shifts into your symbol; your wealth power symbol. Receive this power symbol so that you remember your ability to shatter any limitation. Make sure you use it everywhere you desire to experience success.

10. Continue to run this energy until you sense, feel, know that it is completed. Thank your Divine Support Team and ancestors for their powerful assistance in creating an infinite opening of success for you.

General Magnetizing Exercise

When To Use It

Feel free to use this exercise any time you feel an urge to amplify your broadcast to attract and allow. It is a powerful exercise that I have been using for decades, and in my experience, it always delivers!

Process

1. Go into your relaxation space, breathing deeply.

2. Create sacred space.

3. Call on your Divine Support Team and ancestors to support you.

4. Bring forward in your mind what it is you want to magnetize. Make sure you are very clear and specific about the essences of what you want.

5. Visualize as detailed and as clearly as you can a picture of what you want. Make this a vivid image. If you're having a challenge seeing that—imagine a symbol that represents what you are magnetizing.

6. Take some deep breaths in, focusing your attention to your solar plexus chakra, your power center. See yourself asking this energy center to expand as you take slow deep breaths in.

7. As you allow this amplification in your solar plexus notice the energy that is being generated is forming a coil, see a bright yellow light beginning to circle around and around inside of this power coil.

8. As the energy begins to build you notice the coil extends beyond your solar plexus chakra, out past your body.

9. This golden coil begins to grow and expand and you notice it is lifting,

pointing outward, and you can feel the spinning of your magnetic coil going in the perfect direction for you.

10. Now as you are holding the thoughts of (what you are magnetizing you notice how your magnetic coil responds, it may grow larger, smaller, dependent upon the amount of energy needed to harmonize your energy field with it.

11. You are building your magnetic field and creating a force field around you that is perfectly synchronized with the resonance of what you want.

12. See the symbol or picture of your desire being drawn towards your magnetic coil, as it gets closer, notice where in your body you want to accept it; perhaps your hands, or maybe your heart, if it's wisdom it could be your head, regardless of where, see your item coming to you.

13. Continue to circulate this energy through your coil toward your symbol, image. As you do this imagine what needs to happen for you to have this thing that you desire.

14. Then ask your Divine Guidance "what steps do I need to take to have this?" See, feel, know or sense what those steps are.

15. Ask to see these steps like a staircase—now you can work with the time aspect of these steps by getting a feeling or idea of how far apart they are. If your steps seem too far apart for you, move them closer; if they feel too steep, make them flatter; move them in the direction that feels easiest for you.

16. Adjust your breathing and alignment of your spine to increase your magnetization. Continue running this energy until it feels like it is complete. You may hear or sense a click. Stop magnetizing when you feel the certainty that it is completed.

17. Now ask your Divine Guidance how often you should repeat this magnetizing exercise in order for you to have what you want.
18. Thank your Divine Support Team and ancestors for supporting you and your intention in this powerful energy session.
19. When the energy has subsided, if you received any guidance or valuable messages, write it down.

Money

When To Use It

This is a great exercise to use when you want to understand your relationship with money. Or how you can improve your flow of money. While this exercise is very powerful the first time you use it—it can be helpful to revisit our ancestral beliefs around money when we feel stagnant in our money flow.

Process

1. Answer these questions—use your journal to explore them to uncover your true relationship with money. You can use these questions as **jump starters** for your automatic writing exercises as well.

How do you feel about money?

Is money hard to come by? Do you have to work hard and struggle to get it?

What are the first emotions that come forward around the subject of money?

- Fear
- Anxiety
- Excitement
- Joy
- Overwhelm
- Freedom

Do you believe there will always be enough money for you?

What's the first thing that comes to your mind when you think of money?

What is money to you?

Growing up, how did your family feel about money?

What would an observer say about **your** relationship with money?

If you could change one thing about your experience with money what would that be?

Earning

How do you feel about the money you are bringing in now?

How do you feel about the idea of bringing in MORE money?

Do you believe you can be wealthy doing what you love?

What is your success number? What would you need to earn a month to be able to call yourself financially successful?

Do you believe you have to work hard to earn money?

Spending

Do you spend money and later feel bad about yourself for doing it?

Do you overspend, or do you economize to the point of discomfort because you're concerned there won't be enough?

When you buy something new, do you use it right away, or wait for a special occasion?

Saving

Do you believe you need to have savings to be safe?

Does the idea of investing money to make more money excite you?

Does the thought of working with your money to invest and build your net worth feel like a big task?

Giving

Are you happy giving to others first, so much so, that you have little left to give to yourself?

Are you balanced in the area of giving or are you a little cheap or are you an over-giver?

Use this as an opportunity to get real. Do you give the typical 15-20% tip in a restaurant, or do you just round up to the nearest dollar on your credit card?

What is the one area where you feel you have room for improvement in creating your new relationship with money?

- Saving/Investing
- Earning
- Sharing
- Spending

What new relationship are you creating with money now?

Money Speaks

When To Use It

This is a handy automatic writing exercise to use anytime you want to do what I call, get real with who you are with money and how you treat it. Very powerful indeed!

What You'll need:

- Paper bill/currency of choice

Process

1. Create sacred space.

2. Go into your relaxation space, taking deep breaths in and out.

3. Call forth your Divine Support Team and ancestors for support.

4. Hold dollar bill in your hand and look at it.

5. Using single point focus meditation as you continue to look at your money, begin to look into your money, softening your focus. Notice the energy you sense around the money you are holding. Does it feel alive? It is after all a currency…moving like the currents of our world.

6. Continue to take deep breaths, notice the energy around your hands as you hold this living energy called money.

7. Notice that both the energy of money and your own energy field are connecting, merging, becoming one. As you are in this deep connection with your tool called money, ask to have a conversation with it.

8. When you feel, sense, or know you may proceed, continue by asking your money, these questions. Make sure you pause and listen like with

any conversation listening is more important than speaking. Open your mind to see what you can learn about your relationship with money.

"Money, how do I treat you?"

"Money, how can I attract more of you?"

"Money, what do you want to tell me about my habits with you?"

"Money, I must be honest, as a child you ______________________________ ____________."

"Money, what can I do to develop a healthier relationship with you?"

Sacred Ceremonies

Years ago, I had the privilege to work side by side with Hay House author Steven Farmer. A southern California modern-day shamanic practitioner, Steven introduced me to the incredible power behind ritual and sacred ceremony. This was a big gift to me because ritual and ceremony ceased to exist for me when I stopped practicing organized religion. Steven Farmer gave that back to me—a presence and a feeling of connection I thought was lost forever.

When you take the time to be in ceremony, your intention is significantly amplified. Just like everything in your personal practice, adjust anything to fit what works best for you. Remember, at the heart of the matter is your intention. The language around a ceremony can be complex or as simple as lighting a candle. Ceremony, regardless of length or complexity, require only five things: An opening/beginning, an intention, focus, offering, and an end/closing. If you want to learn more about the power of rituals and sacred ceremonies, there are many shamanic teachers out there like Don Miguel Ruiz, Sandra Ingerman, and Steven Farmer. Trust your intuition will lead you to the perfect teacher.

Things To Consider Before Creating Your Sacred Ceremonies

- Your intention must be crystal clear, not just, "I want more money" because that could be receiving a coupon for 5% off.

- Ceremony work requires big intention and single focus.

- A ceremony doesn't have to be long and drawn out—it is totally up to you. Complex doesn't necessarily mean better. The most important elements are your intention and your focus.

- In preparing for ceremonies, set boundaries, it is important to remember to set a point to know when the ceremony energy will be complete in doing its work. To establish this, we put boundaries around the energy, for example, let's say you set a ceremonial boundary by saying the signal of completion energy is a hummingbird. So, when you see the hummingbird, regardless of its form, (billboard, website, or in nature) it will be the sign that the ceremonial energy is complete.

- When we allow a time for the focused energy to interact with the subatomic particles around us by setting a boundary it creates the type of vacuum nature abhors.

A Cup a Day

When To Use It

This quick little ceremony is a fantastic way to have magic and intention in your life from your first sip of your morning beverage, whether it be tea, coffee, or a magical elixir of your own concoction. It is a powerful way to infuse your beverages daily since water holds energy. You can use this ceremony daily, regularly to your heart's content.

What You'll Need

- A cup of Coffee or Tea
- A Spoon

Ceremony

1. If you brew your Coffee/Tea by the pot or by the cup, matters not.

2. While waiting for the water to boil, keep your attention focused on the ceremony.

3. **Don't get distracted** or walk away.

4. Stay in the moment. Listen to the water as it starts to boil.

5. Focus on your breath.

6. Connect with the properties of your Tea/Coffee

7. Pouring the water and/or as your potion begins to brew, notice how the light changes into darkness, as the clear water transforms into coffee/tea.

8. Add any extras to your brew (Sugar, Milk, etc)

9. As you stir your Coffee:

   Clockwise to **bring** something to you;
   Counter clockwise to **release** something from you.

10. Holding your intention, say over your cup:

    "I ask these things to (come to) (leave) me,
    with a full heart I attract, thee,
    magnetically my intentions fulfilled as I drink this coffee/tea."

11. Then blow your breath (filled with your intentions) into your cup and enjoy your magical brew.

Yummy Brew Additions

Here are some yummy additions to add to your brew along with their properties so you can create your own morning magic

Luck. After stirring your coffee/tea, immediately scoop up and drink any tiny bubbles that may have formed on the top.

Cinnamon. This ancient spice is an all-around amazing magical booster. Sprinkle into your coffee to attract love, boost your power, or to bring success and abundance.

Sugar. For sweetness and love.

Vanilla. Brings love into your life, especially receiving love.

Almond. Pour this in to call in prosperity and wisdom.

Milk. Provides an abundance of personal and spiritual nourishment. Some spiritual cultures believe milk carries and emits subtle vibrations of Divine energy or (Shakti).

Coconut. Increases confidence, intuitive awareness.

Hazelnut. Nourishes creativity, intuition, and mental powers.

Peppermint. Amplifies Divine vision, clears the mind, and the head.

Amplifying Your Offerings

Our "offerings" are the gifts, talents, skills and training we share with the world, our clients, family and friends.

Preparation Before the Ceremony

Magick Money Oil

- Small Green Glass Bottle with Lid or Stopper
- Small piece of Tiger's Eye or Aventurine
- 4 oz. of one of the following: Olive, Almond, or Grape Seed Oil
- Drops of Peppermint Essential Oil
- Gold or Silver Glitter

On a waxing moon or a Thursday add the above ingredients to the Green glass bottle. Shake the bottle 3 times to activate and charge the oil.

Create Your Sacred Sigil

A sigil is a uniquely personal energy signature you draw in order to produce a specific result. Take 1 word that represents your intention — take the letters and develop your symbol from those letters. You can add any embellishments like stick figures, squares, circles, any pictorial elements — whatever arrangement or design that speaks to your intention. It can be as intricate or as simple as you desire. For example, if your focus and intention for this ceremony is "love" — take the letters L-O-V-E and draw them with hearts, smiley faces or anything that conjurs the energy of love. You can't get this wrong, have fun, don't complicate it. This is your personal energy signature of intention.

Preparing Space for Ceremony

What You'll Need

- 1 Broom or Fan
- 1 Bowl
- Saltwater

- Sage (bundled, loose, or incense)
- 1 Fireproof Bowl that you can carry
- Matches/Lighter

Process for Preparing Space

1. The first step to amp up your business and service in the world is to start with a clean slate, this begins with your home environment.

2. Before beginning the clearing process—make sure the entrance to your home or place of business is clear of all clutter and obstacles, assuring the pathway to you is direct and easy to find, place a living plant by the entrance to bring and magnetize life into your space of offering, and make sure there is some sort of light in the space (candle or lamp—just the placement of a light in the space holds the intention of light).

3. Open up your windows and doors, sweep your home with the broom, not just the floor but the air too. Wave the broom through the entire area, side to side, up and down, until you feel you've brushed away all the energetic debris. Some say it's best to sweep in the direction of the sun's rising and setting, east to west. The importance in any ceremony is your intention and how you are representing it. If sweeping the air seems ridiculous to you, don't do it. If it's something you think your 2 year old might get a kick out of, go for it.

4. Always stand in your power to create your ceremony your way, it is completely up to you.

5. Fill a small bowl with Saltwater and sprinkle a little in each corner of your home, flick or sprinkle some in the center of each room as well.

6. Put the Sage into fireproof bowl and light it, blow out the flame and let the Sage smoke. Carry it from room to room, allowing its cleansing smoke to clear the air and restore a clean slate to your sacred space.

Ceremony

What You'll Need

- 9 Sunflowers, Marigolds or other Yellow flowers
- 1 Clear Quartz Crystal
- 1 Green Aventurine Crystal
- 1 Fluorite Crystal
- 1 Amethyst Crystal
- 4 Green candles
- 1 Yellow candle
- Magick Money Oil (p. 446)
- Sacred Sigil (page 446)
- Clean White Cloth

Ceremony

1. Draw your Sacred Sigil on each of the candles with a toothpick, skewer, or knife. As you are drawing your Sacred Sigil, remember to be intentional with your essence of your desire. The intention for this ceremony and focus.

2. Anoint each candle with the Magick Money Oil (on the outside—not anywhere near the wick).

3. On the White cloth place the 4 Green candles one each of the directions (N,S,E,W). Place the flowers in the center of the circle of candles—they represent the success you are attracting into your life. On each side of the flowers place a crystal, so that the flowers are both surrounded by the crystals on the inside of the circle and the candles on the outside of the sacred circle.

4. Place the 1 Yellow candle in front of the flowers and crystals.

5. Go into meditation, pray, focus your attention on your Sacred Sigil, your intention and desire for this ceremony until there is nothing else

in your thoughts but the vision of your Sacred Sigil. When you have created that momentum—light each Green candle, while saying,

"I shine this light into the night
Through the power of fire
I draw forth my deepest desire to be in Divine service
Through my own emergence"

6. Take a moment to activate your third eye vision by gazing into the flame of the Green candles.

7. Anoint your 3rd eye chakra with your Magick Money Oil, circling your middle finger in clockwise motion three times.

8. When you are ready to seal in your amplification of your offering, continue by lighting the Yellow candle in reverence and acknowledgment of the Divine Power within you and repeat these words,

"I call forth my Divine Support Team, Ancestors, Angels, Divine I AM.
Surround me with your wisdom, deep in the dark roots of my lineage,
breaking old barriers and patterns held deep within.
Willingly, authentically I come forth to declare the action I take,
following my sovereign center of Divine Guidance
To share my talents and gifts in this world.
So other's purpose and gifts unfold
Bring them forth with ease and grace
And with thy service I will embrace."

9. Sit and focus on the flame of the Yellow candle, gazing at it until you feel the energy set to a level you are comfortable with. This is just a knowing, feeling, sense. Trust what you feel, see, know, or hear.

10. Then say aloud, "And so it is" or "Amen."

11. When you feel complete—extinguish the Yellow candle first, then the Green candles in the reverse order that you lit them in (W,E,S,N).

12. On the ninth day, if the flowers are still vibrant leave them. Leave the crystals and candles on the White cloth until the flowers are withered. Once withered, remove the flowers and save the petals for use in another ceremony, along with your anointed candles.

Ancestors' Altar

Altars are incredible ways to physically anchor our intentions and magical practices.

Preparation

- To create an Ancestors' Altar, gather photographs, items, or special mementos of the ancestor(s) that you wish to connect with.
- Arrange these items along with other magical items of your choosing around your altar space.
- You may add candles, crystals (Chrysocolla, Petrified Wood, Bloodstone, Amethyst, or Celestite work best for this work), and herbs (Rosemary for remembrance and protection and Sage for wisdom and connection).

Ceremony

1. When you want to connect with your altar, begin by offering your ancestor(s) some kind of libation (for example, if your grandfather loved peanuts, place a bowl of peanuts on your altar).
2. Speak their names aloud, inviting them into your space, sending them love, and thanking them for being part of your life.
3. Sit in the energy with your altar and see what you experience.
4. Ask questions, ask for Divine Guidance, or simply sit and feel their presence.
5. You may want to journal to keep record what you experience.

Attracting Divine Partnership

When To Use It

The intention behind this ceremony is to step into the Divine partnership space. This experience allows you to focus your energy towards having this partnership. Some of my clients say it helped them feel they're building their connection to partnership. If nothing else it soothes the lack and creates a vacuum—and you know how nature abhors a vacuum, so there will be space for that partnership to arrive, in the most divinely aligned form.

What You'll Need

- Crystal Drinking Glass
- Pink or White Flower Petals (preferably rose)
- Rose or Jasmine Essential Oil
- Small Black Obsidian Crystal
- Small verse of love poetry, lyrics from a love song, or your own loving dedications

Preparation

- Gather supplies

- Write down an extensive list of the qualities, values, and characteristics your heart desires for your love partner. It is essential that you are very clear as this ancient love charm is very powerful.

- Create a sacred space, infused with peace and love

- Put pure spring water into the crystal glass and drop 1-2 drops of the essential oil into the water.

Ceremony

1. Go into your relaxation space, taking deep breaths, close your eyes.

2. Bringing your awareness into the now and into your intention of attracting your Divine life partner.

3. Call on your Divine Support Team and your ancestors, asking for support and guidance for your ceremony.

4. Imagine yourself surrounded by Divine energy and light, this energy begins to moves into your crown chakra and from there into your right arm and hand.

5. Create a circle of light around yourself by pointing the first 2 fingers of your dominant hand and imagining a white light emanating from it, like a beam of light from a flashlight, draw the circle in a clockwise direction around yourself 3 times.

6. Place the flower petals in a circle around you.

7. Holding the crystal glass in your left hand invokes the Divine angelic energy, Haniel, by simply asking from your heart to have this angelic presence with you.

8. Recite your love poem, lyrics or speak from your heart, over the crystal glass holding the elixir.

9. Then say,

   "I ask and invoke my Divinely aligned soul partner may come forth with ease and that I easily recognize them and they me."

10. Dip your left finger into the elixir and write on your non-dominant hand, Divinely aligned partner.

11. Place the Black Obsidian Crystal in your right hand, close the circle of light by drawing a counter clockwise circle around yourself three times.

12. Imagine and see your beloved's right hand in your left hand, palm to palm. This is a signal that you will recognize each other and allow the love for one another into your hearts.

13. Thank your Divine Support Team, ancestors, and Haniel for their support and assistance.

14. Walk through your sacred circle knowing your Divine right partner is stepping forward and knowing your Divine partner is also stepping forward and is ready to meet you. Each of your souls created this connection to deepen you and your life, and you both are saying YES to this soul connection.

Attracting Ideal Clients

When To Use It

Use this ceremony when you want to allow more flow into your business, especially in regards to clients. This is a powerful activation that has great success with my clients.

My client and friend Chloe Elgar wanted to do a ceremony to bring in 3 new clients for her intuitive coaching business. So I created the ceremony below. She gathered all her symbols, Sacred Sigil and binding runes and performed her sacred ceremony. The completion boundary she set was that she would know the creation energy of the ceremony was finished when she saw or heard a frog.

On the next new moon, she performed her ceremony quietly in her home. After watching her candles burn down and her herbs finished smoking, she buried the remnants off of her property and looked forward to getting her acknowledgement that the creation was completed by seeing or hearing a frog. A week later she was outside with some friends and she heard a frog croke. It was like she was tingly all over and she knew the energy of her ceremony was completed. Later that day she also saw a frog. And she found that a frog had made his home in their back yard. Boy, she got the message loud and clear. She wasn't missing anything.

Two weeks later she called me excited saying her ceremony worked! She had 3 new paying clients!! Way to go Chloe.

What You'll Need

Gather symbols that represent your intention to have more clients, wealth, and success

- Fireproof bowl, pot or cauldron
- Charcoal—instant light charcoal tablets
- Parsley

- Pepper
- Cinnamon
- Tumeric
- Cloves
- Bay Leaves
- Salt
- 1 Green candle
- 1 Gold candle
- Anointing Oil
- Neroli in carrier oil
- Timing: the New Moon
- Drum/rattle
- Crystals - Citrine, Amethyst, Jade, and any crystals you are aligned with.
- Ancestor symbols—something that represents your lineage

Preparation

- **Intention for Ceremony.** The goal you desire to experience, (ex. 4 new ideal paying clients)

- **Completion Boundary.** Set the symbol or signal as to when the ceremonial energy will be completed. Example: I will know when the ceremonial energy is complete by seeing/hearing a particular animal; a specific sign like money on the sidewalk.

- **Create Your Sacred Sigil.** Take 1 word that represents your intention—take the letters and develop your symbol from those letters. You can also use binding runes or symbols that speak to your intention. (Sacred Sigil p. 448)

- On the Gold candle, carve the representation of the clients you want to attract, it could be stick figures, squares, circles—whatever symbol speaks to you.

- Using a toothpick or skewer, carve your Sacred Sigil into the Green candle.

Ceremony

1. Open your sacred space, call on your ancestors and Divine Support Team while you hold the intention to attract and have your ideal clients for your business.

2. Anoint your candles with anointing oil.

3. Place candles in holders and create 1 circle of salt around both candles. Place your crystals on the left and right of the candles on the salt circle.

4. Heat up the cauldron or fire proof bowl by placing small charcoal in it and lighting it.

5. Light candles.

6. Take your herbs and add to a fireproof bowl or cauldron. Focus on the smoke visually for a moment. Synchronize your thoughts with the smoke that is rising, seeing the smoke as carrying your request for more ideal clients out to the Universe.

7. Then say 3 times:

   "Desiring to serve my purpose without flight;
   My soul is bright as candle light;
   My work is honest and sincere;
   I desire ____ (# of clients) ideal clients here."

8. After the 3rd time say, "*And so it is.*"

9. Continue to watch the flames of your candles and the smoke from your cauldron.

10. Ceremony is complete when candles have burned completely down.

11. Thank your ancestors and Divine Support Team for holding the powerful space of this ceremony. Feel your gratitude for this power they hold for you.

12. Begin to be present to see/hear your completion boundary signal, when you do, you will know the creation is completed! Be present and open to how these ideal clients will show up.

Bubble Magic

When To Use It

This is a delightful and fun ceremony to use with the kids—or even when you feel yourself taking things too seriously. Just because it's fun and easy doesn't mean that it is any less potent so make sure you are clear about your intention and what you desire to manifest.

What You'll Need

- Bubbles
- Talisman or power object [this is an object that feels like it represents power to you, for you]
- Music
- Intention

Ceremony

1. Choose music that is your theme song, that holds your intention and represents what you are creating with this ceremony. If it's freedom you might put on Bon Jovi's "*It's My Life*," if it's love maybe you put on Tom Petty's "*Here Comes My Girl.*" Get creative, make sure it means something to YOU.

2. Place your power talisman, an object you feel energetically connected to on the ground at your feet.

3. Imagine as you take a deep breath in, you are bringing energy in from your power talisman up through the base of your spine, imagine that energy is moving up through your body and chakras.

4. On your exhale, blow your powered-up intention with your breath into the bubble wand.

5. Watch each bubble prayer as it rises up to the sky. See this as your requests being lifted and moved on the energy of the Universe.

6. Recite these words:

   "I make these requests from my heart I say
   I ask these blessings travel through the sky this day
   To reveal and unravel these simple asks I pray"

7. When all of your ceremony bubbles have drifted out of your view and you feel complete, thank the Universe, the sky, the Divine for granting your "wishes." Watch as the Universe receives your intention, through your breath, wrapped up in these delicate bubbles. And remember to be on the lookout for your manifestation— they may first show up as breadcrumbs along your path.

Ceremony For Uncertain Times

When To Use It

This is a powerful ceremony to build energy and focus to amplify our center, the stabilizing force in our body so when things around us, including the world get wobbly.

Recently our world has been turned upside down by the global Covid-19 pandemic. This incredible tidal wave of fear is not only challenging to experience on a human level it is extremely difficult for intuitives who are particularly sensitive to energy, needless to mention a global energy wave.

For the first time in centuries our entire world is focused on the same thing. Covid-19, an unbiased biological pathogen that has changed history in what seems like the blink of an eye. In times like these working with energy and using our intuition seems like the ONLY thing we can do.

I received this Divine Prescription Ceremony to support us in times when we feel less than sure. When we need an amplification of feeling safe, a sense that it will all work out or to create some space for peace, even if it is just a minuscule amount, it matters.

Because this ceremony is intensive make sure you set aside enough time to participate in its entirety without distraction.

What You'll Need

- Black candle
- White candle
- Clear Quartz Crystal
- Smoky Quartz, Black Onyx or Black Tourmaline
- Toothpick, wooden skewer or straight pin
- Rubber gloves—to wear while working with the oil

Preparation

- Gather any symbols that represent feeling grounded, safe, clear and centered to you. That could be graphics or personal pictures that evoke those feelings, or personal items that symbolize it. For me, I often use a Black Hematite that I have because it feels strong to me.

- **Banishing Oil** (see Banishing Oils p. 467,469)

- **Intention for Ceremony.** The goal you desire to experience, (ex. calm, peace, freedom).

- **Your Sacred Sigil.** Create your Sacred Sigil that alignes with your intention for this ceremony. (Sacred Sigil p. 448)

- **Completion Boundary.** You set the symbol or signal that you will see or hear when the ceremonial energy will be completed. For example, "I will know when the ceremonial energy is complete by seeing/hearing a particular animal; a specific sign such as money on the sidewalk."

Ceremony

1. Create sacred space, call in your ancestors and Divine Support Team. Perhaps light some incense, sage, put on some sacred music. Set the tone for your sacred and reverent ceremony. The stronger your participation the bigger the results.

2. With your toothpick write or carve into your Black candle any words relating to the uncertainty you feel, (ex. fear, unknown, anger, scared, it could even be word(s) that speak to the level of your concern. You can write 1 word 1 time or 1 word multiple times, or cover the candle in every word you can think of that expresses your feelings of uncertainty. The choice is up to you.

3. On the White candle carve or draw your Sacred Sigil for this ceremony. A representation of you and your intention for this ceremony.

4. Anoint both candles by spreading a couple of drops of your Banishing Oil on them. (*don't forget the gloves, it's spicy*)

5. Gather your symbols of clarity, safety and strength. Place them next to the candles.

6. Place your Smoky Quartz or Black Tourmaline crystal in front of your White candle. Place your Clear Quartz crystal in front of your Black candle.

7. Take 5 deep breaths in and out, relaxing your body.

8. Pick up the Black candle, close your eyes, imagine you are pouring all of your concerned energy into this Black candle. Feel the words you carved into it. Allow the candle to absorb all of your concerns, fears or uncertainties. Imagine these energies are leaving your body and going into the candle with ease.

9. When you feel you've completely emptied your concerns into the Black candle, put it down beside the Clear Quartz crystal.

10. Take the White candle into your hands, closing your eyes once again, feel your ancestors and Divine Support Team surrounding you, imbuing into the White candle all the balancing universal energy. As you take deep breaths in and out feel your Sacred Sigil being infused with the harmonic and balancing energy from your ancestors and Divine Support Team coming through you into your Sacred Sigil and the White candle.

11. When you feel complete with imbuing the White candle open your eyes and place it down beside the Smoky Quartz crystal.

12. Light both candles.

13. Gaze into the flames of the Black candle and imagine it transforming your uncertainty, fear or concern as it burns away, melting the wax and all the words, feelings and energies you inscribed upon it.

14. Then shift your focus onto the White candle, seeing your Sacred Sigil and all the energy of the Divine being released as it melts.

15. Allow your focus to include both candles, imagine they are working together with the crystals that are in front of them, creating harmony and balancing energy. Imagine seeing an infinity symbol being created from the energy of the Black and White candles.

16. As you look into this infinity symbol infused by your candles imagine it, along with the candles, crystals, talismans (your symbols) transforming your uncertainty into clarity. You feel calm and centered. Imagine the flames of these candles are the Divine power within you. The power that gives you strength and stability, clarity and peace.

17. You can say a personal prayer or recite a poem.

18. Allow your candles to burn down until they go out on their own. If you don't have time to let it burn all the way down, use a candle snuffer to put out the flame and dispose of the candles; do *not* use them in any other ceremonies.

Making Epic Banishing Oil

When To Use It

Use banishing oil to magnify the release of unforgiveness, anxiety, stress or any other energies you wish to dispel. You will use it as you perform the ceremony for uncertain times.

This banishing oil is *very strong* and covers all the bases, head to toe in the letting go department.

What You'll Need

- 2 oz of any oil you like, such as organic Olive, Avocado, or Grapeseed
- Pine Oil
- Cinnamon Oil
- Peppermint Oil
- Rosemary Oil
- Peppercorns
- Thyme
- Lemon Rind
- Garlic Clove, Oil or Powder
- Chili or Cayenne Pepper
- Bottle that will hold all the ingredients
- Rubber gloves—to wear while working with the oil

Preparation

- Please use gloves while handling and working with this oil. **It is not meant to be put on your skin or eaten!**

- Add oil into the bottle.

- Add 5 (the number that represents change) drops of each of the other oils into the bottle.

- Insert the Lemon Rind, Peppercorns, Chili or Cayenne Pepper and Garlic.

Ceremony

1. As you are placing the items in your bottle, imbue the oil by setting the intention for this oil to remove and release anything that diverts or distracts your energy and focus. You may even say a little prayer:

   "I call on my Divine power within, all of my ancestors and my Divine Support Team, to imbue my oil with Divine properties of cleansing and clarity. I promise to use this banishing oil with the highest intent. May it cleanse and support me to discern and release any energy that has run its time and cycle. So that new beginnings may start. And so it is."

2. Put the top on your bottle and let it sit for a week to allow the energetic properties of the herbs to infuse into the oil.

3. After a week, strain your oil through a cheesecloth or a fine mesh colander. Make sure to bury or compost the remnants of the ingredients (Lemon Peel, Peppercorns).

4. Use this Banishing Oil however you'd like, because it is irritating to the skin please use gloves, be present and mindful while using. To use this oil in candle work for release ceremonies only a couple of drops is needed, never near the flame, this is very potent oil, treat it with respect.

Insta Banishing Oil

When To Use It

You will use it as you perform the ceremony for uncertain times. It is not as intense as the Epic Banishing Oil, but still effective, especially when you need some in a hurry. Like when you begin your ceremony only to realize you're out!

What You'll Need

- Olive Oil
- Garlic Powder
- Cayenne Pepper
- Black Pepper
- Rosemary

Preparation

- Combine all the ingredients in a glass bottle.

Ceremony

1. As you swirl the bottle to combine the ingredients say this prayer/ intention:

   "I call forth my Divine power within, with my ancestors and Divine Support Team, asking to imbue this oil with Divine clarity for release. I agree to use this banishing oil with the highest intent. May it cleanse and support me to discern and release any energy that has run its time and cycle. So a new beginning may commence. And so it is."

2. Take a deep clearing breath and blow it onto your banishing oil bottle.

3. The oil is ready to use—make sure not to put it on skin as the peppers are irritating to skin and eyes.

Closure & Completion

When To Use It

This ceremony is extremely helpful in those times when something has activated you and sticks with you—where you can't seem to let it go and move on. This sweet simple ceremony will have you feeling spacious and ready to greet the next step in your life.

What You'll Need

- 1 piece of White Paper
- 1 Pen with Blue Ink
- White Carnations in a Clear Glass Container
- Matches or Lighter
- Patchouli Essential Oil

Ceremony

1. Gather any or all of the following crystals: Black Hematite, Black Tourmaline, Smoky Quartz, Labradorite.

2. Write on the White paper:

   "I now release, forgive and absolve my past or current vows, attachments or DNA alignment to shame, lack and unforgiveness. I now create new, Divine empowering energy to carry me forward, beyond my past limitations, beliefs and resistance. I trust this is for my highest good AND I affirm my commitment to this new path."

3. Fold the paper and place 3 drops of Patchouli Essential Oil onto the paper. Then place it next to your heart as you breathe in your new intentions—calling forth the energy (feeling) of completion and your request to move to the next level.

4. Place the folded paper under the glass container of White Carnations.

5. Place crystals around or next to the flowers. Leave everything as it is until the flowers wilt completely. When you throw the flowers out—burn the paper to complete your release and bury or compost the old flowers outside of your home.

Feng Shui Wealth Activation

When To Use It

I LOVE this ceremony: First because it truly works, and second because you get to combine several different facets of energy work together, including Feng Shui. Use this ceremony when you want a boost the flow of abundance in your life.

What You'll Need

- 3 Red Candles
- 3 Purple Candles
- 1 Yellow Candle
- Clear Quartz Crystal
- Tiger's Eye Crystal
- Your personal symbol or totem of wealth
- Your Sacred Sigil—your intention for the ceremony (Sacred Sigil p. 448)
- Piece of fabric for altar cloth: Green, Gold or Silver in color (the colors of money)

Preparation

- Standing facing inward, at your **most used** entrance into your home, locate the farthest left hand corner of your home. This is your wealth quadrant of your home. Make sure there isn't any clutter in that area, assure everything is organized, free of chaos. This is where you will perform your wealth activation ceremony. Select a place in this area where you can create a wealth altar to amplify and anchor the energy of your ceremony.

- Create your Sacred Sigil for this ceremony that represents your intention and focus for this ceremony. Draw this Sigil on each of the candles.

Ceremony

1. Create sacred space.

2. Call on your Divine Support Team and ancestors to surround you and join you in this sacred ceremony. When you feel you are ready to move forward, all the energy feels set, continue.

3. Place your altar cloth down in the spot you have chosen in your wealth quadrant. Put the Red and Purple candles in a larger circle.

4. Place the Yellow candle in the center of the circle.

5. In front of the Yellow candle place the crystals and your totem(s) for wealth.

6. Take a deep breath in, being present to your intention for this sacred ceremony. On your exhale, light the center Yellow candle and recite these words:

   "Every day
   In every way
   Divine prosperity
   Comes to me."

7. Take a moment gazing at the Yellow candle's flame and your Sacred Sigil inscribed on its side.

8. Light the Red and Purple candles, making sure to light them in a clockwise fashion, starting in the direction of the sun's rising. After you have lit the 6th candle in the outer circle, take a moment and be present to your request, what you are aligning and synchronizing with. Take a deep breath in, hold it for a count of 3, on your exhale recite these words:

"I embrace my abundance
Opening myself now to this Divine flow
Receiving it in all ways
With gratitude and appreciation"

9. Take each of the crystals (Clear Quartz & Tigers Eye), put one in each hand. Sit in a comfortable place close to your altar. Breathing slowly, fix your gaze on the candle flames, watching how they dance and move about.

10. Notice the crystals are feeling warm in your hands, as you continue taking deep breaths, call in your intention, through your Sigil and wealth symbols. Closing your eyes now, if your mind begins to wander bring your attention back to your center candle, the Yellow candle see it in your mind. See the flames of the candle flickering.

11. Sit here for 10 minutes, longer if you wish. When you feel ready, open your eyes, extinguish the candles, beginning with the Red and Purple candles and finishing with the Yellow candle.

12. Carry these crystals with you or place them on your bedside table. They are now charged with your wealth activator—if you feel worried or concerned about money, hold or carry them with you.

Fire Releasing

When To Use It

This ceremony is straight forward and one surely you may have already done while sitting around a campfire. The powerful aspect of this ceremony is the fire as the catalyst using wind to transform and dissolve all that you are relinquishing.

What You'll Need

- Paper
- Pen
- Fireproof bowl, pot
- Matches or lighter
- Glass of water

Ceremony

1. Create sacred space.

2. Invite in your Divine Support Team and ancestors asking for support in this ceremony.

3. Take some deep breaths as you set and declare your intention for this ceremony.

4. Ask to be open to see any and all things it is time to release and let go of. Things that may have run their cycle, whether it is a toxic relationship or fear of speaking your truth allow them to show themselves to you now.

5. Write a list of everything you see, feel or know it is time to let go of, ideas, beliefs, situations, relationships, challenges, patterns, everything you can think of.

6. Take the paper with your list scribed on it, hold it to your heart, feeling your heartbeat as you take a few breaths. Then hold it to your forehead, your 3rd eye area. Lastly take a deep breath in placing on that breath everything known and unknown you desire to release, and as you exhale infusing your paper with your breath imbued with these energies you are inviting to leave.

7. Place your fire proof bowl or pot on a level surface clear of any debris or clutter. Holding the list in your dominant hand place it over your fire proof pot and light that piece of paper on fire and throw it into your fire safe pot or cauldron. As it burns to ashes, circle it clockwise and visualize everything you wrote being cleared away, carried by the smoke up into the sky to be transformed into something new.

8. Then write a list of everything you want and desire which you are calling in to the space you just created. You can use divination tools (oracle cards, runes, pendulums) for guidance on everything that is coming your way this next season/year. Keep a journal nearby to write down any emotions, thoughts, or bursts of enlightenment that come up.

9. Thank your Divine Support Team and ancestors for holding the sacred space for you during this sacred releasing ceremony. Feel the gratitude and honor to have this connection and ability.

Release Old Patterns & Blocks

What You'll Need

- Red Yarn/String (natural no synthetics)
- Knife/Scissors
- Pot or Fire Proof Container
- Lighter

Ceremony

1. Cut yarn into 9" pieces. Knot the ends together of each piece like a bracelet and give each a label of something in your life that you feel is holding you back (lack consciousness, fear, ego, judgment, comparison, bias).

2. Cut as many pieces as you need. Tie each of them around your wrist and say to each of them specifically:

   "(What you want to release, fear), I have carried you and your energy for a long time; Your contrast has been my teacher;
   I receive and accept your lessons completely;
   I now summon the courage, strength and faith to release you entirely;
   For your presence in this form no longer serves me."

3. Then cut through each yarn bracelet with your scissors, your persistence is part of the ceremony. As you cut these symbolic bonds imagine separating yourself from them completely. Then burn the yarn in a pot/fireproof container.

4. When ashes have cooled take them outside and with the wind at your back release the ashes into the air. As they blow away witness this as the sign of your new beginning.

See The Future

When To Use It

Again, you'll see this prescription denotes using this ceremony during Samhain, but you can use it any time you feel called. The combination of candle work and divination tools gives it an extra punch!

Because the veil is so thin during Samhain, it is a perfect time to connect with your ancestors and receive Divine Guidance for your future, but you need not wait for Samhain to do this process.

What You'll Need

- Black Candle
- Matches/Lighter
- Oracle Deck or any divination tool you prefer

Ceremony

1. Go into your sacred space—light candle and place on your Samhain Altar. (* If you do not have a Samhain Altar, or are doing this at another time of the year, simply place the candle on a safe surface where you can connect with it.) Set your intention to contact your ancestors and Divine Support Team to receive guidance on your future.

2. Shuffle your deck of cards—select 1 card and place it face up in front of your candle. Look at it closely and then back at the flame on your candle—stare at the flame as long as you wish, so visions, signs, sensations and emotions rise to the surface. You may even see how the flame dances differently, pay attention

3. Ask your Divine Support Team and ancestors any questions you have about the future. Slowly one at a time allow any impressions, feels, or intuition to come forth.

4. If you aren't receiving anything it maybe because you are attached to what guidance you may receive. Go back to your breath, be present to your sacred space and the trust you have in your Divine Guidance. Then relax and receive.

5. Once you feel the energy is completing, knowing you received perfectly in this moment. Even if it was just breathe. Trust it and follow it.

6. Thank your ancestors and Divine Support Team for holding the space for you to see your future.

Successful Event

When To Use It

This ceremony is a powerful one to focus your intention on having a successful event (even with Covid). This can be anything from holding a virtual workshop to hosting a charity event. If you want to have ease and comfort in being in the spotlight, this is your ceremony.

What You'll Need

- 1 tsp Echinacea Powder
- 1 tsp Allspice
- 1/3 tsp Clove
- 1/3 tsp Bay
- 7-Day Yellow Candle
- Red String or Twine
- Sage
- San Palo Wood
- Crystals—such as, Citrine, Gold, Ruby, Star Sapphire, Tiger's Eye, Amethyst, and Topaz

Preparation

- Smudge and clear the energy of your environment with Sage and San Palo.

- Combine the 4 spices together in a bowl, sit them in the far left corner of your space (cover it tightly).

- Take the Yellow 7 Day Candle (in glass) and bless it as the soveriegn center in your offering. You can do this by placing the candle to your heart and sending love from your heart chakra; or with your breath simply by infusing your energy into the candle. Thank the energy of success for coming to sit with you in your work.

- Take the red string wrap it around the yellow candle—7 times—each wrap signifying the blessing of wealth upon those who come forth and are called to invest in your work. With each wrap say "Om Mani Padme Hum" or any blessing or prayer you feel aligned with. Then tie the ends of the red string together.

- Place crystals around the candle to amplify this broadcast of blessings.

Ceremony

1. Every morning for 7 days prior and including the day of your event, offering, and public appearance, light the Yellow candle and burn a little of your mixture from the bowl in a fireproof container. As it burns recite and read aloud:

   "I am open to allowing abundance and prosperity into my life.
   I am blessed with the energy of life and I love sharing with others.
   I am overjoyed my contribution enriches and supports others.
   The ideal people easily find this event.
   I AM forever grateful for this work and my ability to be the vessel through which the Divine energy flows.
   Thank you, thank you, thank you."

Third Eye Activation & Amplification

When To Use It

As you can see this ceremony is another detailed ceremony which requires more attention and focus. This powerful ceremony will support your clairvoyance being activated and turned up. I suggest using it after you feel comfortable with your Divine vision. This isn't a beginner's exercise, it is for those who have been dedicated to working with their clairvoyance for at least 6 months regularly.

What You'll Need

- 1 tsp of Rosemary (coarsely ground)
- 1 tsp each of Lavender, Ginger, Thyme, Sage
- 9-12 Tbsp of pure Jojoba or Almond Oil
- 4 drops of Frankincense Essential Oil
- 4 Purple or Indigo colored candles with candle holders
- 1 Yellow candle with candle holder

Timing: On a Thursday night during the full moon, if not Thursday any day during the full moon except Saturday.

Preparation

- Blend the herbs and oil ingredients together gently in a glass container.

- Add to your mixture one or any of the following crystals: Lapis, Clear Quartz, Blue Apatite, Azurite, Amethyst, Iolite.

- Cover your mixture tightly and place it on your altar or a place you feel is a place of honor and power in your home or office. Allow it to build power for at least **9 days**.

- Then use this tincture to anoint yourself and your tools in your ceremony.

- On the night of your ceremony, anoint each of your candles imbuing your intention to have an amplified Divine vision of clairvoyance. Simply take your tincture on your forefinger put it on each candle infuse your intention:

  Clear Amplified Divine Vision
  - On the 1st Purple or Indigo candle write: **Clear**
  - On the 2nd candle write: **Amplified**
  - On the 3rd candle write: **Divine**
  - On the 4th candle write: **Vision**
  - On the Yellow candle write: **Ohm Mani Padme Ohm**

Ceremony

1. If possible do this ceremony outside under the full moon, if not, near a window while inside will work.

2. Place each of the Purple/Indigo candles after they are blessed and anointed with your tincture—in the 4 different directions (N,S,E,W).

3. Call forth the energy of your Divine Support Team, Ancestors, and Teachers you work with.

4. Create sacred space for your ceremony. As you do, acknowledge the Divine energy that is present for you with gratitude while lighting each candle, in a clockwise direction, beginning with the east, until all 4 candles are lit.

5. Then light the Yellow candle and place it in the center of your circle. Sit in the center of your circle, if possible, gazing at this Yellow candle infused with the Divine power of your sovereign center of clear Divine vision. Using your dominant hand, middle finger, anoint your 3rd eye with your sacred tincture in a clockwise motion as you breathe it in.

6. Then gaze into your Yellow candle as you acknowledge your Divine sovereign center surrounded by your Divine Support Team, ancestors, and teachers.

7. Asking them now to begin to build this energy for the amplification of your Divine clairvoyance. When you feel the power beginning to build recite this:

   "This light is presence,
   This light is power, It fills me,
   Until I am presence, And that I AM"

8. Repeat this continually until you feel the energy and power has reached its epic peak. Imagine seeing the light from each candle and your Guides being brought in through your 3rd eye chakra with each breath, then call forth your request and intention:

   "I call forth into this body,
   The amplification of my Divine vision,
   This light allows me to see beyond the veils
   With ease, grace and in service of the Divine,
   I receive it now with gratitude, respect AND HONOR."

   (You may also anoint your forehead again if you feel the energy needs an extra boost.)

9. Continue candle gazing until you feel the energy amplification is complete. You will feel a swish, hear a click or just a knowing that it is finished.

10. Before closing your circle tune in and ask if or when it would be beneficial to repeat this ceremony. Also ask for any other guidance you are now ready to **see** at this point in time.

11. After receiving your Divine Guidance, bring your hands together at your heart to acknowledge, paying respect and gratitude for this gift of direction. Acknowledge and thank your Divine Support Team and ancestors.

12. Deep breath in and say, "And so it is."

13. Close your sacred circle, after the energy has receded, extinguish each candle in the opposite order that you lit it, starting with the Yellow candle. As you are extinguishing each candle's flame keep your focus on the acknowledgment of this energy transmission and your gratitude for it.

14. Place these candles in a special place—and only use them for this specific ceremony.

Captain's Logbook

No journey would be complete without recognizing the souls that kept our ship going. A captain is nothing without her crew.

from Lynnette

To my ancestors the lines and lineages, my Divine Support Team, and *Guides,* thank you for showing up and speaking loudly so I could hear and follow my Divine Guidance to create this book.

To my *Mom,* "*Jay*" whose unconditional love and belief in me made this possible. Thank you, mom, for being beside me every step of the way in this creation, for being my person. You showed me what real love is and you never gave up on us, no matter how tough it got, you held on and kept us safe. The best mom and grandmama ever!

My partner in life, *Mike,* I am clear without your contributions of love this book would not exist. Too many to number are all the things you do for me and our family. From your infinite trips to the grocery store, to being the resident chef and ultimate pack leader, you are a true example of acts of service from unconditional love. Thank you, my love, for always saying YES to the wild adventures I put before you. You have made my life extraordinary. Thank you for being my person, the one who believes in me and my intuition without hesitation or fail. *I love you forever.*

Divi, my co-author and partner in crime, thank you for your courage, strength and bravery. You are a beautiful example of trusting your Divine Guidance and living this work. Thank you for your willingness to dive into the unknown with me and for believing in your power and mine. I feel very blessed and grateful to share this journey with you. Thank you darlin'!!

To my family:
Claire, for tolerating me always preaching energy, intuition, and Universal Law. Our connection deepens me and my work. Thank you for being a great daughter and spitfire. For loving me as I am, difficult and otherwise ;) Your love makes this possible, always remember what an incredible contribution you are to us. Thank you for helping my fashion sense and keeping me real. I see the magic within you, even if you don't believe it, I do. *I love you Boogie!*

Ryan, even though this isn't your thing, I am grateful for your love and support. Despite differing opinions, we always arrive at the same place: love. You saved my life by being you and showing me there was good stuff despite all the bad. Your epic commitment and love to our family makes all of us better. Thank you for being a fantastic son, brother, husband and father. I love you. You will always be my hero, just remember, no capes!

Michelle, the best daughter-in-law on the planet, who makes living in the fast lane look easy. Thank you for saying yes to Ryan and to our *interesting* family. You are a striking example of goodness and all that's right in our world. You brought to our family a peace we deeply needed along with two beautiful girls (and soon a little boy) who changed my life forever. Thank you for being a great wife, mother, and friend, truly you are one of my greatest gifts.

Layla, such a sweet energetic child filled with action and curiosity you brought to me this incredible source of energy of "I can do it." Watching you stretch for holds on your climbs that seem out of your reach and whether you stuck or not you gave it your all. Watching you compete, play hard and giving it your all gave me the courage and strength to get this project done. You, my Bear, will have my heart for eternity.

Keira, my soulful, sweet angel, your delicate ease and gentle ways taught me to not be so hard on myself, to see there was something more to uncover, to witness, and to love. Your kindness and creativity show me there are no limits to the joy we can have. Your smile busts my heart wide open. You, my Penguin, will forever have my heart and gratitude for all the laughter and love have brought me and our family.

Nick Eronko, my brother, the person I've known the longest in my lifetime. We have been through hell and back together despite it all we're still here. Thank you for being a practical and logical voice in my world, for saying what needs to be said, every intuitive needs a Nick in their life. I know it hasn't always been easy for you to be my brother, still I am grateful that you are. I couldn't have chosen a better one and thank you for choosing me ;) I love you!

To my dad, *Mike*, thank you for loving me enough to be the one to dish the tough life lessons my way. Dad your influence gave me that grit to be the woman I am today. Someone who can stand up and speak her truth from her heart with complete conviction. Without you it wouldn't have been possible. I love you deeply for being the person to teach me what you did!

My dear friend, *Heather*, whose wisdom is only paled by her incredibly gigantic heart. Darlin' Heather, I know not where I would be without having such a powerful touch stone in my life as you. It is rare to find someone you can trust with **all** of you — the good, the bad, and the ugly, and still feel holy. Thank you for being my midwife in this project — for holding my hand, wiping away the sweat, and cheering me on. Thank you for your incredible art direction and putting your flair into this project of love. You bring to me, the knowing that I am the Divine Feminine, and that I, too, am holy, totally whole, perfect, and complete. Thank you soul sistah! LOVE YOU!!

Gina Anala, thank you for all the years of learning and growing. You are such a powerful inspiration to me of living life on your own terms. A fiery explorer who taught me it was ok to color outside of the lines and like it! Thank you for your big laughs, giant lessons and for understanding me despite the language. Never would've thought 20 years ago sitting on that chair by the pool in Hawaii that we'd still be best buds. Thanks for hanging in with me! You're the best!! I love you!

Chloe Elgar, my weekly writing buddy (pre-Covid), thank you for being real, for trusting me to share our writing time and some awesome lattes too. Thank you for moving to Austin and sharing this crazy Texas adventure with us. I love all your incredible recommendations and suggestions, you've always got something up your sleeve that I'm eager hear about. Our friendship makes being the contemporary monk on the river easier. And while I know your bio family is far away, I claim you as part of our pack, so thank you for joining the family. You're the best lassie (spoken in my broken Scottish brogue)!! Love ya!

Melissa Rohwedder, thank you for believing in my voice on this powerful subject, for your willingness to walk through fire to be that incredible liver of life, teacher of teachers. How you live your life with such compassion inspires me every day. Your heart is bigger than Texas. Thank you for sitting up with me late at night forging titles, linking circles so this project would be synced up. Thank you for loving me and for being there girl! Love ya!

Laura & John Bell, thank you for believing in me, for the incredible invitations to teach and to share this work with the world. You both inspire me each and every day. Thank you for teaching me to not settle for less and how to live life authentically on your own terms. Love you both immensely!

Joe Kudla, thank you for trusting me with your precious business, Vuori, back in the day and for being such a badass great guy. I will always be grateful for the way you came into my world like a whirlwind and said YES! You will always hold a special place in my heart!

Bob Milburn, thank you for being bold and courageously trusting me and this new paradigm with your career and your future. You are a powerhouse!

Jeanne, thank you for your support and faith. Your ease of seeing the good in everything always brings light into my world. Thank you for believing in this project and me! Big Smooches!

Elizabeth Gilbert, thank you for your magic, for teaching me how to connect with my authentic voice and to trust the story that comes forth. Thank you darlin' for being a powerful example of living courageously.

Esther Hicks, thank you for being the extraordinary example of the real deal, for opening up your home and showing me that a powerful spiritual teacher can be "normal" like everyone else (if there is such a thing as normal in this world). With much love, appreciation, and gratitude. Go Spurs!!

Sharon Storoschuk, thank you for your courage and willingness to chart a path in this work. You are a beautiful gift to me and this work. Welcome to the stage darling!

Nancy Villere, thank you so much for your incredible eye—for your talent and artistry. Thank you for always being there regardless of my wild projects you are always a YES! You were a true friend in a time when the bottom was falling out. I will never forget that—ever! Thanks for always making me look good darlin! Love ya!

To all my clients over the past 25+ years, it is each and every one of you that made this book possible. Through our sessions, your vulnerability, willingness, and openness truly made me a better intuitive coach. Your courage allowed me to see that I, too, am courageous. Your faith, showed me that I, too, am faithful. Each and every one of you is in my heart. Even if I haven't spoken to you in 20 years, I see you. I know your heart and I am grateful to have had the opportunity to be blessed by working with you. It is through your grace that I am sharing this work and these experiences. Thank you x infinity!!

To our ICT (Intuitive Coach Training) Peeps:
Thank you for your courage, strength and tenacity. I am convinced and know without doubt your contribution to our world will make a difference. You bless and honor us by trusting us to lead you in this work. I love you all!

To our Editor, *Michelle*, thank you for your easy going nature and not freaking out when I was. Your support was a gift, especially when I was sure I would drown in these pages. Always cheering me on to see the big picture, despite my suggestion of using the book for smudging purposes and starting over. All joking aside, thank you, Michelle.

To my TMLP crew: You **know** who you are and you know it was the possibilities we created together that opened all of this up! Thank you for being a sturdy place for me to stand while I was recreating myself back in the day! (Erin, Nancy, Zach, Roger, Natalie, Christy, et al)

To all my teachers (too many to name), some friends, some exes, some colleagues, some bosses, and some acquaintances, this is your spot. Thank you, my darlings, for being who you were/are in my life to lead me to the great uncoverings of "my stuff." This book is the result of unearthing all of that. I am truly who I am because of you and all that we shared, regardless of circumstance. If I hurt you, please forgive me. If you hurt me, know I still love you. Even if you betrayed me, I love you. Even if we broke our hearts together, know I still love you. And always will. I **thank you** from the deepest depths of my soul, because I know it was me that needed the wake-up call and you were the best alarm ever!

from Divi

Ed Light—my husband and pillar of strength. You put up with me so much! You have watched me daily through this journey of medicine to yoga to intuition, and you supported me the entire time. You never thought I was crazy; in fact, you have been my biggest cheerleader. You have helped me to trust my gifts and you are always supporting me on my next venture, next idea, next thing. Your love keeps me going and smiling every day!

Raj Light—my son. You give me reason to smile every single day. I joke with you all the time because my intuition sky-rocketed with my pregnancy with you. Being your mom is the greatest adventure a person could ever ask for! You teach me every day to live in the moment and truly chill out and smile! You taught me to be a kid again! Thank you for choosing me to be your mom and to support me in everything I do.

Lynnette—my partner in crime. I never thought that an introductory call to you over a decade ago would have led to this! I feel blessed every day to have a relationship with you. You are truly an incredibly powerful person, friend & intuitive who has HUGE passion, gifts, and talents. You have always held the flashlight for me to step forward and for that, I am forever grateful. Even this book—you challenged me. You embody this work and have always held that for me to follow. Thank you!

Om—my dad. Thank you for everything you are. You have always called me "The Great One" and that has always touched my heart so deeply. You have taught me through your example. You are strong and determined, and never gave up and that has landed onto me which has allowed me to follow this path without giving up.

Krishna—my mom. It is because of you that I have any sense of Spirituality. When we were young (and even now) you made us go to the Temple and study the scriptures. As a child, I did not like it at all. It is ironic that I have done a full 360 degrees! You teach me about faith and perseverance and love. You are an incredible mom and human.

Ajay—my brother. You have always brought me such gifts and huge contrast. Despite our head to heads, you are my brother and one of my hugest fans. I am proud to call you my brother! You are a lucky man with an incredible wife and kids. Thank you for being that brother that provided tonne of love and teasing!

Alka—my sister. You are incredible! You have such determination in everything you do, that it blows my mind. Your fierce determination and your passion in PETA have rubbed off on me. Your relationships with animals is something we all could strive for. Thank you for being you.

Bhooma—my sister. Wow! Biggest sister has huge energy and that is you. You are such a pillar for our family and the bond that keeps us siblings close. You are incredible as a mom and grandmother and support to me, your baby sister. Thank you for never doubting me!

Ambereen Quadir—A few weeks ago, in our monthly face-times, you helped me to move through some of my own energy blocks that catalyzed me into this book even more. Your friendship means the world to me. As both of us being physicians and walking this walk—it has always been such a huge gift to have you in my life!

Sharon Storsochuk—You are such a light and I feel gifted to teach with you and have gotten to know you over the last decade. As we have watched each other on this journey, it has been a fabulous ride! Thank you for stepping forward!

Christine Banno—It has been such a gift to watch you step out of the closet and help clients. It has been a pleasure and learning curve to teach with you and Sharon. Thank you for holding that light as we have stepped forward on this journey!

My Yoga Friends and Community—My decade immersed in the yoga world led me to the intuitive world. There are so many friends in the yoga world that there are too many to list here. You have taught me so much through our journey together. I hope this book inspires each of you to take your yoga off the yoga mat and into your world. Thank you for being on this path journey of life with me.

Esther Hicks—I immersed myself in your teachings about two decades ago. It was when I started to truly apply your work that I started to see huge impact. I use your teachings daily and constantly as part of my own journey. I feel blessed to teach the processes that you have taught the world only to impact my life so powerfully!

Michelle—our powerful editor. You have kept us on track, and you have been diligent with us in a loving way. I have loved working with you and have loved the process of seeing you work feverishly on our project. You are brilliant!

Heather—our fabulous graphic designer and friend. Thank you. You have been incredible to collaborate with and to watch you in process has been brilliant! Your ideas for the front/back of the book blew my mind! Funny how the book cover is a picture of exactly that! Thank you for your dedication to this project.

ICT (Intuitive Coach Training) Graduates—Thank you all! Working with each of you has been a joy for me! Watching each of you hone your skill set and heal your lives has been an honor and a privilege.

My clients past, present & future. If it were not for you, I never would be doing this! You have allowed me to help and guide you through your own trials and tribulations. This has helped me to work with my craft Each client I have worked with has provided me so much insight into myself. Thank you all for your dedication and commitment to this work. It takes an open mind to create an open heart—and that is each of you!

Reading List

Meditation:

Zen Mind, Beginner's Mind, Shunru Suzuki's—great for beginners and experienced pratictioners.

Wherever You Go, There You Are is the perfect "modern" meditation guide from the 'father of modern mindfulness', Jon Kabat-Zinn.

Making Space, Thich Nhat Hanh—simple ways to establish a home meditation practice.

The Miracle of Mindfulness, Thich Nhat Hanh—classic introduction to mindfulness meditation.

How to Meditate: A Practical Guide to Making Friends with Your Mind—Pema Chödrön—great book to help beginners start a practice.

Apps: Insight Timer

Online Teachers: Davidji—Davidji.com

Money:

The Abundance Book, John Randolph Price

Creating Money—Keys to Abundance, Sanaya Roman & Duane Packer

The Law of Divine Compensation, Marianne Williamson

The Soul of Money, Lynn Twist

Feel Free to Prosper, Marilyn Jenett

Spirit Means Business—The way to prosper wildly without selling your soul, Alan Cohen

Happy Money, Ken Honda

Energy:
You Can Heal Your Life, Louise Hay

Power vs. Force, David Hawkins

The Astonishing Power of Emotions, Esther & Jerry Hicks

The Subtle Body, Cyndi Dale

Radical Forgiveness, Colin Tipping

Creativity:
The Artist's Way, Julia Cameron

Big Magic, Elizabeth Gilbert

Shadow Work:
The Dark Side of Light Chasers, Debbie Ford

Bringing Your Shadow Out of the Dark, Robert Augustus Masters

Past Life:
Many Lives, Many Masters, Brian Weiss

Your Soul's Plan, Robert Schwartz

Mindset:

Ask and It is Given, Abraham Hicks

A Course in Miracles, Foundation for Inner Peace

A Course in Miracles Made Easy, Alan Cohen

Think and Grow Rich, Napoleon Hill

Return to Love, Marianne Williamson

The Surrender Experiment, Michael A. Singer

The Untethered Soul, Michael A. Singer

Living with Joy, Sanaya Roman

The Right Questions, Debbie Ford

The Invitation, Oriah Mountain Dreamer

The Power of Habit – Why we do what we do in life and business, Charles Duhigg

Universal Laws:

The Kybalion, Three Initiates

The Law of Attraction, Esther & Jerry Hicks

The Law of Divine Compensation, Marianne Williamson

Being of Service:

Belong, Radha Agrawal

Turning Pro — Tap you inner power and create your life's work, Steven Pressfield

Runes:

Lost Teachings of the Runes, Ingrid Kincaid

Notes on Sources

Holographic

"Theoretical physicists and astrophysicists, investigating irregularities in the cosmic microwave background (the 'afterglow' of the Big Bang), have found there is substantial evidence supporting a holographic explanation of the universe – in fact, as much as there is for the traditional explanation of these irregularities using the theory of cosmic inflation.

"Study Reveals Substantial Evidence of Holographic Universe." *University of Southampton,* www.southampton.ac.uk/news/2017/01/holographic-universe.page.

Medium Trance States

A study to examine the state involved in a dissociative state such as mediumship in which a medium is in communication with a deceased person. Spect scans were done to study the brain of mediums when in communication with deceased loved ones - to get a sense of what is happening for them.

Peres, Julio Fernando, et al. "Neuroimaging during Trance State: A Contribution to the Study of Dissociation." *PLOS ONE*, Public Library of Science, journals.plos.org/plosone/article? id=10.1371/journal.pone.0049360.

Theresa Caputo Medium Study

In 2013, on the Dr. Oz show (live), Dr. Oz had the Long Island Medium - Thersesa Caputo on his show. He also invited Dr. Daniel Amen (Brain Imaging Expert of the Amen Clinics) to study her brain during a reading. The results of the scan show that there is a change in blood flow that is not seen in the typical brain when Theresa Caputo is connected in a mediumship session. These results can be found by re watching the Dr. Oz episode.

"Dr. Oz's Psychic Experiment, Pt 2." *Doctoroz.com*, 9 May 2013, www.doctoroz.com/episode/ long-island-medium-inside-psychics-brain.

Tyler Henry Medium Study

In 2019, similar results were found when Tyler Henry (of Hollywood Medium fame) had a brain scan done during a reading. It was shown to have similar results - that his brain scan also reflected changes not seen normally. These results can also be found online and indicate shifts in blood flow which would not be typical to be found. https://www.youtube.com/watch?

Evaluation of Emotional and Neutral Pictures Flashing as Stimuli

When showed positive emotional stimuli, people perform tasks better. Rodríguez, Álvaro Fernández, et al. "Evaluation of Emotional and Neutral Pictures as Flashing Stimuli Using a P300 Brain-Computer Interface Speller." *ResearchGate*, Journal of Neural Engineering, Aug. 2019, www.researchgate.net/publication/ 334980841_Evaluation_of_emotional_and_neutral_pictures_as_flashing_stimuli_using_a_P300_ brain-computer_interface_speller.

Intuition's role on Bigger Purchases

When making big purchases, people are more satisfied when they make an intuitive decision. Readinger, and Wilson. "Intuition in Consumer Decision Making." *ACR North American Advances,* 1 Jan. 1970, www.acrwebsite.org/volumes/12369/volumes/v33/NA-33.

"The Role of Emotions in Our Purchase Decisions." Psychology Today, Sussex Publishers, www.psychologytoday.com/us/blog/behind-online-behavior/201509/the-role-emotions-in-our- purchase-decisions.

Role of Intuition in Large Company and Executive Decisions

How top executives use their intuition to make decisions in their businesses

Bonabeau, Eric. "Don't Trust Your Gut." *Harvard Business Review*, 1 Aug. 2014, hbr.org/ 2003/05/dont-trust-your-gut.

"Psychological Approaches to Entrepreneurship." *Google Books*, Google, books.google.com/ books? id=lpGDw2rh3yAC&pg=PA37&lpg=PA37&d-

q=company+executives+using+intuition+for+diffi cult+novel+decision&source=bl&ots=1JupK0j- Pb&sig=ACfU3U1EqsSVjB8AH-BkAGOwQYv1_5B0iXA&hl=en&sa=X&ved=2ahUKEwiI34q TgYToAhWOJzQIHWFGCjoQ6AEwAHoECAcQAQ#v=onepage&q=company executives using intuition for difficult novel decision&f=-false.

Army Trains their Leaders in Intuition

Intuition is a key skill that the army teaches their troops and leaders.
Jacobsen, Annie, and Phenomena. "U.S. Military Believes Humans Have a Sixth Sense Intuition." *Time*, Time, 3 Apr. 2017, time.com/4721715/phenomena-annie-jacobsen/.

Brain, gut, and heart are intuition centers.

The brain, gut, and heart are the intuitive centers ofthe body.
Soosalu, Grant, et al. "Head, Heart, and Gut in Decision Making: Development of a Multiple Brain Preference Questionnaire - Grant Soosalu, Suzanne Henwood, Arun Deo, 2019." *SAGE Journals*, journals.sagepub.com/doi/full/10.1177/2158244019837439.

Dr. Benson about sympathetic nervous system

Dr. Benson discovered that there was a way to stop the sympathetic nervous system. "Dr. Herbert Benson's Relaxation Response." *Psychology Today*, Sussex Publishers, www.psychologytoday.com/us/blog/heart-and-soul-healing/201303/dr-herbert-benson-s- relaxation-response.

DMT and intuitive abilities

Hamill, Jonathan, et al. "Ayahuasca: Psychological and Physiologic Effects, Pharmacology and Potential Uses in Addiction and Mental Illness." *Current Neuropharmacology*, Bentham Science Publishers, 2019, www.ncbi.nlm.nih.gov/pmc/articles/PMC6343205/.
Gallimore, Andrew R, and Rick J Strassman. "A Model for the Application of Target-Controlled Intravenous Infusion for a Prolonged

Immersive DMT Psychedelic Experience." *Frontiers in Pharmacology*, Frontiers Media S.A., 14 July 2016, www.ncbi.nlm.nih.gov/pmc/articles/PMC4944667/.

Meditation increase DMT production

Miller, Iona. "Pineal Gland, DMT & Altered State of Consciousness." *Journal of Consciousness Exploration & Research*, jcer.com/index.php/jcj/article/view/288.

Science definition of energy and work

Work and Energy, physics.bu.edu/~duffy/py105/notes/Energy.html.

Atoms Vibrating

Staff, Science X. "One-of-a-Kind Spectrometer Reads Vibrations between Atoms to Find Structures of Molecules." *Phys.org*, Phys.org, 15 Aug. 2013, phys.org/news/2013-08-one-of-a- kind-spectrometer-vibrations-atoms-molecules.html.

95% of health ailments are stress related.

"America's #1 Health Problem." *The American Institute of Stress*, 4 Jan. 2017, www.stress.org/ americas-1-health-problem.

Robinson, Joe. "Three-Quarters Of Your Doctor Bills Are Because Of This." *HuffPost*, HuffPost, 22 July 2013, www.huffpost.com/entry/stress-and-health_b_3313606.

"September 2010 - Stress Is The Cause of 90 - 95% of Illness & Disease." *Hypnosis and Hypnotherapy with Deborah Lindemann CHT Fort Collins, Colorado*, www.lpgmindworks.com/ newsletters/september2010stressndisease.html.

Observer is present dynamic is significantly altered.

Hamilton, Antonia F de C, and Frida Lind. "Audience Effects: What Can They Tell Us about Social Neuroscience, Theory of Mind and Autism?" *Culture and Brain*, Springer Berlin Heidelberg, 2016, www.ncbi.nlm.nih.gov/pmc/articles/PMC5095155/.

Made in the USA
Middletown, DE
23 March 2024